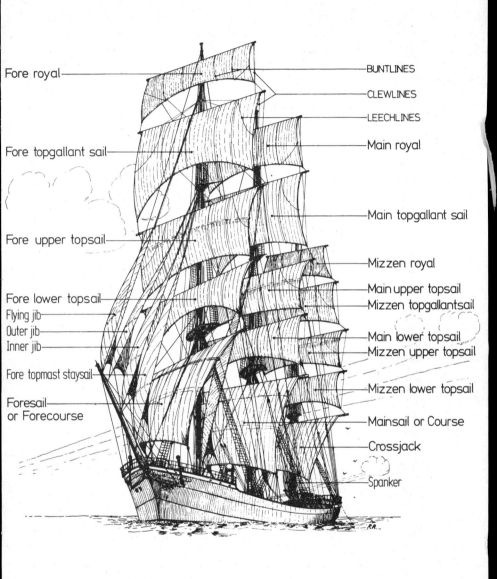

Fore royal

Fore topgallant sail

Fore upper topsail

Fore lower topsail
Flying jib
Outer jib
Inner jib

Fore topmast staysail

Foresail
or Forecourse

BUNTLINES

CLEWLINES

LEECHLINES

Main royal

Main topgallant sail

Mizzen royal

Main upper topsail
Mizzen topgallantsail

Main lower topsail
Mizzen upper topsail

Mizzen lower topsail

Mainsail or Course

Crossjack

Spanker

I REMEMBER THE TALL SHIPS

I remember the tall ships

FRANK BROOKESMITH

SHERIDAN HOUSE INC.

First published in the
United States of America 1991 by
Sheridan House Inc,
145 Palisade Street,
Dobbs Ferry, NY 10522

ISBN 0-924486-12-0

Printed in Great Britain by
Whitstable Litho Printers Ltd,
Whitstable, Kent

drawings by Roger Robinson

To Chiquita

The lady moon is my lover,
My friends are the oceans four,
The heavens have roofed me over
The dawn is my golden door.
I would liefer follow the condor,
Or the seagull soaring from ken,
Than bury my godhead yonder
In the dust of the strife of men.

FOREWORD

Much interest has been shown in the Tall Ships' Race and there are more yacht owners and more people interested in sailing and the sea than ever before. I have thought therefore that both full- and part-time sailors might like to read something of the ups and down of life at sea when still some commercial sailing ships sailed the oceans of the world.

When I went to sea in these ships over fifty years ago, steamers had almost completely driven sailing ships to the breakers' yards. I kept a faithful day-to-day log in my years in two deep water square-rigged ships, *William Mitchell* and *Kilmallie*, which were almost the last to sail under the British flag. That log has enabled me to give an accurate account of my time in them and I hope that this record will be of interest to many. Now these ships and others of their time have passed into history.

Frank Brookesmith

CONTENTS

CHAPTER 1   OF DREAMS

Back in 1911, when I was a boy at school, I was always after seeking knowledge of ships and the sea. A deep water harbour, The Bluff, was about twenty miles from my home in Invercargill in the south of New Zealand and I well remember going there with my father to fish for cod from the wharf. There was a big sailing ship in port and I kept leaving my fishing to go and admire her. I was entranced by the graceful curve of her clipper bow forward, the rake of her bowsprit and of her long jib-boom, her tall masts and her spreading yards, and the clean run of her counter aft. I was fascinated by the intricacy of her rigging and I had to know more about her. A hundred yards along the wharf my father was concentrated on hauling up a fish and I went up the gangway and stepped on to the deck. I asked a man in a reefer jacket and a peaked cap, whom I thought was the captain, if I could join her and learn to be a sailor. He smiled at me kindly and said, 'I think that you'd be a deal better off ashore, Sonny.' I was ten.

I found books and I pored over drawings of ships and their rigging. I taught myself the names of the masts and yards and of the sails. If I heard of a sailing ship being in port, I'd ask my father if we could go fishing to The Bluff. When there, I'd

1

persuade him that the best place to fish was near the ship, then I'd sit there and identify the masts and the standing and running rigging. If I could, I'd slip aboard and talk to the sailors.

They didn't give me any encouragement about going to sea. I remember a bearded giant of a man who said, 'Look my lad, we starve on these ships. We get salted down old horses that have died of overwork, for meat, and you can't get your fork into the gravy, what there is of it. The hard bread, and you won't believe how hard it is, is full of creepy crawly things and you don't get enough water to drink, never mind some to wash yourself. You work like a galley slave for twelve hours a day or more. Most of the time you're wet and cold and *all* the time you're hungry. Anyone who'd go to sea for pleasure would go to hell for a pastime.'

I looked at his thick forearms and his muscular frame and was emboldened to say, 'There must be something about the life at sea which keeps you fit and well, and which keeps you there.'

'Ah . . . well . . .' he said.

I wouldn't believe that they were not just spinning yarns and I felt that when I was a little older, I should be one of them.

Once, a big full-rigged ship *Antiope* went ashore at the edge of the deep water channel inside the harbour and the out-going tide left her with a serious list. Later I learned that seamen were not at all surprised at this accident. They expected her to come to grief one way or another and to bring grief to her crew. They construed her name as 'Anti-'ope'. As far as I know, she is still afloat though without her masts and used as a store ship in Mauritius.

A half-caste Maori who had been a whaling skipper took on the job of salvage. With his sons, he took off all her yards and upper masts and so righted her and re-floated her on the top of a spring tide, quite undamaged. He brought her alongside the wharf and re-rigged her. I followed this operation with absorbing interest and learned a lot more of ships. More

2

than ever I wanted to go to sea in sail.

I learned about boat work for, while I was still at school, a friend and I built ourselves a twelve-foot rowing boat. In it we explored far and wide on the big estuary there and we ventured for many miles up the Oreti River.

When I had finished my schooling and wanted to be apprenticed at sea my family did all they could to dissuade me. They told me what an insecure life it was and how poorly paid and dangerous. My father took me aside. 'I understand how you feel, Son,' he said, 'but you are the only son, and it would break your mother's heart if you were lost at sea.'

My sisters laughed at what they called my romantic ideas of an adventurous life, and they all stressed the advantages of security. In the end they persuaded me into their way of thinking and my father got me a job in a bank.

I can't say that I liked the work, but from a sense of duty to my parents, which I now think could have been mistaken, I tried hard to be successful at it. I was never so happy as when I was afloat and whenever I could I would escape to the wide estuary. I had my first sailing boat when I was seventeen. I bought her cheaply from an old school friend whose family was leaving the area, and I spent all the time I could with her. Most summer evenings and every week-end I was sailing her and learning to handle her in all kinds of weather.

Those were the days before the knowledge of aerodynamics introduced tall masts and high aspect-ratio sails. Boats were built to carry a big area of sail. As much canvas as could be spread was crowded on. My little ship was twenty feet long and she had a beam of 8½ feet and she drew only about a foot of water when her huge centreboard was lifted. Her twenty-four foot mast was stepped eighteen inches from the stem. The gaff was long and well peaked and the boom extended for six feet over the transom. She also shipped a bowsprit which was nine feet long and from which was set a large staysail. She sailed quite fast in the lightest of breezes and in a freshening wind I had to look lively to shorten sail

3

and I learned to heave her to and to put in a reef in quick time.

In her I learned to steer, to trim sail so as to make the most of the wind, to handle ropes and to tuck a splice and to tie at least some of the knots that a sailor needs to know.

All that came to an end when I had been three years in the bank and I was transferred to the branch at Christchurch in Canterbury. Facilities for sailing weren't so good there and I had to live on my small salary, but when I could, I'd go to the port at Lyttelton and dream. A couple of years later I met Sally and my dreams went other ways.

I thought of her as the only girl in the world but I was filled with misgivings. Before, I had always dreamed of escape from my uninspiring occupation and away to sea. Now, I felt that if I were to marry, I would be even more securely chained to an office desk and to a life that I was beginning to hate. She was heiress to a considerable fortune and she made me even more unsatisfied with my secure little way of life. Her parents and brothers and sisters were charming and I got on very well with them but I was not at all sure that the life to which she was accustomed was for me. I was very much in love with her; with her beauty and grace and youth and sweetness. A memory comes to me now of a deserted beach and summer sunshine. After a swim we ran together along the sand. I see again her shapely limbs stretched in effortless speed and her long fair hair blowing free in the wind.

She loved me too. I could have married her and so joined her way of life. I daresay that we could have been very happy but I wanted to be responsible for my wife. I wanted to be able to give her everything she needed and something more. I didn't want her to offer luxury to me. I didn't want to be Mrs Brookesmith's husband. You feel that way when you are two-and-twenty, and so you should.

Then I was transferred to Wellington, a port. All my spare time was spent by the wharves and the comings and goings of ships filled me with sea fever. When I had been there for six months I had a holiday and Sally's parents invited me to spend it with them in Christchurch.

Sally and I walked together on the hills above the town. We sat on an outcropping rock and we talked about my restlessness.

'Look, Frank,' she said, 'We love each other. Isn't that the answer to it all?'

'Yes Sally. It ought to be and it would be if we were on equal terms, but you are a potentially wealthy woman and I am a struggling wage slave. That fact brings a serpent into Eden.'

'Why do you always have to analyse?' she asked with some asperity. 'Why can't you take the happiness that's offered without looking for the grub in the apple? If you weren't such an old darling, you'd make me sick!'

I drew on my pipe and grinned ruefully and I looked out from where we sat, out over the grand panorama of the Canterbury Plains and away to the Southern Alps on that sunny afternoon. 'Maybe because I'm twenty-two and you're only eighteen,' I said.

She looked up unsmiling to the sky and mused, 'A great age he is. So hoary with knowledge.'

A long pause while she studied the little fleecy clouds drifting in from the sea. 'So you think that you must go away?'

'I think that I should,' I answered. 'I have to find myself. I've got to know what I'm doing. I can't be myself yet take the line of least resistance because it's so easy and delightful, without thought for tomorrow and all the other tomorrows.'

'I think you're a fool.'

'Probably, but I like to think that I'm an honourable fool. Let's walk up to Sugarloaf and get the wind in our hair and don't let's talk of this any more.'

I took her hand and pulled her to her feet. She walked beside me with her free and easy stride and we tried to talk of other things but we couldn't avoid the subject. She dropped behind me and sulked for a while so I walked on and wondered if I were really being a fool. A clod of earth struck me

5

on the back of the neck and I turned and caught her and rubbed bid-a-bids in her hair. She trod on my toes and called me an unchivalrous oaf, and the tension was broken and we laughed gaily together. We walked hand-in-hand to the rest house at the top of the pass. When we sat down to tea there we were two young people happily in love with each other.

Still I was restless. If there's anything in atavism this was due to generations of seafaring and sometime buccaneering forbears from Devon who had injected a little salt water into my blood.

When I returned to Wellington and daily watched ships coming and going, I decided that a banker's life held no future for me. I would be a sailor, and because I was too old for apprenticeship, I would serve my time before the mast.

With no further misgivings I threw up my job and as there were no sailing ships in port except a schooner which had a full crew, I signed on as ordinary seaman on an oil tanker which went regularly across the Pacific back and forth between Wellington and Californian oil ports.

CHAPTER II OROWAITI – *AN INTERLUDE*

I soon found that *Orowaiti* wasn't a happy ship. She was on a
special price contract to bring crude oil from America to New
Zealand and she spent no more time in port than her owners
could possible help. Her regular routine was 21 days to San
Luis Obispo or to Oleum, up San Francisco Bay, and she
took 24 hours to load and 23 days back to Wellington.
Forty-eight hours later she was back at sea again. Her crew
had signed on in Falmouth for three years and they were
resentful that they were on British Articles. They said that
they should be on New Zealand Articles because of the trade
that they were on, and then they would draw £14 per month
instead of the £9.10s that they had.

She wasn't well appointed for voyaging across the Tropics
and there was no refrigerator for the ship's stores. There was
an ice box for which we manhandled huge blocks aboard, but
by the time that we had spent three weeks between 35°
South and 35° North with the water temperature overside
85° most of the time, there wasn't much ice left and the
meat was whiffy.

There was a lot of dissatisfaction and general ill-feeling but
I was prepared to put up with difficulties. I wanted to get in
sea time for my 'ticket' and this mattered more to me than

the conditions. My shipmates found me quiet but I tried to be cheerful and willing and I was big enough to look after myself so I got on with them fairly well. After a couple of months I was treated as an A.B. but without change of status and I stood my watch and took my regular trick at the wheel.

The part of the ship that I remember most vividly was the chain locker where the anchor chain was stowed when it came aboard and I had an early introduction to that horrible place.

I had joined the ship as she lay to an anchor in Evans Bay, and mooring lines hove her into the wharf. I stowed my gear on a spare bunk and changed into dungarees. I was told that I would be in the port watch and that my place on mooring and unmooring ship would be on the focsle head with the Mate and the Bos'n. Soon after, I was ordered forward and I helped to haul in the mooring ropes and to coil them down while the carpenter was getting the windlass ready to recover the anchor.

'Go with Sinclair', the Mate ordered me, 'and help him stow the chain.'

I followed the Scottish sailor down the ladder and under the focsle head. He opened a steel door in the forward bulkhead and switched on a light. I looked into a compartment that went down to the bottom of the ship and to where a jumble of great chain lay. Each link was over eighteen inches long and the steel of it as thick as my wrist. A length of the chain reared up from the pile to a hole in the corner of the deckhead where it disappeared up a pipe to the windlass above.

'Doon the ladder ye go,' and he nudged me to an iron ladder fixed to the bulkhead. He followed me down and said 'Here's how ye do it Frank. Ye tak this rope here,' and he put into my hand the end of a rope of which the other end was spliced to a bracket on the side of the ship. 'Ye pass it roond the chain as it comes doon and ye walk it over yon,' and he pointed to the farther dark corner of the locker. 'Hauld it till the chain is agen up an' doon. Let it go an' do

8

the same but a wee bit further aft each time till ye've made a layer an' then ye start agen.'

I looked in horror at the insecure footing of the tumbled links and I asked, 'I walk over that lot? With that heavy chain?'

'Aye. 'Tis naething. Ye'll lairn,' and he shouted up the pipe that we were ready.

Before the windlass started he had time to tell me 'This locker's nae guid. 'Tis away too sma', an' yon pipe should come doon the centre. Because 'tis so sma' and yon pipe comes doon the corner, ye have to stow every link. Else it piles up in the pipe an' could jump the gypsy on the windlass an' kill someone . . . an' us as weel. Whiles, Ah've been in ships whaur there's plenty o' room in the locker an' ye'd have naethin' mair to do on this job than gie the pile a guid kick afore it reached the pipe an' doon it'd all go wi' room tae spare.'

The windlass shuddered above us, the chain rumbled down the pipe and Jock showed me how it was stowed. If I were slow and stumbled over the links, or if I didn't get the rope round it in the best place, he put his shoulder under it and strode sure-footed and flaked down the chain across and across. I helped him as best I could and it was a hard and dirty job. Wellington Harbour mud is known the world over to sailors as a thick slimy grey paste into which anchors and chains sink deep, and it stinks. The cable was smothered in this mud and as the locker filled, the rope was no longer a help and we had to use our hands to push and pull it into place. Embedded in the muck were plenty of broken, sharp-edged shells and blood soon mixed with the mud.

Above the noise Jock yelled 'when ye see anither shackle, ye'll ken there's only aboot ten mair fathoms to stow!' 'How d'you tell?' I shouted. 'There's so much mud you don't know if it's links or shackles!'

There is a shackle at every fifteen fathoms of anchor chain and a Skipper will instruct from the bridge that, according to soundings, so many shackles will be let go when the anchor is dropped. Of the last fifteen, when the anchor is home, some five reach from the anchor at the hawse hole, up over the deck to the windlass gypsy and down the pipe to the locker. I hadn't been conscious of having seen any shackles as I stumbled and fought with the filthy thing but the shackles are marked and Jock spotted that the first one out would soon be back aboard. Those last few fathoms were the hardest of all for we had to lift the links into place. By the time we heard the windlass stop and there was a welcome shout of 'That'll do below!' there was just room for us to crawl to the ladder, we were mud from head to foot and I felt about done.

Jock grumbled, "Tis a cryin' shame that we have to tak all this aboard as weel. There should be a mon wi' a hose oer the bow tae clean it off, but 'tis short handed we are.'

Each time the ship got to Wellington, all hands would go ashore as soon as she docked and that would be the last we saw of them till we were ready for sea. Some might come aboard before we left the oil port at Evans Bay if they had run out of money, but usually we had to go out to an anchorage and wait while the police collected the remainder and brought them out to us. They would all be more or less drunk and it would be hoped that there would be someone sober enough to steer, but the Mate would not have an intoxicated man to stow the cable. I didn't know of this then and I stood by on the focsle head as we moved a mile or so out into the main harbour. The bos'n said to me, 'We'll have to wait for a bit till the police launch brings out the rest of the crew.' As the anchor splashed down and the chain roared out, I thought, 'Dear Lord. Chain locker duty again!'

After the second passage across and across the Pacific, I had the job of stowing the chain on my own. I didn't drink much in those days anyway and in order to qualify for an officer's ticket I had to have a clean discharge when I eventually left the ship so I was usually the only really sober one of the crew.

With experience, I found that I could get the chain over

10

my shoulders and let it with its filthy lubrication slide over my back as I trod the links and I could heave it into place. Fortunately I was a fairly powerful 22-year-old. My special chain locker suit of tough dungarees hung inside its door. These were so caked with mud that I could stand the trousers up and step into them and I banged the jacket against the focsle head ladder to make it pliable enough for me to wriggle into it. It was not worth while to wash them.

That job in the chain locker was always hard and dangerous and I feelingly cursed my drunken shipmates that I should be left to perform this task on my own, but I would not let myself voice a complaint. I had made up my mind that in this life at sea I would take the bad with the good and no one was going to break my spirit.

Once, when I went below to this horrible job, I found a stowaway in the locker. He was a young American who had somehow got stranded in Wellington and he was taking this way back to the U.S.A. He had come aboard with the shore gang and had hidden under the focsle head where there were plenty of dark corners in which to conceal himself. After we had gained the anchorage he had got into the locker, thinking in his ignorance of ships that this was a safe hiding place. I was horrified to think what a mess there would have been if he had gone there before we had dropped the anchor. I could imagine how that heavy chain would smash a man to pulp as it writhed and snaked its way out of its stowage.

This was a shaker to start and I roughly ordered him up the ladder and to report himself. As I slipped and staggered around in that hell-hole I could not help thinking what a shambles it could have been. The thought nauseated me. The chain was heavier than ever, the mud stickier, the shells sharper and my temper shorter. When all was stowed I came up and reported to the Mate as usual.

'All right,' he said. 'Now be as quick as you can. Slip aft and change and then up on to the bridge and take the wheel. There's no A.B. aboard who's sober enough.'

I liked that Mate. He was a big kindly soul who knew that

11

I was serving my time 'before the stick' and he was helpful to me, but this was too much.

'Look at me!' I cried. 'Look at the bloody mess I'm in!' I held out my hands. The knuckles were raw and the palms cut by the broken shells and they were covered with a mixture of blood and mud.

'I'm up to my eyes in shit and you can't even get a hose up to wash at least some of it off before it goes over the fucking windlass!' I glared at the bos'n. '*You* could have done that!' I yelled. 'Instead of standing there picking your arse. I can struggle down there and risk my limbs and you all think that's grand. Frank won't grouse. Well, this is Frank doing a real grouse!' and I stamped off the focsle head and went aft.

I washed and changed and then took over the wheel from the Third Mate. I was seething with rage and a sense of injustice and my feelings weren't helped much by having to spend almost four hours there instead of the usual two before one of the A.B.s surfaced.

Nothing more was said by or to me but the next time we were in Wellington the Mate told me before he sent me down to the chain locker once more that I had been uprated to 'seaman' which meant that I had full A.B.'s pay. The Bos'n was standing by with a hose to wash down the cable.

It was no good to grumble at my shipmates. I didn't blame them for their understandable desire to get away from the ship when they could and it wasn't only the 'common sailors' and the firemen who went off on a binge. One sunset at evening in Wellington, I was making myself a cup of coffee in the galley of the almost deserted ship. One of the Mates looked in at the door, blinked at me with bleary eyes and said, 'Sorry to ask you, and I know that you won't repeat it, but, is that sunset, or sunrise?'

The Scottish Chief Engineer came aboard the morning of one sailing day and he was drunk and dazed into the bargain. He clearly wasn't sure of what he was doing and he blundered about the decks and took erratic walks along the dock before we left. It turned out that he had got into a brawl somewhere

12

ashore and he'd taken a hefty bang on the head that hadn't done him any good.

We'd been at sea barely a couple of days when the Skipper ordered the Second Engineer to take over and he assigned someone to keep an eye on the Chief who had developed suicidal tendencies. His razors were taken away and the Carpenter, who also hailed from the Clyde, was told to keep him company during the day. One of us seamen who were on watch and watch anyway (four hours on, four hours off), shared time in shadowing him if he left his room. He sometimes eluded this guard and was once discovered down the tunnel of the propeller shaft with a two-pound hammer in his hand. He confided to the colleague who found him that there was someone down there who was trying to wreck the ship. Could he have some help to find the sod?

It was a distressing duty to keep an eye on him for he'd come along and mumble to us that he was a hopeless failure and no good to anyone or to himself and he would take an opportunity to jump over the side. He said as much to me one evening. I thought that everyone was giving him too much sympathy and it wasn't doing him any good, so I said, 'There's the rail old chap. You just jump over. I won't look.' He muttered something about lacking courage and he wandered off and shut himself in his room.

There must have been some pressure on his brain as the result of the blow he'd had for this was a complete change in the nature of the man. I thought that if everyone had treated him carelessly instead of watching his every movement, and making it obvious, we could have got him to 'Frisco and to a hospital. Almost all hands fussed over him and Chips would hardly let him out of his sight.

One night, when there were only four days to go to make our port, one of the seamen was sick. He could not leave his bunk and the others of the watch were either on look-out or at the wheel, so the Carpenter was walking the deck outside the Chief's cabin. Mac put his head out of his door and asked Chips if he would go to the galley and make him some coffee.

13

Filled with commiseration for his patient, Chips fussed off. He returned with the steaming mug to find that the Chief was not in his room. Chips looked in the Mess room and in all the lavatories and he shouted below to the Engineer on duty to ask if he had seen the missing man. He looked around everywhere that he thought that the Chief might be and he spent some ten minutes on this. He even came up to see me on look-out to ask if the Chief had come up to visit me for a yarn. Then he reported to the Skipper and a general search was on.

We got no sight of him but we did find that the fall of the wireless aerial was no longer coiled on its belaying pin at the port quarter but was trailing in the water overside and scratches on the paint there showed where a man's shoes could have scraped. We could only conclude that he had lowered himself over the rail to the water and had let go. I doubted if any man could have held on for long against the drag caused by the ship steaming at eleven knots.

A quick conference of officers decided that there was no point in putting the ship about. It was a pitch dark, heavily overcast and windy night and it would have been impossible to have seen a man in the sea. There was little, if any, doubt that from the position he had gone over that he would not have been drowned but that he would have been killed by the propellor. As we were light in ballast, the screw was not fully below the surface. Some twenty minutes had elapsed since he had been missed and it was agreed that there was no hope of finding him alive so the tanker steamed on.

The crew were mostly Cornishmen but there was one Irishman and the rest were from the Hebrides. They were a superstitious lot and all declared that the ship was cursed. Fears of the occult were added to the general depression. Some said that the ship and all her crew were doomed and none laughed at their fears. However, these things were set aside in the general activity of the arrival in San Luis Obispo and in getting aboard the huge hoses to load our cargo. Twenty-four hours later we were at sea again but less two

14

hands who had skipped the ship to avoid what they were sure was its terrible fate.

Crude oil has to be warmed up to make it fluid enough to pump and the ship left port with the oil still warm and thin and she rolled heavily in the long Pacific swell. We left late in the afternoon and Fred, the little Cornishman who went on look-out at sunset, hadn't been there very long before he clattered down the ladder from the focsle head. He ran along the deck and climbed the ladders to the bridge. The officer of the watch asked, 'What are you doing here?'

Fred was trembling and pale with fright. 'I c-can't stay forrard Zur. I'll k-keep l-ll-ookout 'ere. The Chief's up thurr . . . an' -an' 'e's tryin to-to t-t-tell me summat.'

The man was plainly scared stiff and the Mate reported the matter to the Skipper who came on to the bridge and he sent the Mate for'ard to see if he could find any explanation for Fred's terror. He returned to report that he could neither see nor hear anything unusual. They let the Cornishman keep his look-out from the bridge and said no more. I was the next man on look-out and I stood right forward against the rails and let the warm wind blow in my hair. I heard nothing weird and no ghostly form tapped me on the shoulder.

Nothing further occurred and look-outs were kept as usual except that Fred steadfastly refused to go on the focsle head after dark. His very genuine fear was respected and he continued to keep his look-out from the wing of the bridge. The oil cooled and became semi-solid and the ship steamed steadily on through the calm ocean.

Four or five days passed thus and then one evening we ran into a bit of a blow and the ship rolled from the wind on her beam. In the middle watch Mackinnon from Skye ran from the look-out and came on to the bridge to stutter that there was someone trying to talk to him on the focsle head and nothing would make him stay there. He also would keep his look-out from the bridge.

It was my watch on deck at 4 a.m. and my look-out. I started to walk along the foredeck and the second Mate

15

called to me from the bridge.

'Mackinnon's up here. Come and relieve him!'

The Second Mate and I were quite friendly. He was about my own age and we would practise semaphore signalling together when opportunity offered and he helped me to learn something of a sailor's business. I went up to the bridge, and when Mackinnon had gone, he said to me.

'See if you can find what is causing this upset, Frank. There must be some explanation.'

'Sure,' I answered. 'I'll see if I can lay the ghost,' and I went forward.

The ship was rolling quite moderately and I paced the deck from right forward to the after rail on the weather side. I heard nothing. I walked along the lee side and I paused by the windlass. I froze, and the hairs on the back of my neck stood on end. At least it felt as if they did. It felt as if *all* my hair was standing on end. Someone was talking in a hoarse whisper! I took a moment to collect my thoughts. Another stowaway perhaps? I ran down the ladder to the foredeck and I walked into the space under the focsle head. It was all as dark as the inside of a cow but I knew what was there. The bos'n's locker was on the starboard side, the pig-pen to port. Forward were the doors to the hateful chain lockers. I stood quite still and listened. There was no sound save the usual creaks and cracks of a ship in a seaway. I opened the doors of the chain lockers. I shouted 'Anyone there?' there was no movement and no sound save the banging of the chain against its downpipe as the ship rolled.

I went back up on to the focsle head and walked forward. I could hear nothing. I came back to the after rail and I could hear a faint whispering. I could not distinguish words but there was no mistaking the sound. I went to the position near the windlass on the lee side where I had heard it before and here the sound was clearer but I still could not make out any words. My skin crept. I knew that I could easily imagine words but I simply had to find the source of the sounds. I moved about and I found that, the nearer I was to the gypsy,

16

the clearer was the sound. It was an indistinct asthmatic whisper.

I put my hand on the chain where it went down the pipe to that foul locker and I *felt* it!

As the ship rolled the rusty links moved against each other to make this harsh sound. Rub two pieces of rough iron together and you will hear what we heard. Add to it unhappiness and superstitious fears and you will have a haunting.

I went below and got from the bos'n's locker a length of old rope. I brought it up and hitched it round the port and across to the starboard chain, hauled the parts together and lashed them securely to stop them swaying about. The whispering ceased. I went along the foredeck and climbed up to the bridge and reported 'I've found the ghost and I've bound him hands and feet.'

Sally and I wrote regularly and nothing altered the fact that we were very much in love. I used to dream dreams in the night watches on look-out over the moonlit Pacific but I was filled with doubts. I didn't really want her way of life and I doubted if she would be really happy with restless me.

My friend the Second Mate had served his time in a square-rigged ship, the four masted barque *Elginshire*, and he told me much of the life on those grand ships. 'Obviously', he said, 'you don't mean to spend your life before the mast and when you've done your four years at sea, you'll want to sit for your ticket. Do at least a year in sail. Then you will qualify for a square-rig certificate which will give you an advantage when you apply for a job on the bridge. Shipowners are conservative types and many of them are old men who regret the passing of the sailing ships and they believe that they bred better sailors. You'll find that the men on those ships are different. They have more skills, as in the many kinds of splicing they have to do in both hemp and wire ropes; how to make different kinds of chafing gear; how to handle sails and to use a palm and needle, and there are so

17

many things they have to know and which you can learn but you'll not learn them on steamers. The strength of their muscles is the only power available and they work together well for they must depend on each other for their personal safety as well as the working of the ship.'

Here were yet more reasons to make a voyage in sail but sailing ships weren't coming to New Zealand ports any more. I had been ten months in *Orowaiti* and I felt that I should be better away from her and her wretched chain locker. I could take a passage to Melbourne and try there. In those days there were about twenty square-riggers under the British flag and they all came to Melbourne sooner or later. The next time in Wellington I signed off the tanker and booked myself a passage.

Two days before I sailed I saw Sally . . . and all my ideas went by the board. I wanted to be with her all my life under any conditions. She wanted to be with me. Our understanding was so perfect that no ordinary things or circumstances could spoil it for ever and ever. She didn't want me to go away again. I didn't want to go away. Her parents didn't want me to go.

They were taking her to England the following Spring to see the Empire Exhibition at Wembley. I could go with them. When I went to bed that night I had almost accepted but my independence was dying hard. When I had twisted and turned for an hour or more, all the old arguments came crowding back. I wrangled with myself.

'Huh. You'll be a 'yes' man.'

'No! She's not like that. Not that kind of a person.'

'Isn't she? Do you want to be a nonentity, a nothing man, a hanger-on, a kept man?'

'I won't be . . . I'll be very happy.'

'Will you?'

'Of course I will.'

'Oh . . . will you?'

I got up and walked the floor with a devil at my elbow. Finally I slept.

I awoke with a solution. I'd go to Wembley but I'd go under my own steam. I'd see Sally in England. I didn't know how but I'd get there by next Spring. Then we'd really know. It would give us each a chance.

I thought of writing a note to this effect and of slipping off without seeing Sally but I didn't think that that would be very courageous. I called and saw her that afternoon. Several times I wished that I'd written that note and that I didn't have such high falutin' ideas. All the time I hated myself.

I sailed that night.

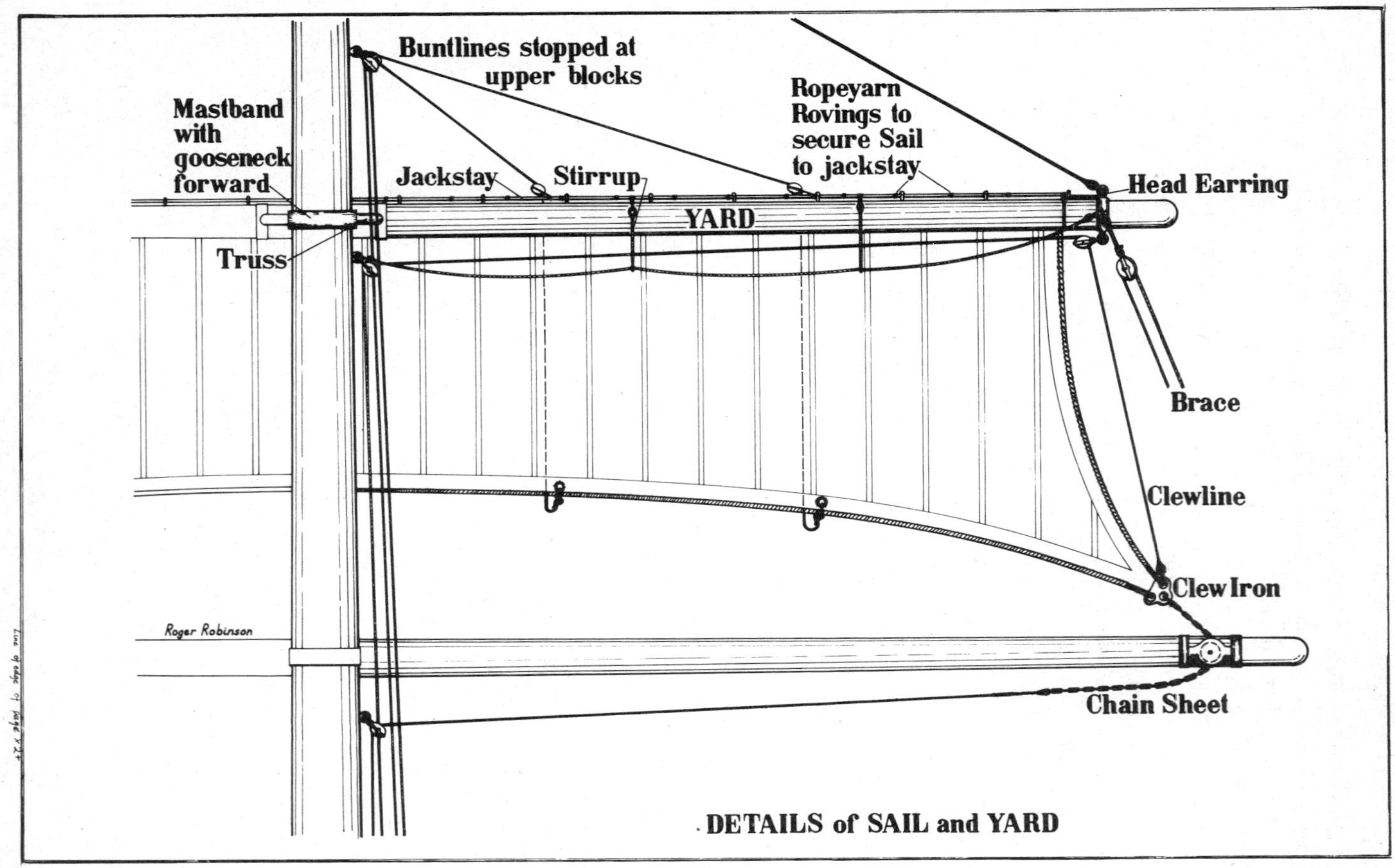

DETAILS of SAIL and YARD

Labels on diagram:
- Head Earring
- Brace
- Clewline
- Clew Iron
- Chain Sheet
- Ropeyarn Rovings to secure Sail to jackstay
- Buntlines stopped at upper blocks
- YARD
- Stirrup
- Jackstay
- Mastband with gooseneck forward
- Truss
- Roger Robinson

Line of edge of page x 2*

CHAPTER III   WILLIAM MITCHELL

Five days later the rising sun was breaking through the mists on the River Yarra as the *Moeraki* slowly steamed into the basin. Through the haze to starboard loomed the tall masts and spreading yards of a full-rigged ship. The uncertain light mellowed her scarred appearance and lent a picturesqueness to her rusty paintwork and grimy rigging. The early sun filtered through and rosily tinted her lofty spars that towered vaguely. I thought, 'There's my next ship.'

Later, I was to know the beauty of those spars straining to their full-bellied sails before a roaring westerly, or swaying gently across a velvet sky in the peace of a Tropic night, and at times, soaked, cold, and hungry, I was to wonder blasphemously how ever I could have seen Romance depicted there. But, on that winter morning in the beginning of June 1924, she represented to me the realisation of boyhood dreams. To serve in her would satisfy a deep and oft-repressed longing.

When as one of a long queue I got through a perfunctory examination by Customs, I went and deposited my sea chest at the Sailors' Home and made my way at once to *William Mitchell*.

Imagine my intense disappointment when, having presented

21

myself and offered my services as seaman, the Mate told me that in all probability the ship would sail no more but she would be sold and the crew paid off. In fact, some of the crew had already been discharged. He gave me some hope by taking my name and address and he said that he would let me know if the ship secured a charter. He looked me up and down with cold appraisal.

'You've a useful looking pair of shoulders . . . . should be able to pull your weight.'

Thereafter I paid a daily visit to the ship and I clung to the feeble hope that she might get a charter. Always I received a discouraging reply. Each day I strode along the wharves and thought that surely today there will be news. Each day I crept back disheartened to my cubicle in the Sailors' Home. Each day my stock of shillings dwindled and I dared not think of the time when they must disappear.

The days went by and I looked half-heartedly for other jobs, just in case, but my hopes were centred in the old wind-jammer. There was a year in which to reach England. Plenty of time to be there in time to meet Sally.

My attempts to find other employment were unsuccessful though I was nearly unfortunate enough to be signed on a small ill-found schooner. I was sitting on a bollard to which one of the vessel's shore lines was secured and I was thinking that in spite of her lack of paint and her general air of dis-repair, her bows were well shaped and she had a nice clean entrance. A big roughly-clad man nudged me and said, ''Arf a mo' mate,' and he stooped and picked up the eye of the mooring rope. As I rose he lifted it clear and asked me to give him a pull. He was moving the schooner a few yards along the dock and I lent my weight to heave her along. I judged him to be the Skipper or the Mate of her and I asked him if he wanted any hands.

'I dunno,' he answered. 'Come along an' ask me agen in a couple o' days.'

'Where do you go?' I enquired.

He raised his eyebrows at that as if it were strange either

that a prospective focsle hand should ask, or that there was anyone who would not know, but he answered a little surlily, 'Across ter Tasmania . . . . an' back.'

I took more interest in the little ship and I looked over her rail. Her decks looked as if they were never even washed down, much less scrubbed or holystoned. A raffle of ropes' ends and dirt cluttered her scuppers. A bleary-eyed sailor was seated on an upturned bucket in the bows as he clumsily tucked an eye-splice in the staysail halliard and, as he raised his eyes and looked in my direction, I didn't feel that I wanted him for a shipmate, especially in so small a vessel.

My thoughts went back to the big square-rigger. I would sit and gaze at her from across the river and try to picture her with all her sails set, close-hauled in the Trade winds, or under lower topsails, running before the wild westerlies of the Cape Horn road.

As she lay there she was not particularly beautiful. She had come out from Fredrikstadt in Norway with a cargo of dressed timber but this was almost all discharged and she stood high out of the water. Her sides were rusty and dirty with the grime of port, and her paint was the more obvious by its absence. But aloft she was as graceful as ever. She was a tall ship and at one time she had been even loftier when she had crossed three skysail yards. From what I saw on my daily visits, the decks were dirty and muddled. Coal dust and soot from nearby steamers blackened her bulwarks and clung in her coiled-up rigging. The deck was unwashed and littered with cargo gear and dunnage. The grubby finger marks of stevedores soiled the white paint of deckhouse bulkheads and generally she presented a somewhat sorry spectacle but beneath all this I could see the ship at sea . . . clean and free.

I felt that a sailing ship is out of her element in a crowded port. She is not at home in its smoky fuss and bustle. Her true place is the open wind-swept ocean where the air is clean and pure and the strife of commerce is resolved to a battle with the elements. Where, together with the good strong winds, the sea and the wide heavens she tends to bring out

23

the best in her men.

Three weeks had gone by and I had already paid a dozen disappointing visits to the ship. Hope had got pretty low. Because I felt that I would receive only the usual negative reply, I kept away from the waterfront that day. Next day, with but two shillings in my pocket, it had to be now or never. So, down to the wharves I went and up the gangway with the thought that I was going through the same business again. I knew that it was useless and I wondered what on earth I was going to do. Prospects were poor indeed. Perhaps I would have to go on that dreary little schooner after all.

The Mate was standing at the break of the poop with feet apart and hands on hips, his head thrown back as he watched an apprentice doing something aloft. As I spoke he turned quickly. 'Why the devil didn't you come along yesterday?' he shouted.

'Why?' I stammered, bewildered by this sudden change of front.

'Didn't you get my postcard?' he asked.

I had received no postcard and I told him so while my heart sank with the fear that it was now all too late.

Some pointed and picturesque remarks hurled up into the rigging and answered by an embarrassed apprentice revealed that the lad had failed to post the card. Fortunately the vacancy had not been filled in the meantime and saying, 'See Captain Wilkie there,' he referred me to a slightly-built man who leaned on the poop ladder by my side.

The Skipper's youth surprised me for he was then under thirty and I had expected an Ancient Mariner. He asked me a few questions about my experience and could I steer and tuck a splice and use a palm and needle. I was able to answer satisfactorily and he gave me the job. I left the ship walking on air. Joyfully I went to arrange about getting my gear on board.

In my youth and enthusiasm I was thrilled no end! At last I was to be a real sailorman and to know what 'running the easting down' really meant. A quite new life was opening before me. A really full-blooded life with men who, when in port, drank deeply and fought and loved in violent manner maybe, but I also knew that they had a deep-rooted sense of right and wrong and that they had their own traditions of the sea.

To them nothing appeared sacred but their friendship was priceless for it never failed. To the outer world these men were 'common sailors' with neither morals nor honesty but among themselves they did not disguise their contempt of the man who locked his sea chest. I was to live and work and have my being among them; to know what it meant to toil and sweat and strain; to freeze and be drenched and go hungry; to exist for months on salt provisions; and I was going to like it.

Late that afternoon I lavished both my last shillings on the owner of a small handcart who put my sea-chest and bag aboard. With mixed feelings I came over the side, made my way forward and stepped into the focsle. Would I fit into this life? I was very conscious that my speech and ways were different and I wanted to be accepted and be part of the life of the ship. My manner had not caused any serious friction with steamboatmen and I was more than ready to adjust myself.

Most of the men were out on deck at work though someone snored drunkenly from a bunk. An old man with a thatch of white hair and a moustache like a paint brush was busily clattering a collection of enamel mugs about on the table and arranging them in some obscure order. There was an upper bunk unoccupied with the advantage of a port over it to give both light and air and I asked the old man if it had been claimed. He said 'Nah. Grab it.' so I dumped my kit on it, shoved my sea-chest under the lower bunk and looked about me.

I was in a nearly square deckhouse which stood just aft of the foremast with the galley at its after end separated by a steel bulkhead to which were fixed a row of hooks from which clothes hung. I learned later the value of those hooks

25

for behind the wall was the galley stove which kept it warm. Wet clothes would dry there. Also, the chill was taken out of our quarters in cold weather for there was no other means of heating the place. Two tiers of bunks were round the other three sides and a table and benches stood in the middle. Steel half-doors, as in a stable, led on to the deck at either side over high steps.

The old fellow looked up from his occupation of pouring tea from a large coffee pot and he peered at me from under his bushy brows.

'Arfur 'Ill's me name. Fish aht yer mug an' 'ave some tea,' he invited in fruity Cockney.

'My name's Brookesmith,' I said. 'But call me Frank.'

'Frank'll do me,' he answered. 'I carn't remember the ovver,' and he filled my mug with strong black tea.

Now work was over for the day and my new shipmates filed in. Tired and dusty dungaree-clad figures took their particular mugs from the assortment while old Arfur brought in a steaming kid of stew.

'My name's Frank,' I introduced myself.

The statement was greeted with a few nods and grunts and voices of varying accents said John, Paddy, Bill, Bert, etc., which I failed to associate with faces at the time. I knew that only time would tell if I were accepted. It was up to me.

I took the proffered seat at the corner of the table and I ate my meal with the rest. There was little or no conversation. Eating was far too important an occupation to be interrupted by small talk. Opposite me sat a tall Swede who, when he had finished his meal, asked 'You bin in these sailing ships before?'

I said, 'No. Only in steamships, so I've much to learn. I know the ropes but I don't know where they are on deck.'

'Come vit' me,' he said and we rose and I followed him out.

Thus my first evening on board was spent in being instructed in the function and position of the endless collection of ropes. I knew the name of every sail and rope and of their function aloft. I had known them since I was that boy at school but where the ropes came down on deck for us all to haul on was something I had to learn. The formidable array sapped some of my confidence but my new-found friend was very helpful.

Most illustrations of square-rigged ships give the impression of acres of billowing canvas and little is shown of the many ropes with which to work these sails. As I walked along the deck I passed fathoms of rope of all sizes. These hung in coils by the standing rigging and at the 'fife rails' at the foot of the masts, where ropes were secured to belaying pins thrust into holes in this heavy teak rail — fixed at waist height to strong posts set into the deck. A cascade of more ropes hung down the masts and rigging, and aloft they made an intricate network.

The standing rigging which supported the masts, alone ran into miles with its swifters, shrouds, backstays and its many forestays and these I knew. It was the location on deck of the running rigging for setting and stowing the sails that I needed to discover. There were the sheets, to hold the lower corners of the sails to the yards; halliards (originally haul yards) to heave the yards aloft to set the sails; clewlines to lift up the clews at the lower corners of the sails when they were taken in; buntlines to bring up the bunt, or middle of the sails, up to the yards; leechlines to pull in the leech or side of the sail; downhauls to haul down the fore and aft sails and brails to bring them into the mast or stay. There were the many braces which led to the ends of the yards and which were used to pull the yards round to the required angle and so to trim them and their sails to the wind.

Although there was much to remember, I found that it was really quite simple. Ropes for the lowest sails came down the forward shroud in a fixed order. Those for the next sails up the mast came down the next shroud in the same order and so on. Clewlines and topgallant and royal sheets came down to the fiferails. I learned where sheets and halliards were belayed and generally I made myself conversant with the

27

positions of all the hauling lines. Another step forward was being made in my education as a square-rig sailor.

I was preparing my bunk for the night by installing a skimpy mattress and by putting in it a feather pillow which some good friends in Melbourne had given me and for which I became so very grateful that it stayed with me for all my years before the mast. Another of my shipmates lurched through the doorway. He suffered quite happily from an insatiable thirst for he had sold almost all his clothes for beer and he was dressed in only a singlet under his dungaree jacket and trousers. He had no hat and he wore a pair of self-made rope-soled slippers on his feet. Even his blankets had been sold to buy drink and the only thing left in his bunk was his 'donkey's breakfast', a long bag of hessian stuffed with straw. He cut an extraordinary figure and although as drunk as any man could be while still able to remain upright, he was in the best of spirits. He drew his sheath knife, without which no sailing ship sailor is complete and an ancient coarse proverb emphasises this. He slit open one end of the bag and as he wriggled down into the straw he said cheerfully, 'If the Lord knew of anything better than beer, He kept it to Himself.' A few seconds later he was peacefully snoring.

I lay awake thinking of the months to come. Men drifted in by twos and threes and were soon in their bunks. The last to arrive were old Arfur and a wizened little old Welshman who was his particular chum and who occupied a bunk above the Cockney. From the chorus of snores I thought that everyone was asleep and I was just dozing off when there was a yell from Arfur.

'Gawd bleedin' blimey! Yer dirty ole barstard. Yer've pissed yerself an' it's orl comin' dahn on me!'

Tatty leaned over the side of his bunk and said calmly, 'Indeed then, what are 'oo making such a fuss about? 'Twill make 'oo smell like a MAN!'

28

CHAPTER IV   INITIATION

Next morning I was told that I would be in the First Mate's or starboard watch and I was sent down the main hatch to work at the bottom of the ship. To compensate for her comparatively light cargo of planks, tons of broken iron railway chairs has been stowed in the spaces between the floors. Scrap iron had a good market in Melbourne and our job now was to remove these by hand and to put them into huge baskets which the cargo gear swung out of the hatch and ashore. I well remember the bitterly cold and clammy feel of those chunks of iron. They were coated with rust, slimy from the filthy bilge water and icy to handle. They had been put there when the fjord alongside had been frozen and it seemed to me that they had retained that Arctic cold. My hands had grown soft from the inaction of the past weeks and they were so little used to such rough work. They soon became seared and raw. After an hour it was agony to scrabble at those jagged pieces jammed in the frames and to claw with stinging hands at their foul chilliness. No Romance there!

After two days of this misery we had got the iron out of the space under the hatch amidships and we started to load ballast to take us round to Newcastle, New South Wales. There we were to take on a cargo of coal for Iquique in Chile.

The first thing to be done was to rig shifting boards fore and aft and athwartships and to build them into the form of a great box amidships to contain the ballast. This 'stiffening' as it is called is very necessary on a large sailing ship because of the great weight of the masts and spars. Without several hundred tons in the hold the vessel is quite unstable. This ballast was composed of some of the refuse of Melbourne. It was largely building rubble but it contained a generous quota of odds and ends of pots and pans and ancient tins. A great deal of it was wet and sloppy and the remainder was just earth. After tons of it had been hoisted aboard we had another day of horror when we got the last of that revolting iron from the bilges under the fore and the after hatches. Then we were given shovels and sent down the main hatch to trim the mucky ballast . . . and Romance received another jolt.

Was this the work for which I waited so long? In my dreams I had seldom if ever thought of below-decks. I had pictured myself swinging aloft on those dizzy spars before a mighty wind, standing at the wheel to steer, or hauling on ropes while the oldest sailor sang a rousing chanty. Still, obviously a ship has to be got ready for sea and there was nothing I could do but get on with the job in hand and be patient. The Third Mate was shovelling with the rest and working beside me was an apprentice lately from the *Worcester* training ship. Why should I grumble? I should not have been human if I had not thought with some regret of the comfort I had forsaken for an idea.

A few days later our work in the hold was complete and we bent all sails except the royals. Now I was working aloft and the ship took on a new meaning. I learned to haul out and secure a head earring, a short piece of rope which holds the head of a sail taut along the yard; to pass the intermediate rovings which tied the head of the sail to the jackstay on the yard; to shackle chain sheets to clew irons; to pass the buntlines and leechlines through bull's eyes on the fore part of the sail and to make them secure to the foot or the leech

30

with a backing hitch. Then to furl the sails in a neat 'harbour stow'. The uncongenial work of the past few days was forgotten. Soon we would be putting to sea!

A new main royal backstay was fitted and I learned from the A.B.s who did the job that *William Mitchell*'s mainmast was 150 feet from deck to truck. Further, her main yard was 98 feet long, hung 65 feet from the deck and it weighed three tons. She had been built in Londonderry and launched in 1891 which date was impressed on a heavy brass plate on her capstan head. I found recently from the National Maritime Museum, that her length was 273 feet, her beam 41 feet and that she drew 23 feet when loaded and this gave her a freeboard amidships of only five feet. I was amused to read in the information that they sent me that '... she was always noted among seamen as a workhouse.' Who among those who had sailed in her and handled her heavy gear could doubt it?

A tug took us clear of the Yarra and we lay at anchor off Williamstown overnight but a week was yet to pass before we got through Port Phillip Heads. We were due to start out to sea at dawn the next morning but the winds were light and variable. Though we sailed twenty miles towards the Heads that day we were still a long way from the open sea. Three times we made the attempt and three times we set all sail to a fair wind only to get a couple of miles on our way and to have the wind fail or draw ahead. Each time we dropped anchor and fathoms of chain. Each time we trudged round the capstan to heave it all in again. The strength of our limbs and backs was the only power available on the ship. There were no other aids.

'Man the Capstan!' shouted the Mate. Long heavy capstan bars were taken from their stowage, thrust into their sockets in the capstan head, on the focsle deck and we leaned hard against the bars. Once round hove a bare six inches, or half a link aboard, and there could be fifty fathoms to take in.

'Come on,' we called to each other, 'Dig your toes in!' as we walked what seemed miles round and round, heaved at the bars with straining backs, brought the anchor into sight,

31

shackled on the heavy three-fold tackle from the crane and hoisted the 'mud hook' to hang it off at the cathead ready to be dropped. To a succession of orders we hauled on halliards, sheets and braces, sweated and pulled and pulled again only to have to undo it all.

Within the hour we heard the anchor splash and the cable we had striven so hard to bring aboard, go rattling out again. We slacked off sheets, let go halliards, and as yards came down we hauled on clewlines, buntlines, and leechlines, went aloft to stow the heavy sails, came down to the deck to square the yards and to coil down all the ropes ready for running.

For me it was an exhausting but useful education. The recurring sail-drill taught me by actual practice the position of every rope on the ship. It was not long before I could lay my hands on whichever rope that was required without more than a moment's thought.

For three days we lay a bare mile within the harbour entrance. Although the breeze was favourable for sailing out, it was dead ahead for our purpose of getting to Newcastle. Doubtless the Skipper decided that we were more usefully occupied quietly at anchor, than in tacking to and fro in Bass Strait and wearing out our gear to no advantage.

One of the apprentices caught a small shark while the ship lay here and he opened it to see if its stomach contained any strange article — for these creatures have a catholic taste and have been known to have all sorts of things in their tummies. In this one we found nothing more interesting than a partly digested fish. Further incisions discovered several young sharks and the parent must have been very near her time for these were quite lively. We put them in a tub of seawater and they swam around and each dragged after it by a short umbilical cord an object identical in size, colour, and appearance, to the yolk of a hen's egg.

On the fourth day the Pilot came alongside and called to the Skipper that he would take us to sea. The Captain agreed though no-one thought that the wind had altered its direction. Nevertheless once more we prepared for sea. Big John, the

32

Swede, said that 'de pilot vas fed oop vit' seein' us layin' dere an' 'e tink 'e send us avay to sea.' We hove round and round the capstan as the chain rasped through the hawse holes, hauled and pulled at the many ropes to set sail and get under way.

We sailed through the narrow entrance of Port Phillip Bay on a beautiful clear evening, close-hauled to a light easterly wind. It was quite dark when we backed the main yard and dropped the pilot.

For the next six days we sailed across and across Bass Strait. Now we went about near King Islands off the coast of Tasmania, and again we sighted Port Phillip Heads before we went about on the next tack. The sailors called it 'darning the water'.

At eight bells of every other watch, the Mate would call, 'All hands wear ship!'

Time after we laid hold of braces, tacks, and sheets, brought her about before the wind, and lost all the advantage we had gained. *William Mitchell* had the reputation that she could not be tacked satisfactorily, that is, brought about into the wind. Wearing ship involves turning the ship's head 'down' or 'before' the wind. When beating to windward a considerable part of the ground gained may be lost by this manoeuvre. This was particularly true of those square-rigged ships, for they would never lay closer to the wind than six points and the course made good would not usually be better than a point to windward because of the leeway they made and the lighter the wind the greater the leeway.

Rightly or wrongly, I could never accept that she could not be tacked. She was a very manageable ship and later, when I had spent more time at the wheel, I thought that I would have liked to have had a try at bringing her about into the wind. It may not have been successful in a light wind but I always felt that she could have been tacked in anything of a breeze. My little vanity perhaps?

It was all new and interesting to me and I took to it like a duck to water but at the same time it was disappointing that

33

day after day all this effort was being expended to no purpose. The Skipper paced the poop deck and his frowning face expressed disgust. Some of the hands grumbled at the lack of progress. Others said, 'Wot the 'ell. More days, more dollars.'

Because all things, good or bad, come to an end sooner or later, on the sixth evening, at sunset the longed-for wind came with a will. All that day it had been almost completely calm with only faint airs from the west. All hands were more cheerful that the yards were square and at the thought that all this beating to and fro could be coming to an end. As evening fell we were gradually stealing out of the Strait with the help of the tide. The breeze was scarcely enough to keep the sails 'asleep'. To port, five miles away, was Wilson's Promontory, the southernmost point of the continent, and as we looked there we could see a white line of broken seas before wind-darkened water. Before it reached us we could hear the rush of the gale. It hit the ship with a WHOOSH! Before anything could be done it filled the sails and light in ballast as we were, she laid hard over to the pressure. Then she leaped ahead like a startled animal.

Brisk orders were yelled from the poop but they were lost to my ears. Everyone was suddenly active. Paddy yelled to me to stand by the fore t'gallant halliards and I dashed for'ard, fumbling in my mind for the position of the gear. I slid across the deck with heel of the ship and fetched up right by it. I threw turns of the rope off its belaying pin and the Mate who was running along the deck, shouted, 'Lower the yard!' I started to ease the rope round the pin. He shouldered me aside and flung the turn off the pin and the yard came down with a run.

'Clap on to the buntlines!' he roared and he thrust the ropes into my hands. Taking clewlines, buntlines and leech-lines together, we pulled and hauled with a will and the t'ga'nts'ls were soon up in their gear. It was getting dark as we ran aloft to furl them.

I was beside Big John at the weather yardarm and it was fine and exhilarating up there with the roaring wind. John

34

picked up the heavy sail as if it were a pocket handkerchief and I helped him to smother it. I passed the gaskets for him as he rolled up the canvas and banged it into a neat stow with his forearm and together we made the sail fast. It was not till later in the voyage when I had to stow the sail with an ordinary seaman to help me that I really appreciated how his great strength and skill had made light of what was a heavy task.

Before descending I paused a moment to take in the scene. Below us were the bellying topsails and the foresail and below them the cleaving bows parted the waves in bright phosphorescence while the last of the daylight caught the jibs and showed clearly their graceful outlines against the dark sea.

The wind held and took us along in fine style all that night and the next day but during the following night it fell light and gradually drew ahead. Daylight showed us Sydney Heads on the port quarter and we lay close hauled on the port tack to a north wind. We had but seventy miles to go to Newcastle and after this good run, here was the wind foiling us again. It was a beautiful day with a calm sea and a fine breeze for any ship desiring to go the opposite way and we all felt that the Fates were against us that she should be headed off like this. About midday a tug put out from Sydney and steamed towards us. She slowed up on our weather quarter and, after some parleying about price, the *St. Olaves* took us in tow.

Then we had one of the worst jobs in stowing sail that I ever had to experience. Furling sails at sea in a howling gale with the sails wet and hard is difficult and dangerous work and it calls for terrific and sustained effort. The sail is flapping and surging above and ahead of you on the yard and your every effort is exerted to subdue its wild antics. You grasp it where you can or you slam your forearm down on it to make a fold which you can clutch while the wind does it best to make you release your hold. On this job however the sails were quiet enough but they were held flat against the yards and blown out under and abaft them by the pressure of the

35

strong head wind added to the speed of the tug. The foot-ropes, on which a sailor stands when working on the yards, were lost in the folds of the canvas and we had to kick about and find them while the sails fought against us and tried to tangle our feet. Then it was a matter of reaching far out over the yard and grabbing at reef point or bull's eye or anything we could grasp and which, as soon as we took hold, strove to drag us right over the yard. It was perilous work and we managed it with much struggling and profanity. I was work-ing beside the man who had sold all his gear for beer when the Mate yelled up from the deck that we were fumbling 'like a lot of soldiers' and taking a long time about it. To my amusement, my shipmate bawled down at him, 'Aw shut up! Ye're never happy unless ye're shoutin' at someone!'

In spite of the conditions, we put a good harbour stow on the sails for we knew that it would be some weeks before we threw the gaskets off again. Gaskets are lengths of rope which are passed round the yard and the sail to keep it secure when it is furled and which modern yachtsmen will call, deplorably, 'tyers'.

The rest of the passage to Newcastle was uneventful. It was Sunday and we were relieved of the usual tiresome jobs of chipping rust blisters off the steel of bulkheads, deckhouses and ladders, or of washing the grime of port off the paint-work. Some of us leaned at the rail and watched the coast while daylight lasted. Others lay on their bunks and read or caught up on sleep. At the end of a long tow we stole into a sleeping port under a bright moon and anchored in the stream about midnight.

Next day we made fast alongside the dock and the fore and after hatches were opened. A crane lifted a big coal truck off its chassis and swung it over the hatchway. A burly stevedore with a heavy hammer gave one blow to a toggle, the hinged bottom of the truck fell open and twenty-five tons of coal dropped into the hold at one swoop. Ten trucks in the fore, and ten trucks in the after hatch and we were quickly stiffened with part of our cargo against the discharge

36

of our ballast. A diminutive tug towed us across the river to Stockton where we went back to navvies' work, shovelled the rubbish from Melbourne into baskets and dumped it into the river.

Over the next few weeks we painted the ship's sides a light slate colour above the water line and with thin, evil-smelling anti-fouling below. Her appearance was much improved. She carried no figurehead but about the bows there was the outline of some elaborate scrollwork cut into the plates. I was given the job of painting this in from a small stage suspended from the deck railings. I filled it in carefully in white and then I picked out in black and gold the builder's coat of arms on the stemhead. This was a convex shield with a castle and a dagger on its upper quarters and the lower half pictured a skeleton seated on a rock. Rather a grim character to have in the family, I thought as I gilded his ribs. The Skipper took a lot of interest in my work here and he was repeatedly coming along to see how the operation was going. I got the impression that he would have loved to be doing the decoration himself.

Stockton lies opposite Newcastle on a sandy strip of land between the Hunter River and the sea. We spent many of our evenings at the Seamens' Institute there, where the Rev Vickery did much to entertain lonely sailormen by arranging socials and concerts which even the most hardened shellbacks would attend and enjoy. No matter how rough and tough they all enjoyed a good sing-song and 'Onward Christian Soldiers' or 'If you were the Only Girl in the World' were sung with equal gusto.

Mr. Vickery was a man all seamen admired, while many deep-water sailors and apprentices of those days would tell you enthusiastically of the charming young ladies who assisted him in his good work. One little thing endeared him to many, both on ships and in homes far away. He would always have letters sent aboard with the least delay and he encouraged all and sundry to write home. Before we sailed he sent aboard a large box of good books for which we were

37

more than grateful. It was a relief from the austerity of our lives to read Galsworthy and Locke or the adventurous tales by Rafael Sabatini or P.C. Wren.

I had written to Sally from Melbourne and I had a letter from her before we sailed. It was full of thought for my comfort and wellbeing, of fears for my safety and with some gentle and so sweetly worded reproach, but through it all, anticipation of our meeting in London.

I wrote again before we left and I told her something of the life aboard and more of the zest of this life. I told her of how she was always in my thoughts, how I looked forward to being with her in England and of how I felt that, in spite of difficulties, we would have a wonderful life together. With this experience, I would get this salt out of my blood and love meant so much.

A few of the crew were paid off here. I was sorry that the man who had gone to bed in his donkey's breakfast left the ship, for, in spite of his drunkenness in port, he was a fine sailorman and a good shipmate and altogether a different man when at sea. The little Welshman also left. We signed on some who had sailed in a schooner from Wellington. I cannot now remember that vessel's name but she was a good looking American built four-master which had been arrested in Wellington for debt, sold for some paltry sum, and started in the intercolonial trade between New Zealand and Australian ports. I had tried to get a job in her to work my passage over to Australia but when I heard the experiences of those men who joined us from her, I was glad that I had been unsuccessful. Life aboard her had been far from pleasant. The food was poor and badly cooked and she had worked heavily on a bad weather passage. A considerable portion of each watch on deck had been spent at the pumps and I cannot imagine any more back-breaking toil than this. It was truly one of the horrors of a sailor's life.

A young Australian of about my own age and build joined the ship here. I learned later that there was only a fortnight between our birth dates. I was immediately attracted to this

38

man, William Porteous, and we became fast friends. Although he first went to sea as a radio operator, he was, I should think, about the finest British seaman afloat in those days. He was then, like me, twenty-three years of age and he had already made two voyages in deep-water sailing ships. He had 'jumped' the ship *Mount Stewart* because the Skipper, who was a hard man, refused to pay him off in his native country. Doubtless the Skipper knew that Porteous would leave the ship anyway and he'd save the owners the expense. In passing, *Mount Stewart* was a splendid ship, the last of the Australian wool clippers with some very fast passages to her credit. Bill told me much later when he had made many voyages in square-rig, that she was the best ship to steer that he had ever known. Even when running before heavy seas she was as easy to handle and to keep on her course as when close-hauled in the Trades.

Bill Porteous and I remained great pals and the last time I saw him he was home from a voyage to Antarctic seas with Sir Douglas Mawson's expedition, the last voyage of the old *Discovery*. He sailed again in *Discovery II* to meet with a tragic death in the Falkland Islands.

We have clung side by side on a pitching yard to fight a maddened sail; pulled together on icy, sodden ropes; sweated in the Tropics; chilled in the region of Cape Horn; pitted our strength against one another in the many physical contests we had in the dog watches. We have walked and talked and drunk deep together in many ports of the world and he was one of the best fellows it has been my good fortune to know. There was not a skill of seamanship he had not mastered and I learned much from him. He was thoroughly at home in any vessel but the tall ships of sail were his delight and they had an everlasting charm for him. He threw his heart and soul into the work aboard and he laughed at hardship. He was one of those people whom one meets perhaps once in a lifetime and with whom there is an immediate accord. He was such a happy shipmate and even under the worst conditions of toil and cold and hunger he had a joke and a cheerful word. I

39

well remember one pitch-dark night when the ship was rolling rails under, down to lower topsails, and hove-to to a roaring gale, he yelled in my ear, 'What if the bottom were to fall out?!'

CHAPTER V   WE SET OUT

Now the ship was towed across the river and the rest of our cargo was loaded and on Monday, 4th August, we moved from the wharf and made fast to the Farewell buoy. On the next day we took on the remainder of our crew and got all ready for sea. Early on the Wednesday morning we were towed about two miles off shore and with a good breeze and square yards we stood away for our next port, Iquique in Chile, 7000 miles away.

In these days of rapid transport, people unfamiliar with the sea in general, and with sailing ships in particular, may find it difficult to realise just what a voyage of 7000 miles could mean. For this passage, the greater part of our course would lie below the 40th parallel of latitude, that region which is referred to rather vaguely as the 'Roaring Forties'. Those of us who have known it from the deck of a sailing ship will think of long rolling seas with breaking crests; red dawns and raging winds; wet decks and shortened sails. We remember long grey days of poor visibility when the rain joined with the spray from the tops of those great waves; longer nights of howling winds and grumbling combers which broke over the rail and drenched us to the eyebrows. There can be few of us left.

On that journey we would see nothing for weeks but those huge Pacific rollers under the wide heavens and no other living things save the gracefully soaring albatrosses which might relieve their and our loneliness by following us for days. There would be weary days and nights of hell let loose when we hungry sailors clung aloft to stow gale-tormented canvas, or soaked and shivering, we hauled on soggy ropes on decks half filled with water. There would be a few days and nights of heaving, oily, maddening calm when the Skipper paced the deck with short impatient steps and whistled for a wind. Nearly two months would pass before we would hear the cry of 'Land!' and after weeks of nothing but the ocean that call is electrifying. It means life, other people than those you have seen so much of for so long, firm ground to tread and fresh food and drink. A thousand things spring to your mind. Even then it may be but a lonely island which is passed with a wide berth.

But all that was to come and we hoisted the yards with a will and set all sail to the fair wind. I was glad to be off again and back to the ordered routine of a ship at sea. It was good to get to work with a broom and buckets of sea water to get the coal dust and dirt off the decks and to know that the clean wind and rain would soon get it out of the rigging. Good to be away from the disorganisation of loading cargo, of shore leave, taverns, and waterfront life. Nothing I have ever experienced is more filled with promise than that curtsey of a ship leaving port to the first of the deep sea rollers. Then, if at no other time, a ship takes on personality. She greets the sea with a buoyant gladness and she shakes from her the bewilderment of the land, and she spreads her wings to the wild wind and the ever distant horizon.

There was much to be done in preparation for our passage across the stormy south 'Pacific' ocean. The anchors were hove in and secured by many turns of light chain. Their cables unshackled and stowed below in the chain locker. In this one there was ample room. The hawse holes were plugged with big pieces of wood shaped to the purpose as were also the scupper holes. Everything moveable about the deck was either stowed below in the forepeak or in the bos'n's locker or lashed down.

Bill and I found some holystones forward and with a boyish grin he said, 'We don't want these things. There's no good in being on hands and knees on a wet and sandy deck pushing to and fro with a piece of gravestone. It'll only get us housemaids' knees. Better see if the buggers'll float.' When neither Mate nor Bos'n was looking, we tried.

About midday the wind fell light and by one o'clock we were quite becalmed. While all this activity was going on the ship was idly drifting about. With the evening a light breeze sprang up and light winds continued to spring up and to die away from every point of the compass all through the night. To each and every air and catspaw, we hauled the yards around.

'Lee fore brace!' shouts the Mate, and it's out you get from whatever corner you've been hiding or dozing, haul up the courses and clap on to the braces. One man gives the time so that all pull together.

'Wey — hey — a — HEY!' the first three noises, often inarticulate, are a warning, and all pull together on the last. The Mate encourages, 'Haul 'em round! Walk away with it!' Then, 'That'll do! . . . Belay'.' The man nearest the belaying pin catches a turn, calls 'Come up behind,' and as he makes further turns to secure the rope he calls 'All fast!' and we ease our hands from the rough rope. Now this one.

'Oh — a — hey — PULL you! Heave — and — POINT 'em!' One after another pull, pull, pull, pull, till your shoulders ache and the hard ropes make your hands sore. Then the Mate shouts, 'Steady tight the weather braces!' and we have a couple of 'dry' pulls when we gain barely an inch on the already taut ropes. Then it's 'Sheets and tacks!' when we reset the courses and then coil all down ready for running.

When it's all done we slip into the focsle for a quiet smoke but pipes are just drawing nicely when two whistles are heard and the Mate's voice.

43

'Square the cro'jack yard!' Aw . . . what the hell!

Still, it had to be done and while we grumbled we got on with it. I was feeling my muscles harden and my confidence grow as I put into more actual practice all the things I had learned in preparation for this experience which had been in my dreams for so long.

We kept 'watch and watch', four hours on duty and four hours off. These periods were broken by two short watches known as the 'dog' watches of two hours each between 4 and 8 p.m. The origin of this term is obscure though some joker has said that they are so-called because they are cur-tailed. I suspect that it is a corruption of 'docked'. These short watches ensured that each period on and off duty were changed every twenty-four hours. A bell was struck on the poop at each half hour and during the hours of darkness, the man stationed on the focsle head on lookout repeated the time on the bell there and reported, 'All's well!' He, and the man at the wheel, were always glad to strike four bells, for that indicated that half the watch was passed and a shipmate would take his place for the next two hours.

During the four hours of the watches on deck at night, three men were always awake. One was for two hours at the wheel, one for the same time on lookout, and one 'police-man'. The latter was usually the man to take the second lookout and for the second two hours, the man who had come off this duty. The rest of the watch could steal a sleep on their bunks or elsewhere, if they were lucky. If the Mate blew two whistles, which meant that he wanted the watch on deck to haul on braces to trim yards, to set or to shorten sail, or for any other duty, the 'policeman' would call the sleepers. He also called the watch below at one bell, which was struck a quarter of an hour before eight bells when all hands mustered aft, the First and Second Mates counted heads and the watches were changed.

About this time we found that we had hordes of hungry shipmates . . . fleas. The older hands said that it was not unusual with a cargo of coal but that was no comfort to me

44

for fleas have an eager desire to suck my blood. There must be something about my particular brand, for, if there's one within 100 feet, it'll find me. My shipmates didn't seem to be bothered by them. Darkie said proudly, 'They never bite me,' and Bill answered, 'No. Your skin's too thick.'

They attacked me with unrelenting viciousness and for some obscure reason, mostly on my feet. When it was my turn to be policeman, I would sit at the focsle table and read by the faint light of the dimmed lamp and I'd catch the hungry little beasts as they hopped on to my bare feet. I'd crush their bodies with glee and I'd line them up on the table before me. If we had been undisturbed by the Mate's whistle, there'd be dozens of corpses before I called the watch below.

They collected in scores at the foot of my bunk and they kept me awake with their attentions. When I turned the blankets off my feet there'd be a hopping crowd of them at that end.

I said to Bill in the next bunk. 'Cor! Just look at these little sods!'

'Lot of friendly little buggers you have there, Frank.'

'I could do without their friendship. They're only here for my blood.'

'Tell you what, Frank. They can't stand kerosene. My mother used to sponge the floors with it at home if any of us got a fleabite.'

So I lined my bunk with old newspapers and wet them with oil from the lamp, and enjoyed peaceful sleep.

Through the next few days the wind held fair and light and just enough to keep the sails asleep while the ship slipped along gently at three to four knots. Now we had been ten days at sea and we had some heavy rain. Each of us collected a bucket of the fresh water that ran off the deckhouse roof. Scupper pipes from deckhouses on those ships ended about two feet above the deck so that this could be done. We had the first good wash that we had had for more than a week. Though there was only a bucketful each in which to bathe ourselves, we counted it pure luxury.

45

'Shure,' said Paddy Delaney, who was prone to malapropism, "Tis this that makes me flamboyant.'

One of the real hardships of those times was the lack of fresh water. We were rationed to two quarts of water per man per day but the cook had one of these for cooking, coffee and tea and the rest was put in the storage tank in the focsle and carefully hoarded. Once a week we were able to draw two-thirds of a bucket each and we were able to wash at least our underclothes. The remaining soapy water was kept beneath our bunks for washing hands before meals and by the end of the week one could just about cut a piece out of it. When later, we sailed in hot weather we drank most of the water and washed even less. Fortunately it was a clean life.

Now the wind drew to the south and we continued to make steady progress full and by on the starboard tack as we made to pass around the north of New Zealand. As there was little sea running, the ship sailed smoothly, and it was comfortable to work about the deck or aloft while the sun shone brightly from blue skies only lightly flecked by small clouds. Squally weather came towards the end of this week. During one middle watch, a sharp gust came out of the night, carried away the fore royal sheet and tore the canvas from the roping. Two of the apprentice boys stowed it and in spite of the wind and the rain and a wildly flying clew iron, they made a good job of it as Darkie and I found next morning when we went aloft to unbend the sail.

To stop the sail from flapping about, rope yarns were tied about it at intervals before the gaskets were thrown off. A rope was rove through a block above the yard and made fast to the bunt and by this means, after rovings were cut and sheets, etc., were unshackled, the sail was lowered to the deck for the sailmaker to repair.

While on the yard we saw a violent disturbance close to the bow and a wide black back rose from the water and dived with an almighty swirl.

'A whale shark!' called Darkie, and I was amazed by the size of it. I have not seen a larger one before or since except

46

years later, in the North Atlantic.

The following morning when we came out of the focsle for our watch on deck the Mate greeted us with 'Square the cro'jack yard!' and we hauled the yards round to head away before a fair wind. The fore royal had been repaired and we sent it aloft, bent it to the yard and set it.

All day the wind gradually and steadily increased. We carried on and made good progress and canvas was not reduced till the second dog watch when the fore and mizzen royals were stowed. Our watch was on deck for the first watch (8 p.m. till midnight) and I had the wheel from 10 p.m. It was a dark night and by now the wind was strong but there was little sea running and it was fine to have the feel of the ship as she slipped along before the steady sou'-wester and she gently heeled to the pressure of the wind and the lift of the long easy swell. Towards the end of the trick there came a black squall from windward which hit us with a rush and sent the ship along at speed. It was gone in a few minutes but a peculiar feature of it was that, as it left us, the wind drew ahead about three points. The weather clews of the royals lifted and banged as the wind spilled from them.

The Mate was standing at the rail and he yelled.

'Watch it now! Look at the bloody compass! Ye're away off course! Ye'll have her aback!'

'I'm not, you know,' I said. He strode to the binnacle as I put up the wheel and let her off a couple of points and he looked at the card and saw that I spoke truth. In less than a minute he said, 'Ease her up. You can lay your course again.' I edged the ship gradually to windward and sure enough, the wind had veered to its original direction and it held steady. It freshened during the middle watch and we came on deck again at 4 a.m. to a gale and hard work.

The main royal had been stowed and the watch on deck had clewed up the mainsail. Now all hands went aloft to furl it. It was a heavy job though we had fifteen foremast hands to do it but I came to realise that it was but child's play compared to what was to come.

Generally speaking, after the royals, i.e. the topmost of the sails, the mainsail is the first to be taken in at the beginning of a blow. This huge sail, the lowest on the main, or middle mast, is a fine driving sail when the wind is not too strong, but it cannot be left set when the wind is increasing as it might easily be damaged or even blown away when being taken in. Inevitably a sail thrashes about when being hauled up in its buntlines and before it can be furled and securely snugged along the yard. This is the time when it is most likely to be damaged.

On *William Mitchell* this sail was about 90 feet long on the head and 50 feet deep at the bunt and in those days it cost between £300 and £400. Apart from its economic value, it took a tremendous effort to stow and consequently it could not be left set till the last minute, or the operation of furling it might well be approaching the impossible. By that time all hands available would be required for more pressing tasks. In earlier days when small ships like, say, *Cutty Sark*, carried 50 focsle hands, this was not such a problem. We carried 25 men all told and these included the cook and the Captain's steward. To compare with the figures that I have given earlier, *Cutty Sark* was 963 tons Gross, less than half our tonnage. Her length was 212 feet, her beam 36 feet. Her main yard was only 78 feet long though her main mast was only five feet short of ours at 145 feet but at that height we did not cross a skysail yard. One can see that we were thinly manned compared with that famous clipper.

That was a wild weekend. We spent most of that morning watch (4 a.m. to 8 a.m.) standing by t'gallant halliards ready to let go. The ship flew along at about her maximum speed of fourteen knots in a series of violent squalls. Spars and rigging groaned and cracked at the strain, the wind howled about us and spray flew in stinging sheets. With daylight the gale steadied to a hard blow and we stowed the fore and mizzen t'ga'nts'ls which were hard struggles in that weather but when we came on deck at midday, we stowed the main t'ga'nts'l.

48

William Mitchell, unlike many vessels of her size, didn't have double t'ga'nts'ls, but she set big single ones and this main one, and the largest, was made of cotton canvas. On a previous voyage the vessel had been to New York and while there she had acquired this cotton sail. Such sails were usual on American ships but rare on British where sails were made of hemp canvas. Every sailor knew only too well how hard cotton canvas gets when wet. Hemp gets as hard as a board but cotton takes on a rigidity that beggars description. Paddy said, ''Tis as 'ard as a hoor's heart.' We all came to curse that sail with bitter emphasis.

Four of us were up on the yard to furl it and it swooped above us like a great white bat. It came back and struck at us as if trying to knock us off the yard, and we punched and clutched with balled fists and stinging hands. It refused to fold up neatly and it ruckled and buckled in lumps and bumps and it was as easy to furl as sheet metal. God damn the parsimony, we said, that doubtless bought that American sail for a song. Let our sails be made of good Irish linen for in those days no one had heard of the beautifully strong and light sails of man-made fibres that yachtsmen of today know. The sea was running heavily and the yard swung dizzily as we strove with the maddened thing. It swayed and thundered in the gale but we stowed it as snugly as we could and we made it securely fast though we would have been glad to have seen it go with the wind.

Now the gale drew ahead a little and we came down on deck not to rest but to heave and pull on sodden braces to trim the yards and to bring the ship closer to the wind. She was taking green seas aboard and we were all washed about the decks. I admired the old Mate who stood with hands gripping fife rail or rigging screw, feet apart and legs braced to the weight of water as he disappeared from sight under a wave and when it passed he would be standing there, water streaming from him but without even the least change of expression. I tried to emulate him but found it impossible with the wild torrents swirling about my hips and I was

49

flung against hatch coamings or into the scuppers and I got bruised and thoroughly drenched. When caught like this in waist-deep water sloshing around and with nothing to hold on to, one is completely helpless. The water washes one every whichway so that one feels to be a confused jumble of arms and legs twisted in every direction. I was bashed against the corner of the deckhouse and as the ship rolled, my battered and semi-senseless form was about to go over the rail as the welter poured back into the ocean. A huge fist seized the collar of my jacket and I was almost strangled as Big John held me against the roaring cataract. As the worst of it passed he caught me up and put my hands to the lifeline which was rigged fore and aft the length of the ship. I gripped the rope instinctively and I turned to give him a gasping thanks. His leathery face wrinkled and his gap of a mouth fell open to his ear-splitting laugh.

In one of the lulls I tore off my seaboots and soggy oilskins and for the rest of that day I went about the work of the ship in trousers and singlet only and cared not how soaked I became. What did it matter to me? I couldn't get any wetter.

While the weather was not too cold, there was much greater freedom in working like this for the sailor who wishes to keep dry in stormy weather is encumbered with heavy gear. Over thick clothing he wears an oilskin suit. The ends of the trousers are tightly lashed with several turns of sennit outside his seaboots to prevent the water from entering them. More lashings at the wrists and a towel or heavy muffler around his throat stop the sea from getting up his arms or down his neck. Then the 'soul and body lashing' around his waist and under his crotch from back to front keeps the jacket close around him so that it doesn't fly over his head as he works aloft. Well secured like this, in new oilskins, he can be submerged and washed into the scuppers and come up with no more than a trickle sneaking down his neck. Even in oilskins which are old and chafed, these lashings keep out the worst.

50

The cook was the only man in the ship who had no need for oilskins. He was a weedy undersized Negro and very dark of skin. Some of the hands said unkindly that he wouldn't be so black if he washed more often. He carried on his operations, 'grub spoiling' we called it, in the galley at the after end of the deckhouse. This place of work lay athwartships and it had heavy doors at either end made of solid teak, two inches thick. The weather door was kept bolted in this sort of weather and we grabbed our food as opportunity offered at the lee door.

That afternoon two men were making a dash to collect our evening meal when we shipped a tremendous sea from focsle head to poop. A huge green wall of water appeared, the length of the weather beam, and crashed aboard with a thunderous roar. It splintered the weather door of the galley to matchwood, raged through and rushed out of the lee door like a breaking wave. Riding the crest, arms and legs flung wide, was our cookie. His eyes started from his head, his lips were drawn back from his yellow teeth in a ghastly grin of abject fear. As he fetched up against the bulwark and clung immobile to a stanchion, he was no longer black, but a dirty grey colour! After him hissed a dense cloud of steam from the quenched fire and a clattering medley of pots and pans. The poor wretch huddled trembling in the scuppers, clung to the stanchion with shaking hands and gasped, 'By Golly, I looked Deaf in de face.'

He shivered there, terrified and half drowned, far too scared to move while the water swirled about his puny waist and scrawny limbs. His grey face worked and his yellow eyes rolled at his beloved pans as they rumbled from scupper to deck and back again and we slipped and slopped on the heaving decks to rescue them. Not until the Second Mate and a couple of us had blocked up the galley door with stout planks, would he re-enter his domain, or did his colour return to its normal black.

By good luck our potatoes were ready for us in a kid and they had been washed high and dry on to the coal locker.

51

They were still warm! However, the rest of our hot meal was gone to the fishes and we had to be satisfied with slabs of cold bully beef. With the help of Big John, cookie set to with a will to clear up and to get the fire going again. Eventually we had our coffee pot filled with hot tea but seawater had got into the water cask and it had a pretty awful taste. At least it was hot and why grumble at an extra ration of salt?

During the night the wind eased a good deal but there was still a heavy sea running. It was wet and difficult work to pull on hard, stiff ropes, up to our knees in water on a wet and slippery deck which had lost all sense of stability. It was a weekend of watery discomfort and endless toil but when it was passed, we were clear of the Three Kings Islands and the north of New Zealand and we were heading south for the strong westerlies.

Now that we had been ten days on salt provisions, the regulation on British ships to issue lime juice to all hands was applied. This requirement, as a preventative to scurvy, is the origin of the soubriquet of 'Limey' which Americans have given us and British ships were known as 'Lime-juice ships'. For the rest of the passage, at the change of the watch at every midday, the Mate stood at the after hatch, or on the poop if the weather was too bad, with an oaken bucket of lime juice. It was his duty to see that each man brought his cup and received a measure and he saw that it was drunk. It was dark of colour and strong and not much like the pleasant cordial that one can get under that name.

There followed a week of uncertain and unfavourable winds that gradually increased to gale force and the weather grew colder hourly. By the end of the week we had shortened sail to five topsails and we crashed close-hauled through mountainous seas. The screams of the wind in the rigging were like the shrieks of all insane things and there was the continuous accompaniment of the roar and thunder of breaking waves. There was nothing around us but foaming swirling water and howling wind till it seemed that the elements had gone mad. It was not easy to keep one's feet, and anything on deck that was not securely lashed in place was gone.

As I stood one night braced at the wheel while the ship tossed in the fury of the great rollers, stung by hail and spray that flew blindingly, the thought that Sally in New Zealand lay only three hundred miles up the wind came unbidden to my mind. Before me stretched over five thousand miles of the loneliest ocean in the world. Would it all be like this?

CHAPTER VI   SHIPMATES

With all this stormy weather and the wild motion of the ship, meals were taken with anxiety and we were kept busy while eating in retaining the food on our plates. It was difficult enough to keep the dish on the table; it was even worse to keep things like potatoes and gravy on one's plate. When all things rolled towards one, the only thing to do to avoid the lot pouring into one's lap was to lift up the plate and to hold it level till the ship should right herself.

One evening when we were having our supper, the ship took a particularly severe roll. Everyone seized his plate and mug and held them off the table and with an anxious expression waited for the ship to get somewhere near level again. The earthenware jar of pickles, which was a new issue and almost full, shot across the table. The man in the line of its passage, with a plate of sloppy hash in one hand and a brimming mug in the other, tried to save it with elbows and body. It smartly evaded this effort, smashed on the deck and scattered shards of earthenware and a gallon of mustard pickles under the bunks. I joined in the general rueful merriment till I suddenly realised that it was my turn to be 'Peggy' that week and so my job to clean it up.

We had no ordinary seamen in the focsle of that ship for

they had separate quarters at the forward part of the half-deck. The duties of daily sweeping out the focsle, getting the meals, tea, coffee, etc., from the galley and giving the deck a weekly scrub and generally keeping the place tidy, usually fell to the youngest of the ordinary seamen, who became known as 'Peggy'. These chores were therefore necessarily performed by us and we took weekly turns to do them.

I crawled under the bunks and slopped and scraped the slimy mess off the deck, urged on by many coarse comments and much laughter. Someone said, 'Now you'll know how to clean up after the baby.' I answered, 'It looks as if a whole creche of the little bastards have been here with diarrhoea.'

When I had collected the horrid mixture of pottery and pickles in a bucket and hove it over the side and cleaned up after the disaster, I hoped that I would never see mustard pickles again.

These pickles were issued to us once in a passage and they were regarded as something of a luxury. They were mostly cauliflower, preserved in a harsh acetic acid, but there were a few onions. These were greatly sought after and Bill and I had a game at times when one hove in sight. We sat opposite one another across the table, each with a spoon in his hand, and we contested with much hilarity for the prized onion. It was fair to knock it off the other's spoon, but once one of us had it out of the mouth of the jar, it was clearly the prize of the owner.

There was one unsavoury occasion when we opened the new issue to find the pickles covered with a thick crust of mould. Two men were deputed to take the jar aft to the steward and to ask for another. The steward demurred and the Captain came from the saloon to see what the discussion was about. He took one look at the mould and said, 'Steward, fetch me a large spoon.' He took the spoon and thoroughly stirred the contents of the jar, handed it back to the men and said, 'There you are. There's no mould there. Take it for'ard and be grateful.'

The days of the week could be told by the meals we had

and the menu recurred with unvarying regularity. Paddy Delaney said that 'it gets sort of motonomous.' Take breakfast for instance. On Sundays and Thursdays it was haricot beans cooked with molasses. Tuesdays and Saturdays it was porridge and a spoonful of treacle. On Mondays and Wednesdays we had curried bully-beef with boiled rice. I've no idea where the cook got his curry but the meat took on a distinctly green colour and the dish was known as duckshit and hailstones. On Fridays we had dried and salted fish but we smelt it coming on Thursdays. It stank of ammonia and Bill said, 'You always get this bloody fish on these belly-robbing ships. I'm sure it's cured in piss, an' horses' at that.'

Life could have been a misery with the cold and wetness and hunger and the terrible toil but we always got a laugh out of it even if it was against ourselves. The food was poor and there was never enough but we would make it the subject of a joke, albeit a coarse one. Every dish that came from the galley was christened with a name calculated to put our shipmates off their meal. Vain hope! The life was rough in the extreme and the focsle of a sailing ship was no place for refinement but we were a cheerful lot.

We were a very mixed crowd. There was Big John, the Swede, a tall and powerful man whom nothing could daunt. He had sailed for years in British ships and mostly in square rig. His full name was John Holldin. I asked him one day if his name had not a British sound. He said, 'Ya, de grandfader of mine he come from Scotland to 'elp built de sheeps for de king of Sveden.' He showed me a photograph of his family all seated round their dining table. Two large parents looked proudly at five strapping sons and three buxom daughters. John was well over six feet tall and his brothers were no less. I said to him, 'You've lost weight since this picture was taken.' He answered 'Ya. Dot vos after de t'ird dose of pox. Den I get ever so t'in.'

He was still an enormously powerful man which he demonstrated one day while the ship was in Melbourne, by picking up a blacksmith's anvil. When he lent his weight to haul on a

57

rope or to heave on a capstan bar we felt the advantage. He was a happy soul. I've seen him anxious in times of stress, intense in argument, mischievous in teasing or in practical jokes, serious in propounding a theory, but hardly ever angry. If something, such as an injustice, annoyed him it would not be for long. He would make some facetious or philosophical remark and laugh it off.

His laugh was something to hear, and to see. His lower jaw would drop and his great trap of a mouth would open wide to emit a deafening 'HAW . . . HAW . . . HAW!' and his little eyes would be lost in creases of mirth. The sound did not grow. It suddenly exploded on one's eardrums. The first time I heard this stentorian bellow was soon after I joined the ship in Melbourne. It was late at night and most of the hands were in their bunks and asleep. I was just dozing off when he came aboard with a couple of others who were all happily half-drunk. There was a lot of sniggering and shushing for the newcomers were making an elaborate business of ensuring that the sleepers were not disturbed. I watched them amusedly as they crept about and finally crawled into their bunks. John's was opposite mine across the square room and he was pulling his blanket up to his chin when a memory of his exploits ashore was too much for him and he suddenly bawled, 'Vot a gurl! Did ever you see such lofly beeg teets!' and then came this sudden guffaw. I jumped as my body stiffened with shock. Men stirred and muttered and one grumbled, 'Carn't a bloody man 'ave a kip in peace?' Big John mumbled an apology and pulled his blanket over his head.

He served in sailing ships because he felt that that was the way to go to sea. There was an essential association of the wind, the sea, and sails. The hardships of the life in bad weather he took in his stride and laughed at them and he appreciated the good times when the skies were clear, the sun hot on his back and the sea calm. He proudly showed me a superb fisherman's jersey that his girlfriend, Berta, had knitted for him. It was of thick navy blue worsted and it must have been made on quite fine needles. An intricate pattern gave it an added density which would have been a real protection against a Cape Horn winter but he never wore it. He thought that it was too good to run the risk of being soaked in salt water and he was too proud of it to subject it to such a hazard. He told me of this girl, 'Oh . . . my Berta is a bootiful BIG gurl,' and he outlined with his hands her billowy figure. 'She so fat that ever' time she laughs, she farts!' Over his bunk he had fixed a vividly-coloured photograph of her clad in only a pair of black stockings and one red garter.

Old Arthur, whom I have mentioned, was past seventy but he was extraordinarily active. He was from Whitechapel and his thick hair and luxuriant moustache had grown white in the shadow of the Red Duster. He could tell of the days of the smart clipper ships of the Aberdeen White Star Line, Shaw Savill and the New Zealand Shipping Company. Those fine little ships that made consistently fast runs out to Australia and New Zealand with general cargo and came back with the wool clip and later, with frozen meat; their names are now only history. He told us that in those days seamen signed on a ship in London for what was then the going rate, £2.10s per month, 'jumped' her in New Zealand and signed on a homeward-bounder for £10 per month. Such was the demand for sailors out there in those days for many men signed on a ship simply as a means of emigrating to that country.

He told us how he was paid off a ship in London after a three year voyage and he did not get more than fifty yards from the shipping office before he was bludgeoned and robbed of the pay he had earned by three long weary years of hardship. He would shake his old head and say, 'You young fellers don't know 'ow lucky yer are.'

On the other hand, he told us of how, after a long voyage back in 1900, he had gambled half his pay on a horse, had won £250 and had lived 'like a bleedin' lord' for two years before he had to go to sea again. Doubtless his standard was

59

not quite the same as many others but it goes to show what one could do with a few pounds in those days. I couldn't help wondering why he didn't take the opportunity of giving up a sailor's life with all its hardships. He said, 'Well . . . it gits in yer blood yer know.' 'It must do,' I answered, 'or you wouldn't be in one of these ships now.'

His Welsh shipmate had left the ship in Melbourne.

'Svensk' was a Swede who had come out to New Zealand in a windjammer twenty years before. At times he had taken a berth in a coastal schooner but more often, he swung an axe in the bush. He stood no more than five foot three, but he had the arms and torso of a powerful man of six feet or more. A good shipmate, always cheerful and willing and a useful member of the watch where brawn and sinew meant so much.

There was Jock, from the Isle of Skye. He had never been in sail before except for small fishing boats off the Hebrides, and he always spoke of *William Mitchell* as the Big Ship. I remember that when we left Newcastle, he was aloft on the upper topsail yard and the Mate sung out to him overhaul the t'gallant buntlines. Jock stood up on the yard, grasped the foot of the t'ga'nts'l and started to overhaul the buntlines from this precarious position. A shake of the sail would have shipped him off to certain death below. It should be explained that those buntlines are led through blocks above their respective yards, over the fore part of the sail, and are made fast on the foot. When the sail is set, they are overhauled so that the otherwise taut rope will not chafe the canvas and they are stopped at the block by a turn of sail twine. When it becomes necessary to take in the sail, a sharp pull on the rope from on deck breaks the twine and the rope is free. Naturally, the Scot could not keep the rope slack from where he was. He was nowhere near the block to stop off the buntline and, as soon as he let it go, the weight of that part of the rope which led down to the deck drew it tight again. After a while the Mate saw him and stopped dead in his tracks. He made a funnel of his hands and yelled, 'What in hell are ye doing up there, man! Don't ye know *anything* about a sail?'

Jock looked down with a very worried expression and, to the Mate's puzzlement, replied 'Wull ye see, Mister, I've nefer been in a Big Ship befure.'

In passing, it has surprised me to see in photographs of what has become known as 'The Tall Ships' Race', that the buntlines on those square-riggers which take part, are not overhauled. Could this omission account for the quite high loss of sails on those ships in not so very hard weather?

Paddy Delaney had run away from his home in Cork and had joined a ship bound for Australia when he was only ten years old. That must have been a very tough experience for such a child but he was made of the right stuff and nothing could get him down. He had been in many and varied wind-jammers since then and he was a thorough good sailorman, always ready with a joke and a grin under the worst of conditions and nothing was too much for him to do for a shipmate. His distortion of English was something to hear. He was as coarse as a sack in some ways, absurdly sensitive in others. He would give to the food the foulest of descriptions, yet, when one man took out his false teeth to remove a hard crumb, he rushed out on deck, leaned over the rail and was sick. He was quite unpredictable but always cheerful. He had a way of striking an attitude and quoting some bawdy rhyme. As when we left Newcastle and had just dropped the tug, he pointed dramatically towards the town and declaimed, 'Mary on the quay, she farted at me and the wind from her arse blows this ship out to sea!'

Porteous I have mentioned. A shipmate I shall always remember as one of the best.

Then there was 'Darkie', a New Zealander from North Auckland where his father had been a farmer and part-time kauri-gum digger. He was a slim, very sun-tanned young man of about my age. He was small and slender of build but as hard as nails and we sometimes wrestled together but he was as slippery as an eel to catch and hold, wiry, and deceptively strong. He claimed that he had run off to sea to get away

61

from his father who was always trying to get more and more work from the members of his family. He had spent much of his seafaring life on schooners among the Pacific Islands and he knew his job. He was, to the sorrow of his shipmates, one of those persons who have no ear for music, but he *would* sing. He knew the words of many popular songs and he would make valiant efforts to render them but he had a range of four notes and the results were awful. However, he was not readily abashed.

Paddy Murphy hailed from Waterford originally but he had shipped out of London for many years and he had been for a long time in small sailing vessels trading around the coasts of Britain. Consequently he was used to bad weather and hard conditions. He enjoyed his beer and when in port we could hear him coming aboard when he was yet a quarter of a mile away. After a day spent in slaking an everlasting thirst, he sang at the top of a full-throated voice as he rolled along, lurched into the focsle, fell into his bunk and was immediately fast asleep. He would sleep soundly and sing lustily all through the night. He was always smiling and good-tempered but hardly ever had anything to say for himself.

Fredriksen was a young Dane, some eighteen to twenty years of age. His full name was Christien Hovgaar Harald Fredriksen. We called him Dansk. He had joined the ship one dark night in the middle of the Skaggerak. *William Mitchell* had left Fredrikstadt loaded with dressed timber and had set out for the North Sea in January. This was of course before I had joined the ship. She sailed through three long nights and short days of wind and snow and ice. It was dark and bitterly cold and for most of that fateful night she had been pushing floe ice before her. There was a heavy sea running and the ship was sailing with square yards at about eight knots when the lookout reported a red light fairly close on the bow. Exactly what happened then I do not know for I could never get a clear account of it nor have I since been able to obtain any record of the subsequent inquiry, and Dansk would not talk of it.

Obviously it was the duty of one or the other vessel to give way but the visibility was poor and possibly there was no time for a manoeuvre. There was a sickening, splintering crash. The ship's jibboom took the masts out of a little Danish schooner and she must have been cut nearly in two. Dansk was the only one on her deck and he seized the bight of her anchor chain and swung himself aboard.

Valiant endeavours were made to lower a boat but the falls were frozen in the blocks and they would not budge. The Second Mate and two men performed the impossible that night. Desperation lent them such strength that they picked up the heavy boat with all its gear and swung it bodily out of its chocks. The Skipper forbade the launching of the boat in that awful sea. The main yard was backed and the ship hove to for a while but there was no sign of the wreck or of any survivors. The yards were squared and she stood on her course. Young Fredriksen was taken aft and looked after and when the ship called at Falmouth later to report the collision, he signed on for the voyage as able seaman.

An inquiry would have to be held but it was arranged that it would take place when the ship returned to England as such a probably lengthy business would delay the voyage considerably. The Authorities agreed that *William Mitchell* could sail on. Dansk was the only witness from the schooner and his presence was assured by his joining our crew. He had picked up English of a sort with the help of Big John who seemed to be able to get by in almost any language, and it was lurid and none too intelligible. I suggested that I could teach him to speak more fluently, but he said, 'Vot I care so long you unnersten me? I no go barstar Engleesh sheep no more.'

There were four ordinary seamen in a deckhouse aft of whom we saw little except when working about the ship. Also four apprentices lived in the half-deck aft.

The Skipper was quite young and did not appear very robust and I cannot say that anyone in the ship ever got close

63

to him. He kept himself very much aloof.

The First Mate was a big broad man from Dover. He was past sixty and he had been Master in sail for years. He and the Captain did not get on well and there would be flaring rows between them. It wasn't very sensible, and certainly not good for discipline, when the Skipper would criticise the set of the yards and the Mate would yell, 'God damn it man, don't tell me how to trim sail! I was master when you were still in swaddling clothes!'

He maintained a bluff and hearty manner to us all but he was a kind-hearted soul. I well remember a very cold day on this passage when I stood shivering at the wheel, that he took over the steering from me and gave me a drink from his mug of hot coffee. I was just taking a sup from it when the Skipper stepped on to the poop. The Mate grabbed the cup from me, pushed me against the wheel and shouted, 'Mind your steering!' Only because he disliked the idea of being thought soft.

The Second Mate was popular with us all. He was twenty-two years old and just out of his apprenticeship when he signed on in London. As he was in charge of the other watch, I did not come very much in contact with him. He grew a thick bushy brown beard which was the envy of others who had given up shaving.

The Bos'n and the sailmaker were 'daymen', that is, they did not keep watches like the rest of us forward of the main-mast. The Bos'n was large and fat and I never knew him to go aloft.

'Sails' was a pint-sized Welshman who plied his trade under the break of the poop in fine weather and under the focsle head in bad. I would yarn with him at times always with the idea of picking up some useful knowledge but it wouldn't be long before he would be telling me that in time all these sinful sailormen would be frying in hell but he had a seat reserved for himself near to the Golden Throne. He wanted me to be 'saved'. Big John worked with him at times and John took a wicked pleasure in making the most outrageous remarks in order to see Sails' horror-stricken expression. I remember him pottering about in his suit made from canvas. It wasn't made from an old sail that had been scrapped and the cloths of which had been softened by the rigours of Cape Horn weather and the roaring forties. No. He claimed as his right to make a jacket and trousers of new and heavy canvas. When they got wet as they were bound to do at times, they grew so stiff that he could hardly walk. He waddled, but he had his rights.

He would never lose an opportunity to tell us how sinful we all were and what a horrifying prospect we had for the hereafter. He promised us eternal joy and happiness if we would see, as he put it, 'the beautiful light'. He didn't believe, he *knew* that the Lord would take a terrible revenge upon us and we would suffer torment in eternal fire if we did not repent, mend our ways, and 'come to the arms of Jesus'. I tried to tell him that he was preaching a religion of hate and fear and that I had always understood that Christianity was a religion of love. I wasted my breath.

His next favourite subject for discussion was the decline of the sailing ship as a means of transport, and the numbers of sailmakers' jobs on those square-riggers that were still afloat that were filled, not by properly apprenticed, fully qualified and experienced tradesmen but by sailors who had worked as sailmakers' mates at some time in their career at sea. He contemptuously described them as 'only handy with a palm and needle'. He maintained that they were keeping real tradesmen out of jobs and he couldn't or wouldn't see that there were very few men left who had served a full apprenticeship to sailmaking for it had been a dying trade for a quarter of a century. Shipmasters would be only too glad to sign on proper tradesmen if they could get them. He was jealous of his knowledge. While he was happy enough to have someone to help him in the monotony of straightforward stitching, he'd never let anyone see how he cut the cloths, nor did he like to have anyone watch him do any special job like fixing a bull's eye or a cringle, or even roping a sail. I asked him once, how a sailmaker's splice at the head of a sail was made but he wouldn't tell me. I learned it from Bill Porteous.

I have told of the cook, and the Captain's steward was also a Negro. He was long and lean and we saw little of him except when he came to the galley to have long and bitter arguments with the cook. The cook would shout, 'Wot de good of dis? I got twennyfive men to do de cookin' fo'. Dis no good. Yo tink I Jesus Christ to feed 'em wit' some little loafs an' fishes? Yo long black nigger yo! Go get me some mo'.' The steward leaned down to the cook and said silkily, 'Yo undersized little runt yo. Effen I give yo good rations yo make a mess o' dem. Cook, yo call yoself! Yo couldn' cook no mo' dan yo mammy. Ef she could a cook yo'd a grown to de size o' a man!'

CHAPTER VII   SOUTH PACIFIC

Now we had made good way to the southward and were heading east. The wind blew fair and strong and we roared along before it. A big sea was running and it worked the ship so much that the Skipper feared for the safety of the main upper masts. The topmast backstays were new and they had stretched. We could tighten them no more for the rigging screws were screwed up to their limits. So we put a frapping on the backstays by passing a heavy rope across and across from port to starboard about ten feet above the deck and we hove all tight with the main deck capstan. Without this frapping, the upper mast jerked at the top as the ship rolled from side to side.

There were three days here when the wind moderated and we set the courses and t'ga'nts'ls but the breeze freshened and we furled them in the yellow light of a foul sunset when the gale was audibly increasing. At eight bells of the second dog watch all hands took in the foresail. It was then blowing with hurricane force and we were all crouched over the yard, clawing at the maddened canvas, fighting with muscle and sinew and determination as the ship made prodigious rolls, a tearing rain beat upon us, penetrated oilskins and drove under sou'westers. It is a nightmare memory; that night of stretching out over the yard straining every ounce of energy to hold and smother that devil-possessed sail; doing it but feeling that it was almost beyond humans to do.

That night stands out as one of the most violent nights I have known at sea. It was pitchy-dark. The ship reared and plunged with wild abandon. Hail and rain stung as they drove before the howling wind. Great seas crashed aboard with stunning force and the old hooker trembled from stem to stern. Everyone's quarters on the ship were awash and no one had dry clothes. We had to yell in one another's ears to be heard above the awful din.

The man at the wheel had great difficulty to keep the ship on her course, and at the Mate's two whistles we fought our way aft to set the mizzen staysail to steady her and to help the steering. What with the mad lurching of the vessel and the waist-high water, we had the devil of a job to hook on the sheet tackle. Porteous and I engaged it at last but the foot of the sail was full of wind and it lashed about wickedly. Try as we might we could not get the sheet right aft. The Mate bawled 'Try it at that!' so the others clapped on to the halliards to hoist the sail. As it went up the stay and the wind caught the slack of it, it shook and flapped wildly and the steel ring at the clew was marked by great sparks which it struck from the hook of the tackle.

'Get that sheet aft!' shouted the Mate.

While Bill took a turn on a belaying pin, and held on to the fall of the tackle, I jumped at it and held it close to the block in the hope of bringing it down. Of course there should have been more men at the sheet and the wild slamming of the sail was far too strong for me alone. It picked me up like a straw and flung me hard against the rail and then back with a whack against the poop ladder. Bruised and sore, I crept behind the poop ladder out of harm's way with an excruciating pain in my right knee. The Mate saw that it was hopeless to set the sail, and he had it hauled down again. I gritted my teeth and got about somehow for the rest of the watch. At eight bells all hands set the staysail successfully.

The knee was very stiff and painful the next day but the ship was snugged down under short canvas and we could only stand by in that terrible weather, so I was able to go easy and it didn't bother me all that much. But cold and wet hadn't helped and when I got out of my bunk at the end of the afternoon watch below, it almost brought tears starting to my eyes to put my weight on the leg. It was my trick at the wheel and I struggled aft to the poop and spent two hours of agony there as I wrestled with the ship to keep her near her course while she yawed and corkscrewed about before those huge seas. It went against the grain that I would not be able to take my share of the working of the craft in its fight with the elements, but I felt that I would have to 'go sick' and rest the knee. I could not get about usefully at all and the least movement gave me exquisite pain.

Paddy said to me, 'Git along aft wid ye and tell the Old Man. Ye'll be creepin' round like a bluddy cripple an' won't be anny use to us at all at all. Ye'll 'ave to rest it or it might go maligint.'

When I crawled aft, I got thoroughly wet because I could not be active enough to get out of the way of the seas that came aboard. I showed the Captain my swollen knee which by this time was the size of a small football, and he declared that I was suffering from gonorrhœa rheumatism.

'Gonorrhœa be damned!' I answered indignantly. 'I'm not such a fool as to lay myself open to that sort of trouble. I tell you that my leg was struck by the staysail sheet and the tendons have been strained.'

There were some men at sea who blamed all a sailor's ills on venereal disease, and, in all fairness, with some justification.

'Well, it's rheumatic gout,' he persisted. 'If you'd been hurt there'd be some bruises.'

'I thought that one had gout as the result of high living,' I said drily. It was useless to tell him that I do not bruise easily.

That wretched knee kept me in my bunk for a week and then, though I did my best to do my part of the work of the ship, it was a month before the pain left me.

Thereafter we had a strong fair wind for a fortnight and we had a splendid run. We averaged 220 miles a day for eight days here. Day after day we drove on, now setting sail, again shortening it, straining at braces, hauling on sheets, up aloft on the swinging yards to fist the sails, or up to our waists in water on the reeling slippery decks. We took our tricks at the kicking wheel or we dreamed of home and beauty on lookout on the focsle head.

One night, when all hands were furling the upper topsail, I found myself on the upper yard beside Old Arthur. The wind tore through the rigging and shrieked at us. Together we fought the mad canvas. Arthur's sou'wester had blown away and as he cursed the wind and rain that strove to tear us from our perch, he groped blindly for the gaskets. I hove up the sail as he passed the rope and I banged the hard canvas down with my forearm as he hauled it tight. When he came to the last turn, he did what we all knew was the wrong thing to do. He leaned back and with both hands pulled on the rope to get the last turn tight. Gaskets were made from any old rope that was available and with only his inconsiderable weight the rotten old hemp parted. He'd forgotten the proverb, 'One hand for the ship and one for yourself', but Big John used to add, 'At times 'tis bot' 'ands for yourself an' fok de sheep!'

As I felt, rather than saw him go, I instinctively flung out my hand and grabbed at him. I caught a generous handful of his thick white hair and hung on for all I knew. My body was braced between footrope and spar and my other hand gripped the jackstay. In spite of desperate effort, I felt his wet hair slipping from my hold and I yelled to him to reach up and grasp my wrist. To my horror it seemed to me that he was trying to break my hold and I could feel his gnarled fingers fumbling at mine while furious shouts were flung away on the gale. They were only inarticulate howls to me but in a momentary break in the roar of the elements, I could hear him scream, 'Leggo me fuckin' 'air carn't yer! Gor' bleedin' blimey d'yer want ter bleedin' well scalp me? I'm sittin' on

70

the fuckin' yard!'

By great good fortune he had swung forward under me on my hold and he had landed astride the lower yard but a few feet below us.

The following day we set that fore upper topsail again, and, rather than call out the watch below, the Mate had us hoist the yard by taking the fall of the halliard tackle to the main deck capstan. We trudged round this, now helped by the heel of the ship, and again climbing up the deck's steep slope as the ship rolled the other way. After a long struggle there there was about four feet between the two heavy blocks of the tackle, which meant that the yard was almost up, when there was a sudden jar and the capstan ran free as the fall broke. By remarkably good fortune the end of the rope flew across the cheeks of the block and jammed the turns so the yard came down only a few inches.

'Under the focsle head, you,' shouted the Mate, 'and fetch a chain stopper and that gun tackle!'

With these we hove down the upper block till we could free the rope and with these and a handy billy on the end of the fall, we hauled up the yard till the blocks were together, when we stopped off the halliards.

'We'll have a long splice in that fall,' said the Mate. Then, grumpily, 'Stand by for'ard out of the rain, all of you. I'll do it. Don't suppose any of you could tuck a splice anyway.'

He knew that we all had had a hard time of it just as he knew quite well that any one of us was perfectly capable of tucking a good splice, but the kindhearted old chap had to make the sneer because he couldn't let us feel that he was giving us a break.

During the next three weeks we made very good progress. The average day's run for sixteen days was over two hundred miles. She could sail with a good wind. There was one half hour of a wild squall when the log showed that she covered seven miles, but the Skipper dared not carry t'ga'nts'ls for longer. On her outward passage, when running the easting down she had made good 296 miles one day and 298 miles the next. She was not a slow ship yet I never heard that she ever made a fast passage, simply because she was unlucky in getting a wind. The voyage after I left her (and her last) she took 156 days from Wilmington, Delaware, to Melbourne. The passage was not so lengthy because she was mishandled or in any trouble, but only because she could not get the wind to send her along. Even down in the 'forties' she caught only light and even head winds.

The heyday of the sailing ship had gone and freights were poor while the costs of sails and gear was such that ship-masters could no longer afford to hold on to canvas and drive their ships for fear of losing sails that possibly would never be replaced. The wool clippers in their day commanded freights of £6 to £8 per ton for the voyage to and from Australia and it has been said of them, in fact some of their masters boasted of it, that they left a trail of light spars and gear from Land's End to Bass Strait. I believe that if some of the latter-day ships had carried the canvas and had been driven as those ships were, they would have made passage at least approximating those of older days.

One evening when we hauled down the outer jib, I went out to the boom end to make it fast. I stood a moment before coming in and from this vantage point I looked aft at the ship. She presented a scene that I hope I shall never forget. There was a broad band of yellow light still in the western sky and every rope and spar stood out clearly against it. The sails on the foremast, piling one on the other, strained at their sheets before the gale. As I clung there she buried her lee bow to the cathead in a huge sea and in the surge of parted water a sheet of snowy spray was flung across the crouchinc oilskin-clad figures that were making sheets and downhauls fast. It was a picture of shining wet figures on a shining wet deck, grey sails towering against a grey sky, purest white foam at the forefoot frothing over a sea of nidnight blue, and over all a soft yellow light.

Now and again we would have a few hours of bright sun-shine and the lifelines would be hung from end to end with blankets, bedding, seaboots, and every and any article of clothing. All hands seized the opportunity to dry out their possessions. Sometimes they would be getting nicely dried off when a shower of flying spray would undo all the good work. The man at the wheel would be sure to be blamed and colourful remarks were made about 'that there farmer wot carn't keep a ship steady on 'er course but must go splashin' about an' wettin' 'ard workin' sailors' gear.'

Soon our course trended to the northward and the weather grew a little warmer and the winds less violent. Now we unbent the hard weather sails and sent the fine weather suit aloft. Then, on Saturday 27th September, fifty-two days out from Newcastle, there was a call from Svensk, who was working on the fore yard, 'Land ahead!'

It lay on the horizon under our jib-boom, a big blue mountain, still many miles distant, the Island of Mas-a-fuera. It was a fine bright day with very little wind, and as we drifted over the calm blue sea, the island made a dome shaped smudge of a lighter blue. We drifted on with virtually no wind through that day and night and we passed the island the next day before a light wind that gave us three or four knots.

Mas-a-fuera is a most impressive sight. The western coast towers sheer for thousands of feet from the lonely ocean and it terminates in rocky crags and pinnacles. The cliff face is scarred and split, a huge wall of rock. After days and weeks of the level ocean, this colossal rampart, a distant outpost of the mighty Andes, was an inspiring sight. The island falls away from its eastern coast and lower down it presents pleasing grassy slopes dotted with patches of thick vegetation to low cliffs scarcely a hundred feet in height which show promise of sheltered bays and coves. It is a hundred and twenty miles from Juan Fernandez, the original Robinson Crusoe island where William Dampier marooned Alexander Selkirk. He lived there for five years and from his story Daniel Defoe wrote his classic tale.

That day the Mate's bird escaped. In Australia he had acquired a long-tailed, brilliantly plumaged bird like a macaw.

Probably he wanted to follow an old tradition and to bring home a parrot for his wife. In cleaning out the cage, he had inadvertently let the bird go and it had flown up to the mizzen royal yard. The Mate sent an apprentice after it and the bird watched him with droll seriousness until it was almost within grasp when it flew over to the main. Down to the deck and up the mainmast went the lad with a confident, 'That's all right. I'll catch him,' to the Mate. The same thing occurred. The bird watched with mild interest as the boy ran up the rigging and it cocked its head and eyed the lad in the amusingly friendly manner of the parrot family until it appeared that capture was imminent. Then, in a bored way it flapped over to the fore t'gallant yard.

The apprentice started down but it seemed to him to be senseless to go all the way down to the deck only to come up again, so the active youngster swung over the yard and went hand over hand along the fore t'gallant brace. He was half way across to the yardarm when the bird flew down to the main yard. He struggled back along the sagging wire rope and he sat astride the yard to recover his breath. He looked down and saw the creature unconcernedly preening its feathers below. He got round to the opposite side of the mast out of sight of his objective and went down the rigging. At the main yard he very gradually worked his way along towards the bird who affected a lack of interest and went on with its toilet. When within a few feet of the bird, the youngster rested there, held out his hand invitingly, and made foolish clucking sounds. With a distinctly nautical roll the bird took a few steps towards him and bowed. Encouraged, the lad moved nearer. The bird retreated and bowed again. The boy twittered to it. The bird advanced, bowed twice, and flew up to the brace where the brassbounder had recently swung. Up the ratlines ran the apprentice and at the t'gallant yard he saw that the sail screened him and the bird from the Mate's eyes. He seized the standing part of the brace and shook it violently, and in subdued tones he called heaven and hell to witness the terrible things he would do to the thrice blasted bird

74

once he had caught it. This amused the hunted one for it teetered with the agitated rope and when it could no longer keep its balance, hovered over it and alighted when it could, and it performed the most absurd gyrations rather than let go.

Much to the amusement of us on deck, the boy tried subterfuge. He lowered himself and sat on the footrope to bring the sail between himself and his quarry. The bird stood a moment or two in perplexity to find itself suddenly alone. It put its head on one side and then on the other and it gazed at the place where the lad had been. Then curiosity overcame it and it rolled and swayed and fluttered along the rope and jumped on to the yard. The apprentice sensed it close to him and he put his head above the yard to look straight in the creature's eyes. He made one wild grab at it which nearly lost him his balance. The bird easily evaded this and flew aft to the mizzen mast.

Down from aloft came the boy in an atmosphere of perspiring profanity and avoiding the Mate's eyes, he sweated up the poop ladder and was climbing into the mizzen rigging when the old Mate said grimly, 'Let it be.'

The Mate left the open cage on deck with some seed in the hope that the bird would return of its own free will. It had other notions and it spent the afternoon aloft and explored the masts and rigging. Then, as dusk was falling and the island began to fade into the sunset as we drew away before a freshening breeze it evidently thought, 'Well, here goes. I don't go much on a life at sea,' and to the Mate's disgust and the apprentice's delight, it took off and flew towards the land.

After we left Mas-a-fuera the weather was delightfully mild and all hands were cheered. There was more joking and sky-larking in the dog watches and we would sit around on the main hatch and sing sea-songs and shanties or wrestle and pull against each other. Yarns would be spun about other ships and ports and of men and women and that best of all ships, the last ship.

Then we ran into light winds and periods of calm and we were interminably pulling and hauling on braces to trim the yards to every little fitful zephyr. It was hard work on a heavy and short-handed ship and nothing is more liable to fray the nerves and tempers of officers and men than this continual dragging at the gear in an endeavour to make the most of every little puff of wind that came from here and there and was gone in a matter of seconds.

The Mate had a slight 'breeze' with his watch about this time. One night of these variable and short-lived airs we were constantly on deck and pulling on braces to trim the yards to each change of wind and I suppose that we weren't putting our backs into it as we might. He wanted to know in the name of the Seven Sozzled Sisters why we egg-bound, stuttering bloody landlubbers were fumbling round the ropes 'just like a lot of twittering old ladies at a tangled ball of wool!'

We resented this. We went dumb. It really annoys an officer to have the men fail to sing out when pulling on the ropes. It indicated a lack of co-operation and of willingness and no doubt the Mates regarded it as a lack of that respect which they felt was their due.

Next time that he blew two whistles and called 'Lee fore brace!' we came quietly along and lined up at the lee rail. There was none of the usual chaffering and banter. He threw the weather braces off their belaying pins and called 'Haul away!'

We hauled but only the rattle of the sheaves in their blocks told that we did so. We pointed the fore, main, and mizzen yards. We sweated up the halliards. We took a pull on the sheets. He had us take a pull on every rope that he could think of but still no one called 'Oho . . . pull . . . you!'

Later that night the wind drew so much ahead that we wore ship and the whole complicated operation was done in grim silence. We could *feel* the Mate growing fierce. Finally we went forward to take a quite unnecessary pull at the fore sheet. We hauled it tight and waited for the Mate's 'Belay!'

76

It didn't come. We took another pull and gained a bare half inch. Still there was no word from the Mate. He stood on the moonlit deck with his hands in his jacket pockets, his short pipe in the corner of his mouth and he said not a word. Svensk was the first on the rope. He braced his foot against a stanchion and hove with his great strength and we pulled with him but the rope was as tight as a bar and we gained nothing. He sat down on the deck. Darkie was the next and he followed suit. Bill and I sat down almost together. One by one the watch sat on the deck. The Mate took his pipe out of his mouth and spat. 'All right,' he growled. 'Belay'. He stumped aft while we coiled all ropes down ready for running.

There was one custom on those ships that was welcome to all and I have thought at times that it was worth all the hardships of the life to have, at five o'clock in the morning, the cook poke his head out of the galley door and shout 'Coffee!'

The watch on deck would have been on duty from eight till twelve the night before, possibly called out in their watch below, from 12 till 4 a.m., when they came on deck again after inadequate sleep. It was disproportionately pleasing to hear that call, to line up with a pint mug at the galley door, and to collect steaming strong coffee. Once in three weeks we had an issue of a 14-oz tin of condensed milk and most of us kept it specifically for this drink. At other times we could have it as it came but this mugful deserved a spoonful of milk.

The cook wasn't the most popular man in the ship but we were for ever grateful that no matter how hard the weather or how much the roll of the ship slammed things about in his galley and made his footing precarious, and when things were so bad that he couldn't manage hot food, he hardly ever failed to produce the five o'clock morning coffee.

Old Arthur told us that in the days of wooden ships, the galley was often a separate structure. It was no more than a great sealed box which contained the stove and all the cook's gear. When the vessel was in port, the galley was hoisted overside on to the dock so as to have clear decks to facilitate the handling of cargo in and out of the ship. The cook would perform his operations there for those officers and crew who were working on the ship and they would send a man ashore at the appropriate times to collect their food at the stable-like upper half of the door. When the ship was loaded and ready for sea, the galley was hoisted aboard and lashed down at its four corners to strong ringbolts on the deck.

Old Arthur spun us this yarn about such a ship in which he had sailed as a young man.

'We wus ahtward bahnd fer Ostralia an' we'd rahnded the Cape o' Good 'Ope several day afore. Least, the Old Man sez we 'ad. We never seen it 'cos we went away souf of it. Then we gits inter bleedin' awful wevver. The decks was alwys full o' worter an' I never seen such big waves. We wus dahn ter two lower tops'ls an' I reckon we should 'a bin 'ove to but I fink the sea was so bad the Old Man wus scared to.

Anywy, I wus at the wheel in the mawnin' watch an' it wus comin' up ter two bells. I wus finkin' that I 'oped me mate wouldn' fergit ter tell the cook ter keep me coffee 'ot till four bells, w'en orl of a sudden like a bleedin' big green sea breaks aboard by the mainmast an' fills up the decks. Orl I c'n see forard is the foscle'ead an' free masts and the top o' the galley stickin' up aht o' the worter. Then she rolls 'ard ter loo'ard an' the worter spills aht of 'er. But . . . Blimey! As the worter goes over the rail, the lashin's give way, an' the galley floats over wiv it! I spose the poor perishin' cook 'ad got sorter used ter seas crashin' orl arahnd an' 'e didn' know wot 'ad 'appened, 'cos as the galley drifts past the poop, 'E puts 'is 'ead aht the 'arf door, an' 'e yells 'COFFEE!' '

In spite of the never ending work at the braces and the slow progress of the ship, we were all pleased at the prospect of soon being in port, of having fresh meat and vegetables, and that much looked for reward of the deep water sailorman, all night in.

This is a very real pleasure for after many weeks of watch-

78

and-watch, four hours on duty and four hours off, eight of unbroken sleep is sybaritic luxury. When he has only four hours for sleep, the most a sailor gets is three and a half hours even if he falls asleep at once on turning in and does not wake till called fifteen minutes before eight bells when the watch is changed. Quite often, in bad weather, this watch below may be interrupted by the cry 'All hands on deck!' and out he must go. Or, at the change of the watch, all hands might be required to take in sail. So a whole night to sleep through means quite a lot. Nowadays sailors enjoy four hours on watch and eight hours below and they know nothing of the toil and hardships of those earlier days. And a good job too.

The next Sunday afternoon the ship drifted on an oily sea. Two of the hands idled on the focsle head. At the wheel, I watched the sails flap against the masts and fill again as the ship rolled. She had no steerage way and it was useless to do other than keep the helm amidships. The westering sun turned the sea to gold that was shot with green in the shadow of the long swell. A burst of laughter came from the halfdeck and a profane exclamation.

'Come up here, boy,' called the Mate from the head of the poop ladder.

'Yes, Sir,' answered the apprentice as he stepped on deck, still smiling.

'What d'ye mean by using such language?' burst out the Mate. 'Get up on the mizzen top till eight bells. Perhaps that'll be teaching you to be more decent in your speech.'

This from the old Mate who never hesitated to use to all and sundry, the most astonishing combinations of swear words and blasphemy and who, only the night before, in reproach to this same apprentice, had 'damned his soul to hell'.

The ship rolled on. Little eddies swirled at her stern and the water gurgled and chuckled round her rudder post. About four points close on the bow I could see something which might be drifting but which looked like the triangular fin of a

79

shark. I gazed hard at it but I could not see that it was making any such movement as it would be if it had belonged to one of those ferocious fish. It would disappear for a moment or two and reappear but keep its position. The ship was drifting crabwise and she should come up on the object before long. I seized an opportunity while the Mate was in the charthouse to point it out to the boy on the top. Something to relieve his monotony.

Gradually the distance between us lessened and I could see that we would just clear the object. As it passed under our counter, I could see what it was. The point of the wing of a giant ray and a horrible looking thing. Twenty feet from its nose to the end of its long tail and fifteen feet across, it lay just below the surface. Its eyes were the size of a motor car's headlamps. Elsewhere, only in octopuses, have I seen that baleful, coldly wicked stare with which the creature looked up at us and sent cold shivers down our spines.

Again, while standing at the wheel one morning of calm while the ship stood motionless on a glassy sea, I watched the swift flight of numbers of 'Mother Carey's chickens', or stormy petrels, that flew about close to the stern. I was very interested in these little birds with the remarkably clean cut to their wings. In later years, Mr Mitchell must have had the shape in mind when he designed the Spitfire aircraft. I had studied these birds when we had been further south in the west winds and I had noted that they flew close to the water but they did not alight. All old sailormen had emphatically assured me that they never did sit on the water and that they couldn't swim though we met with them when we were a thousand miles from land. It puzzled me how they fed, for they always ignored any scraps which we threw overboard. I had observed that they often swooped close to a wave crest and as they glided but an inch or so above the water, they dropped one foot and skated it over the surface of the sea and at the same instant they stretched they necks and lowered their heads. I formed the theory that they were feeding as they did this and the lowered foot

80

splashed up some of the tiny crustacea that float on the surface of the sea.

I leaned on the teak wheel as the ship drifted in the calm and I looked over the stern to where the roll of the ship spun little whirlpools. One of the diminutive petrels made short darting flights, fluttered a moment, then settled on the water! Another and another joined it. Soon four of them swam together in the wake of the ship.

On Wednesday 8th October, we sighted the mainland some fifty miles away. A chain of barren mountains towered into a cloudless sky and as we sailed north and drew into the coast, their sterility was the more apparent. Here we had a steady though light wind from the south and this with the strong Humboldt Current which sweeps this coast from Cape Horn to the Equator, gave us such progress that we sighted the lights of Iquique at midnight the following Saturday. At daylight, the town was plainly visible eight miles off, scattered over a strip of flat land at the base of the dusty yellow hills.

We positively loafed along till eight o'clock when we were off the harbour entrance and we took in all sail as a Lilluputian tug came out and took us in tow. We were as much as she could manage and as the ship lifted on the long Pacific swell and brought the towrope taut, the tug stopped dead and stayed still until the swell passed and it could pull us down the slope of the next.

Slowly we came up to a mooring buoy and took a wire rope from it to our bollards forward. The tug pushed us into position and another wire was passed through the ring of another buoy aft and we were secured.

So the ship came to her anchorage as we lay along the yards once more to put a harbour stow on the sails on Sunday 12th October, sixty-eight days after leaving Newcastle N.S.W.

CHAPTER VIII   IQUIQUE

There were about twenty deep-water sailing vessels in the bay and that day was so calm that the ships stood straight on their reflections. Their spars and rigging were outlined against the desert hills, or to seaward, they were pencilled in a clean cut tracery against the pale blue sky in that dry clear air. Small boats made widening arrow heads on the calm, their wakes straddled by successive rings where their oars had dipped. The town half-circled the bay and buildings sprawled up the rising ground to where a railway cut a long zig-zag to climb the drab hillside. And how drab it was! Up and down the coast the land showed a dull khaki colour. Unrelieved by any sign of vegetation, it stretched as far as the eye could see. To the north, cliffs rose straight from the sea to about 3,000 feet, dusty, brown, and lifeless. Here was the vast Atacama Desert which lies between the Andes Mountains and the sea for nine hundred miles from Southern Peru far down the coast of Chile.

We lay not far from the little barque *Garthneill* of the Garth Line of London which had been in Newcastle with us. She had made a better passage across. *Lawhill*, a big four-masted barque with the unique feature of having her t'gallant masts stepped abaft the topmasts, once British-owned but

83

now under the Finnish flag, lay on our quarter. Ahead was *Pommern* a big black stump t'gallant four-master. A Frenchman from Dunquerque had a sweet sheer. She looked very trim with her white spars and hull with ports painted along her sides, compared with the black hull and spars of another Flying P liner and a couple of grey painted Finns. Bill and I stood at the rail and admired her. He said to me, 'I'd like to make a passage in her.' 'Me too,' I answered. 'By the look of her she should sail and handle well.'

Something we often said to each other when we liked the look of a ship. Or, when we read of, or saw, an illustration of a clipper, 'I'd like to have signed on her for a voyage.' What romantic souls we were. We didn't think of the inevitable hardships, but of the pleasure (?) of pitting our skill and strength against the elements in what we appreciated as a well-built and smart vessel.

We were soon surrounded by small boats, some of whose occupants offered to sell us goods but most desired to get a fare for the shore. It was Sunday, the ship at anchor and the canvas stowed, and the time was our own. Porteous, Delaney and I each had an Australian pound note which we had saved from money drawn in Newcastle. After our midday meal I suggested that, as the ship by then had been granted pratique, we should ask the Skipper if we could go ashore.

'No,' said Paddy. 'Doant be doin' that. He's shure to say No and 'tis the sails he'll be havin' us unbendin'. We'll just go ashore.'

We dressed in our shore-going clothes and called one of the small boats under the bow. We made fast a jib sheet and dropped it to the boatman who held it taut while we went down the rope hand over hand. The oarsman sent his little craft shoreward with long powerful strokes.

They were all built to a pattern, those light double ended, canoe-like boats that plied from ship to shore in Iquique Bay. They were safe and swift and the boatmen handled them with great skill. Our man told us that he was a German who had left a ship there fifteen years previously and he had

84

made his living as a ferryman ever since.

We were soon alongside the landing steps and we strode out into the sunlit dusty streets. We were almost immediately accosted by numbers of bums. They were mostly Scandinavian sailors who had left their ships here or at other ports along the coast and were 'on the beach'. They were pretty cool about their begging too. One, who saw that we were unwilling to take him into the nearest bar and to treat him to unlimited drink, said, 'Vell, if you don' buy us a trink, you' got to give us some money.' 'Got to . . .!' We liked that.

We wandered about and tried to find a place where we could change our money into pesos. Of course all shops were closed on a Sunday afternoon but eventually we were directed to a café and sailors' boarding house run by a Norwegian. It was here that the bums collected for he provided them with food and lodging, of a kind, and he provided seamen for those ships whose crews had deserted and were now ready for sea. If the men were doubtful about going, he did not hesitate to drug them and send them. He took at least a month's pay for each of them and he must have done well out of the business. It certainly did not cost him much to keep the men the way he fed and housed them and he did not keep them longer than he could help. We did not know this then and the rascal changed our notes for twenty-eight pesos each. It was not until later that we found that the ruling rate was thirty-eight pesos to the Australian pound. 'The repobrate!' said Paddy.

After a drink there we went to look over the town. It never rains there and nothing grew save in the Plaza Arturo Pratt and the Plaza Condell, two squares named after famous Chilean national heroes of Irish parentage. A few sorry shrubs drooped in the dry air. The houses and shops were for the most part, except for some more modern business places, built in the old Spanish Colonial style of thick adobe walls and jalousied windows but many were built of planks that were twisted and shrunk in that arid atmosphere and their frames hung crazily.

85

We sampled beer, wines, and pisco in various establishments. We went to one shop where we were served by an ancient Chinese whose wrinkled skin fell in yellow folds, hung below his lean jaws in skinny dewlaps and folded about his scraggy neck. One eye was closed and all his teeth had gone save two mossy fangs. He looked as old as China itself. We finally gravitated to the back room of a foul-smelling wine shop where we could buy a litre of wine for one peso and I have seldom seen such a villainous clientèle. The unquenchable thirst of a little old dried-up English beachcomber, who had attached himself to us, led us to this unhealthy spot. He told us that he had lived in the town by his wits for twenty years.

We feared that if we stayed too late ashore, our action could mean that all shore leave might be stopped for our stay in the port and moreover there was a meal waiting for us aboard. So we spent our last pesos in the purchase of vino and pisco which we stowed about our persons and we made for the landing stage. As we had no money left, we paid the boatman with a bottle of vino and were hoisted uproariously aboard. When we produced our bottles of pisco in the focsle we were hailed with delight. This spirit is distilled from grape juice, is quite clear and fairly potent, and, as Jock described it, 'Goes doon ye're thrroat like tin tacks.'

The next day the mail came aboard. There were letters for almost all of us. Letters for me from my family but . . . none from Sally. I couldn't believe it. Of course, there was one ashore for me with the shipping agent. It would come along tomorrow. Letters with news and gossip from home only partially interested me. I wanted to hear from my love. I was worried and very sorry for myself. I assured myself that mail was very uncertain across the Pacific and I'd hear any day. I feared that something terrible had happened to her. I was sure that she would have written if she could. The whole world was grey. There was no light in the sun nor gleam on the sea. It was all dull and horrible.

After a couple of days spent in unbending sail and rigging

cargo gear, we started on the work of discharging coal. A donkey engine had been brought aboard in Newcastle to work out the cargo and now it was unlashed from its stowage abaft the focsle head and trundled down to a position near the main hatch. Here it was lashed to the deck by way of convenient ringbolts and the bulwark stanchions, watered and fired for its work. Whatever we may have thought about cargo handling being the work of a sailor, we had no choice but to get on with it. As sailors said in those days, 'Growl you may, but go you must.'

Two days passed as we toiled in the heat and shovelled the coal into great baskets, three to a ton, which our wheezy engine swung up from the hatch to a stage rigged over the bulwarks, whence they were tipped into waiting lighters and over ninety tons went overside every day.

There was still no word for me from Sally and the work was doubly hard. I felt no joy in my strength and no spring in my step. Why had I persisted in my foolish idea of going to sea? However, I kept my feelings to myself and did my share of the heavy work.

In the mornings we worked from seven till eight o'clock, had an hour for breakfast and then we worked on till twelve. There was an hour's break for our dinner, after which we worked on till five. At each of the four corners of the hatch two men worked to fill one of the baskets. Porteous and I worked together as always. Each pair shovelled energetically to be sure that their basket was full and ready when the hook from the cargo tackle came down to their corner, and in those first two days close on two hundred tons had been discharged.

On the third day we turned to as usual and we had put out fifteen tons before breakfast, when we knocked off for what we regarded as a well-earned meal. It consisted of steak cut into small portions, each of which would go easily into the palm of one's hand. There was not enough to go round and there was nothing else. Two men were left with no meat. They went aft to ask the steward for more and the Skipper

87

saw them and told them to get for'ard out of it as they had had their 'whack'. A sailor, in port or at sea, was entitled by the regulations of the Board of Trade and by the Articles he had signed to a certain scale of provisions which was generally known as the 'whack'. As Jock said, 'Ye get ye're whack an' ye get nae mair.'

The Captain's statement that we had had our full ration was obviously wrong and feelings ran high. No one had had sufficient and we felt that we could not be certain to what lengths this parsimony would go. Life anyway was bad enough without having to shovel coal on short grub. We formulated a plan. We would not strike or stop work but we would show 'em.

When we started again at nine o'clock we all sat listlessly about in the hatchway, picked up lumps of coal one at a time and slung them carelessly into the baskets and with frequent rests for recuperation. The Mate came to the hatch coaming and looked as if he could not believe his eyes. He roared to us to know what in the name of all that was lurid did we useless heaps of good for nothing think we were doing. We replied that we were engaged in discharging cargo. He uttered dire threats of the awful things he would do if we did not get on with it. We replied that we were working as hard as we could on the food we got.

'You had steaks for breakfast!' he shouted in a tone that implied that they had weighed a pound each.

'Shteak!' yelled Paddy Delaney. 'Shteak is it? Wud ye call that ignificent little thing a shteak? Well I know whut me mither wud call it!'

No doubt the Mate would have liked to have dealt with us in the 'good' old way but the days of two-fisted discipline were gone and that was as good for the officers as the men especially in a ship where the men held together as well as we did. He stumped aft and fetched the Skipper who came along and declared that we were malingering, and that he would have us all arrested. Big John's mouth fell open to his deafening guffaw.

We indignantly and vigorously denied the accusation and we even went so far as to ask him if *he* would like to shovel coal all day in this bloody heat if he had had no breakfast and did he think that there was any nourishment in the coal dust that we were forced to breathe? After some more in the same vein he declared that he would put the matter before the Consul and we could be sure that we would hear more of it. We said that we thought that a good idea.

We carried on as before.

There was plenty of food for all at midday but we kept up the go slow tactics for the rest of the day and the total output was forty tons.

That evening the Skipper sent for Porteous, Delaney, and myself and we lined up opposite him in the saloon. He accused us of inspiring the crew to what he called mutinous behaviour and no protests from us would convince him that the day's action was due to the generally held feeling of all the foremast hands. He stubbornly persisted in his belief that we three were the leading spirits in defying him, probably because of our unapproved shore leave. He asked us what we were going to do about it.

'Why shud ye be intoggerating us?' asked Paddy. 'Shure an' we're on'y three of the crew!' The Skipper ignored him.

We told him that it was up to him and that no doubt the hands would make no difficulty about doing the maximum work if they had enough food.

He admitted that we had had short rations at breakfast time and he said that it would not occur again. There the matter ended as far as we were concerned. He was as good as his word and thereafter we always had enough to eat (while we were working on cargo) and we had no further cause for complaint. The coal went out to the tune of about 100 tons per day. The old donkey engine was kept going without a stop and we could do no more. I do not think that the Skipper ever forgave us three and I fully believe that he remained convinced that the whole thing had been arranged by us. I would have liked to have known if he really did go to the Consul and, if he did, what that official said to him.

Day after day we shovelled away down in the bowels of the ship. Hour after hour we carried on the monotonous job of filling up a basket and hooking it on to the fall of the cargo gear for our puffing-billy of an engine to hoist away into the sunshine. Sweat and coal dust combined to make us as black as the coal. Once we got down to the floors, it was not particularly hard work for the coal could be made to fall into the basket but it was heavy and hot and there was coal dust everywhere from our hair to our boots and it clung in our sweaty waistbands. It penetrated eyes, ears, noses and lungs. Our teeth ground on it and our very souls felt gritty. At evening a tribe of black and weary humans came up from below, drew each a bucket of water, slipped off their filthy rags and bathed on the foredeck. Often after this I would dive over the side and refresh myself with a swim.

The Skipper generously allowed us to draw money each week for he was not obliged to let us have any if he did not think it advisable. Each week we could have one hundred pesos which was as much as we earned at our pay of £9.10s per month. He was also very kind in letting us for'ard have the use of the ship's boat in order to get ashore. She was a handy craft and often I would act as ferryman and put my shipmates ashore at the landing. Then, because I wasn't all that keen on the drinking that they all indulged in, I'd go off and prowl about the bay. I'd visit the many ships and then at sunset, I'd go to the landing place and collect those men who did not stay ashore for the night. The boat was easy to scull and I stood at the stern with a long steering oar and manoeuvred her about the harbour and thoroughly enjoyed myself.

Iquique was then a very busy port and there were many ships coming and going day by day. There were big steamers of a Dutch Line whose ships were built after the style of the Blue Funnel Line of Liverpool and these I often visited because their larders were well stocked and with an eye to a Cape Horn passage, I was able to buy little extras like cocoa, cheese, condensed milk, etc., from their stewards who, when they heard that I was from a sailing ship, were always very helpful. Good tobacco could also be got from them very cheaply. Sometimes these ships had let their deck space to a banana merchant in Central America who loaded up with the green fruit so that all the space available was stacked high with them and they were sold down the coast as they ripened. I could buy a stick of bananas which was as much as I could carry for six pesos. I would hang the stick by the head of my bunk and lie there and read and eat and my shipmates appreciated that there was over a hundredweight of fruit for all to help themselves.

Sometimes I would join the rest and prowl about the town and drop in at sundry cafés and swop yarns with the men from the other sailing ships in the harbour. A favourite place of resort was called the Radical Club and it was approached by a stairway that went straight up from the street. There was a large, airy and well-lit room with chairs at small marble-topped tables and a bar opened out of it. There was another door which opened out of this bar and which gave on to a landing on the outside of the building and a stairway which led on to unexplored regions.

One evening we were all in the big room with some Scandinavian members of the crews of *Lawhill* and *Pommern* and there were also numbers of Chilenos who were mixing with us and we were all talking, drinking, singing, and playing cards. Paddy Delaney had been drinking deeply and he went out to the outer stairway for a breath of fresh air. He was away for some time and his pal Jock got worried at his absence and went out to look for him. He found Paddy huddled on the stair, feeling miserable and not too sure of his surroundings. He also found a Chileno going through Paddy's pockets.

Jock gave one wild Highland yell, 'Ye dirrty Chileno bastud!' and went for the robber, knocked him into the bar and sailed in after him. Everyone leapt to his feet at this irruption and in a moment there was a free fight. The floor of the room was one glorious mix-up. Any dark skin you saw you hit before he could hit you and you aided any fair skin. The proprietor was a short, fat, sallow individual whom I saw dancing about the edge of the mêlée with a squat black bottle in his hand which he brought down smartly on any fair head that he saw with a muttered 'Hijo de puta'. Just as I spotted him, Svensk was thrust out of the scrap right by him. The Swede's massive fist shot out straight from the shoulder and that fellow's heels came up to the level of his chin before he crashed into a limp heap. Presently when we were beginning to feel that we were doing some good, one of the Chilenos darted downstairs to the street, and we, expecting reinforcements or the police, gathered our wounded and departed. No one was seriously hurt but we were all more or less marked and we left one or two senseless Chilenos on the floor. We learned later that they came round all right and we visited the place several times after that, so my shipmates told me, and no one appeared to bear any ill will.

My shipmates were a drunken lot but who could blame them? I have attempted to describe the hard conditions in which they worked; the crude accommodation, poor food and cruelly hard toil through long hours and many days at sea. There were no facilities for recreation and neither time nor energy for it anyway. Was it any wonder that they sought escape when they could in the one simple means available to them.

Late one afternoon I strolled through the town alone. I was dreaming of Sally and I was very unhappy but I tried to be hopeful for a future for us together. She was very much in my thoughts and I was hurt by her unexplained silence. Out to the west the sun was drowning in the Pacific and giving to the bare brown hills colours they could never possess of themselves. They towered above the houses and filled the end of the dusty street up which I walked. They rolled up and ever up to the great Chilean tableland, their drab sides crying their barrenness. Forbidding and sterile, they soared to high heaven and hung like a threat over the port and the houses scattered over the sandspit at their feet. All things were parched and dry. Nothing grew. Scraggy hens scratched in the roadway and I idly wondered what they sought.

The sun set and the shadows climbed the mountainside. I strolled another two hundred yards and passed a man who sold measures of water from a cart. Already it was dark. Dim lights from candles and oil lamps appeared at windows and at open doors. The windows were often unglazed and the doors hung crazily on twisted frames that the burning sun and arid air had warped and shrunk far from their original shape.

I wandered aimlessly on, filled with romantic thoughts of my beautiful beloved. An old toothless crone sat at an open doorway and she held out a soiled and skinny hand.

'Deme poco plata, buen senor?' she lisped.

I loafed on.

Suddenly my hat was snatched from my head, and whirling, I saw a slender ankle and a high-heeled shoe disappearing past the old witch. I swung back in fury to the doorway, brushed aside the trembling hand of the old one, but I saw her leering grin.

I strode into the house. There was only one room but a curtain divided off a part of it. I swept it aside, and there, across a double bed, two dark eyes laughed at me from under a mop of delightfully towsled black hair. She held my hat behind her and two red lips parted over pearly teeth in a roguish smile. But I was angry.

'Deme mi sombrero!' I demanded fiercely.

She looked at me maddeningly and put her head on one side. Black brows lifted over two big eyes in which the lamplight gleamed. Her clear ivory skin was only slightly flushed.

'Venga acqui. Come an' take it, senor.'

Little devil, I thought. 'Give it to me. Pronto!'

'No, senor. It is 'ere. Come an' get it,' and her smile showed the wiles of centuries.

I vaulted the bed and, before she could dodge round the

93

end I had my arms round her from behind. My fingers pressed into the softness of her rounded breasts as she strained away from me. Her heels hacked at my shins and she scratched and bit. I swung her off her feet and made to grasp my hat but she flung it over the bed and reached back over her head with both hands, seized my hair and pulled with all her strength. I could feel the muscles of her lithe young body tense with the effort and it felt as if she would scalp me.

Then she was suddenly limp in my arms and as I relaxed my grip she swung round to face me, put her arms around my neck and looked up at me and laughed. I was breathless from the whirlwind struggle but she was cool and her voice was only faintly hurried.

'You are strong, senor.' Her hand slid caressingly over my shoulder and felt my arm. 'Si, very,' she whispered and again the big eyes smiled, as she said softly, 'You do not want your hat . . . yet . . . my strong senor?'

Her shapely form was pressed to me. I could feel the vitality throbbing in her and my own blood leaped in response. I held her close and bent my head to kiss those full red lips. Another moment and I should have crushed them passionately on mine but in that moment I saw all those other lips that must have kissed hers. Drunken, lewd, callous, and lustful, I saw them all and with a curse I flung away from her and round the bed. As I bent to pick up my hat I saw her stoop and lift the hem of her skirt but I was too mad with rage and disgust to realise her intent. I had all but reached the door when I felt a blow and something seared into the small of my back. I lurched forward and, with a hand on either doorpost, I turned to face her. The girl was half crouched a few feet from me. The knife was in her hand and I remember wondering that there was no blood on it. She must have withdrawn the blade at once. She stood there with hunched shoulders and stared. Hate and resentment glared at me from under the black brows.

'You damned little cat!' I gasped and in my fury I wrenched at the doorway and the whole fabric of the frail wooden

94

house cracked and swayed. The door fell inwards against the girl and knocked the knife from her hand and the old woman shrieked and made to rise but I kicked the stool from under her and slipped down an alley beside the house. I winced and felt faint as I climbed over a wall. I stumbled in the darkness over what seemed to be a dump, crawled through a broken fence and was away before the screams brought the neighbours to interfere.

In the shelter of a deep doorway in the thickness of an old adobe wall I tore up my shirt and bound a wad of it over the flowing wound. A shirtless man was not unusual in that climate and I got back aboard the ship. I asked the Skipper to wash the cut with antiseptic and, as he stuck some cotton wool over it with some plaster he said, 'You *will* go to such places. But don't worry. It's gone with the sinew channels and not across them. It's only a flesh wound though fairly deep.' It felt more like a deep bruise than anything else and the discomfort was gone in a few days.

Through the town and down by the outer beach there was a park of sorts and a picturesque restaurant known as 'Chalet Suisse'. Sometimes Porteous and I and one or two others of the crew would retire to these more peaceful surroundings where we could sit in a sunlit window and look out over the restless Pacific. Here we could eat crisp, crusty pancitos with butter and good coffee or have a meal of 'biftek' or 'hamneck'. There I remember Mike, one of our ordinary seamen, who had no Spanish, and in order to explain to the waiter, who had no English, gave a detailed pantomime of how to milk a cow so that he might have milk in his coffee.

One Sunday, Porteous and I went to the races. We did not back any winners but it was as good as any show. The course lay at the back of the town and it had originally been covered with tan. In time this had disappeared or had been ground to a powder and over all lay the ubiquitous fine white dust. This dust overlay everthing in Iquique. Whether it blew overland from the Atacama Desert or whether it was volcanic in origin and drifted up on the prevailing southerly winds from the mighty Aconcagua, I do not know but it was fine and white and it lay on all things.

The horses, small lean animals, paraded in a fine show. Glossily groomed, wiry little beasts with their jockeys in bright coloured silks, they walked around and the crowd would look them over and rush off to the parimutuel to lay their bets. The horses lined up with many prancings and curvettings on their part and to many shouted instructions and earnest looks from their backers. As there were never more than five in a race, they usually got away well and then all that could be seen was a great cloud of white dust going round the course after the fore part of the first horse. The horses started as bays, blacks, whites, and roans, but they finished as one general dirty white and at least at the front of the jockeys' gay shirts the colours were indistinguishable.

The finish was tremendous excitement. The crowd threw their canes and straw hats in the air and yelled like mad. We saw one Chileno tear off a brand new hat with a joyous whoop, throw it to the ground and jump on it with howls of delight. I said to Bill, 'Let's watch him collect. He must have made a fortune.' We followed him to the pay-out window and he took his winnings with his coppery face wreathed in smiles of unalloyed joy. Five pesos.

We spent some evenings aboard other ships in the harbour and we frequently visited *Garthneill*. She was then the only other British vessel in port and she was manned mostly by cadets though there were one or two older men in the focsle and all declared that the food on board was awful. There were some pigs aboard her and one of the crew who was putting in square-rig time in order to qualify for a Hull Pilot's certificate, told us that the food that went to the focsle was the same as that which went to the pig pen.

Paradoxically, they all agreed that their Skipper was a splendid man. My chum Porteous sailed in her later from London to Melbourne and he also said that Mr Thompson

96

was as fine a Skipper as he could wish to sail with. *Garthneill* looked a trim little barque, but on board she appeared to be in a sorry state of disrepair.

We also made friends with two of the crew of *Lawhill* who were a very mixed lot and who all left the ship there except these two Australians who were making a passage to Europe. One of these was a deserter from the Australian Navy, and though I took an immediate liking to the other, I cannot now remember his name. On those ships under the Finnish flag they had the hardest biscuits it is possible to imagine. They were roughly elliptical in shape, about nine inches long with an irregular hole in the middle. The colour was that of old Jacobean oak and they were about as strong. I 'borrowed' a couple and took them aboard our ship and though we had some powerful fellows among us, not one of them could break one with his bare hands. After I had broken one up by hitting it with an iron belaying pin, I soaked it in a cup of coffee for four hours. It could be eaten but it tasted like sour sawdust. I nailed the other at the end of my bunk as a frame for a photograph of Sally, and even at the end of the voyage after months in that moisture-laden atmosphere, it had not softened or grown mouldy.

A big German auxiliary four-masted barque *Magdalen Vinnen* came into the port and one evening some of us visited her. It was her maiden voyage and she was, to us, a wonderfully well-appointed ship. She was manned wholly by cadets who told us that they were all destined for the Norddeutsche Lloyd Company. They were a fine healthy lot of lads and though they had no English and we had no German, we got on quite well together with sign language and graphic pantomime and they showed us over their ship. With her auxiliary diesel motors and refrigerated storeroom she combined the pleasures of sail with the comforts of steam. In those days we had not the remotest idea of the comparative luxury that the lone sailor Chichester could enjoy for a voyage in sail.

There was a Finnish training vessel lying close to us named *Glenard*. She was a little, once British, stump t'gallant barque, i.e. she carried no royal sails and she was resplendent in white paint and gleaming brass. She had been in Newcastle when we were there and I had heard that some of her apprentices had cleared out and that she had had some difficulty in making up her crew. A couple of Scots lads from Leith had shipped aboard her and very fed up with the ship they were. They declared that they were worked very hard and starved to death. They were neither of them very robust and I did not think that they made the best of things. However, they made up their minds that they would leave the ship and as they had no money and could not draw any of their pay, we had a 'tarpaulin muster' for them. This yielded enough pesos for them to get away up to the nitrate mines where they hoped to get a living. From what we heard of that place we did not expect them to be there for long.

Eighteen months later, when Bill and I were strolling along Lime Street in Liverpool, we met these two on their way home. They, like all sailors who jumped their ships there, found that there was only short commons and hard work at the mines and they had drifted back to Iquique. They had managed to get a job on a steamer bound through Panama for Jamaica, and after spending some time in the West Indies, they had been able to get a berth on a ship bound for England and had been paid off in London.

Then there was *E.R. Sterling*, a big graceful six-masted barquentine, which had at one time been the British four masted barque *Lord Wolseley*. She had been built for, and had spent, many years in the jute trade from Calcutta to Dundee until she had been sold to American owners, re-rigged and sailed under the Stars and Stripes. Old Arthur had sailed in her for years when she had sailed under the Red Duster.

We visited her and met most of the crew, none of whom thought much of her Skipper. They said that he tried to be a hard case but he had not the strength of character to carry it off. She had uncomfortably crowded quarters and a very mixed crew and they were certainly a hard-bitten lot. They had nearly all deserted from other ships and had been ashore

98

in Chile for some time. I was surprised to hear one of them speaking good English in an educated voice and he told me that his people were prosperous merchants in Sydney but that he had kicked over the traces and was seeing life from the other side. He was getting a good look at it.

There was another full-rigged ship under the Finn flag which had particularly sweet lines and lofty spars. She was an ex-British ship with a good record but the thing that interested me most at that time was her makeshift crew. All hands that had brought her out had left her there, and they swore that never again would they sail in her under any circumstances. The waterfront of Iquique had supplied her with a crew and such a mixture!

Men from fourteen countries were in her focsle. We visited her the day before she sailed because there were a couple of Britishers aboard whom we had befriended ashore and Bill and I had collected some odds and ends of warm clothing for them against a Cape Horn passage. We did not envy them their shipmates. Few of them had any language but their own and a great hairy-chested Spaniard feelingly cursed one of his mates about the occupancy of a bunk and was answered in voluble Russian. Sweden, France, Italy, Germany, Bolivia, U.S.A., Chile, Japan, Australia, Finland, and Norway were all represented and the place was a babel of what sounded like angry tones.

Of course all the ships were not like these but there was a large proportion under the Finnish flag and they had the reputation of being cruelly hungry ships. The main article of diet was sweet soup which was fairly solid and something of the order of Scotch broth but with a variety of dried fruit added. I have already described their hard bread. The accusations against them could not have been without some justification for as soon as one would make port it was the general rule for all or nearly all hands to clear out and to get as far away from her as possible. Although they knew that most likely they would be forced to ship aboard another Finn before long, they swore that at least no other ship could be as bad as the one they had left. Doubtless the owners, who should be restless in their graves from the curses that were heaped upon them, were only too glad to have these desertions, as there would be an appreciable amount of wages that they would not have to pay, and possibly they encouraged the masters in this meanness.

Aboard the British ships in the harbour, complete harmony reigned or as nearly approaching that state as could be expected under the conditions. I do remember one Sunday afternoon when there were only three hands aboard our ship that one of the ordinary seamen stood shirtless on deck in a pugilistic attitude and shouted drunkenly to the cook to come out and get what was coming to him. The darkie stood just inside the door of his cabin and beckoned the young man in, while I, who had seen the razor behind his back, lounged unobserved with a heavy iron belaying pin, ready to stop any bloodshed. It fizzled out with an astonishing exchange of insults and really we were a very happy crew.

The cook had spoken to me that afternoon when I was sitting with my back against the deckhouse, reading and enjoying the warmth of the sun after a swim. He said, 'Yo' don' go shoah much?' I said, 'No. Neither do you Cookie.' He answered, 'Ah well, now Ah'm married an' Ah save ma money, but w'en Ah was yoah age Ah was at de fandango joints all de time. Ah'd git Madam judge o' pricks to give me de bes' gal in de whoah'ouse. In dem days Ah 'ad a prick 'at spat fiah!'

I believe that we were about the last sailing ship under the British flag that was manned by a crew who were nearly all sailors experienced in sail and who knew the ways of ships and the sea. We were very different from those few later ships which carried crews composed almost wholly of boys whose only reason for being there was to put in time for a square-rig ticket.

There was one Sunday when we were visited by a Salvationist, and the Skipper sent him forward with some hymn books. He looked an ill-fed, down-at-heel individual

100

but he was treated with the outward respect that I have often observed that the roughest of men will show to the disciple of almost any religion. There were more of us aboard than was usual on a Sunday and we were findings things a trifle dull so I slipped into the focsle and put on a collar and a waistcoat back to front. There was an ancient bowler without an owner kicking about and with my sheath knife I removed the brim, cut an inch and a half off the crown and put it back in place. This caricature of a shovel hat with a navy-blue serge jacket passed me off as a comedy clergyman and we held the most awful farce of a service.

We sang hymns with spirit and provided other words than those in the books. They were full of local colour and of comments about the ship that were neither polite not complimentary. I kept an eye on the Salvationist for fear that he might take offence but he appeared thoroughly delighted by what he may have put down to our religious fervour. He was spared the truth for his English was confined to 'Good-day', 'Yes', and 'No', and I admired his devotion to duty against this difficulty. When we crowned this performance by taking a collection and handing him a handful of centavos, his pleasure gave us some cause for shame.

In a mild way, the joke turned against us afterwards when we found that when he had come aboard he had made arrangements with the Skipper that those of us who would care to, could make a donation to his cause by signing a sheet against a certain amount and have the money deducted from our pay. We all paid up.

CHAPTER IX   TO CAPE HORN

In the meantime, our cargo was disappearing and when two-thirds were out we prepared to load some eight hundred tons of nitrate as stiffening before we discharged the rest of our coal. A space under the main hatch was cleaned and carefully swept, for coal dust and saltpetre make a highly explosive and dangerous mixture.

When this nitrate in gunny sacks was neatly stowed, rumours were frequent and varied as to our next destination. Some said that we would take a cargo back to Australia and some that we would be bound for the Continent of Europe. *Garthneill* had just sailed for Australia with nitrates and *Garthgarry* had done the same not long previously. Those who thought, and possibly hoped, more days being more dollars at the payoff, that we would follow this example, loudly quoted these precedents. The thought that we might do so appalled me. It was all right for my good shipmates, but I wanted urgently to get to England to see Sally and to know why I hadn't heard from her. I needed to look in her lovely eyes and to see her gleaming hair and her pretty mouth. I wanted to know that there was some silly ordinary reason why I had not heard from her and to ease the anxiety in my heart.

We completed the discharge of coal five weeks later and it was not long after that the news came that we were to load a full cargo of nitrate and to sail to Falmouth for orders. Now everyone was well pleased for it meant home for the majority aboard. For myself I was overjoyed. There would be scarcely more than four months of lime-juice ways and I should be in England in April. If Sally were not there when the ship arrived, I had long promised myself a walking tour in Devon in the Spring. Also it meant that we would round Cape Horn in midsummer and that was vastly preferable to sailing that stormy region when it is lashed by wintry gales as would have been the case had we made another passage across the Pacific.

One is accustomed to reading and hearing of the 'dreaded Horn', the 'stormiest and most dangerous of the world's headlands', etc., but I did not anticipate the passage with the least feeling of fear. Had anyone asked me, I should have said that I had supreme confidence in the Master's handling of his ship, and of his navigation, in our ability to cope with difficulties, in the ship herself and in our own good fortune, but the thought did not enter my head. If I thought of it at all it was with pleasurable pride that I should round Old Cape Stiff in a sailing ship and join the company of those ancient mariners who had fought their way round that storm-swept cape and whose souls, if their beliefs came true, have entered into those splendid albatrosses and still run their easting down round the world. It also would give me a reputed ability to piss to windward. Most of all I was on my way to see Sally.

A gang of Chileno stevedores now came aboard and the tiny tug was kept busy as it towed the nitrate-laden lighters out to us. The sailors could work out the dirty coal, but only Chilenos handled the clean sacks of nitrate. While they were loading, we painted the ship's sides. First we took a punt around her and with long scrapers did our best to clean the barnacles and marine growth from her bilges while she was still high out of the water. A flat-bottomed punt held alongside

104

a ship to a line run fore and aft is an insecure place at best in any swell and those who know the Pacific coast know what a swell runs in there. Also when we had this job to do there was always a fresh wind and a nasty short chop. It was a hard task to try from this bobbing craft to thrust a scraper down against the ship's side under water. We shoved a tool shaped like a Dutch hoe against the weeds and things but this action pushed the punt off. At the same time a playful wave tipped up the other side and we made desperate grabs at the line which held us and whose swaying motion caused us to make the wildest gyrations in our efforts to keep our balance till a more kindly disposed wave put us right. Then we had to paint with thin, sticky, evil-smelling anti-fouling paint. We had some illicit recompense when we found that, from the shelter of the counter, safely out of sight of the Mate's questing eyes, we could barter with cruising boatmen one pot of paint for one bottle of vino. It took as long and as much paint to paint that area under the counter as it did to paint all the sides.

The ship *Monkbarns* made port as our loading neared completion and we paid interested visits to her for she was also one of the few full-rigged ships still afloat and the only other British one and she belonged to the same Company as our ship, John Stewart, of London. So quickly had steam ousted sail that in 1924, there in Iquique, the last two full-riggers under the Red Duster met. At that time there were some eighteen deep-water sailing vessels under the Red Ensign, but the others were barques. At the beginning of the century they had been numbered in many hundreds.

At length the last few lighters came alongside and before long the loading was completed, hatches battened down, sails bent, and we were ready for sea.

I wrote to Sally before we sailed. I sent her a long letter that told her of our life aboard and of Iquique and of the people there; of their lives and ways; of the harbour and of the ships and of their men. I also told her of the brilliant sunshine on the bright sea and on the drab and barren land.

I wrote nothing of my concern at not having had a letter from her, but I wrote in glowing terms of the things that we should do when we met in England. We could not know where the ship would go from Falmouth but I asked her to write to me at the Sailors' Home in London. There was plenty of time. We could not expect to be there in less than three months at the very least.

The tug struggled out with us at about ten in the morning of Thursday 4th December and we set every stitch of canvas to the light breeze. To get away from the strong current that flows to the north we headed off shore and we made slow progress for the next three or four days till we picked up a stronger southerly which held us on a westerly course for a week. It was delightful weather and we found it cool and pleasant in the south wind which accompanies this Peruvian Current. Except for the daily 'sweat-up' we did not touch a brace and, during the night watches, the 'farmers', i.e. those who had neither to keep look-out on the focsle head, nor to take their trick at the wheel, could sleep in peace during their watch on deck.

On the tenth day out we sighted *Glenard*, the Finnish training ship which had left Iquique the day before us, and we did not lose sight of her for a week. Day after day she hung there, hull down on the weather beam, and we could not shake her off. Every morning the Old Man would come on deck soon after dawn and scan the horizon, and when his eyes sighted her sails, he would look daggers. No sailing ship master liked to think that his ship couldn't show a clean pair of heels to most others and he was riled to see a little bald-headed barque holding its own with us. When, one morning, there was nothing to mar the clean line of the horizon's vast circle, he held his head higher and stepped more lightly.

Soon we ran into a belt of calms but they did not last long and we found a useful easterly and for days we headed away south under clear skies and a hot sun. By Christmas Eve we had made a long way to the south and well to the west. It began to grow cold at nights and we started to dig down to the bottoms of sea-chests and bags for heavier clothing. There was a school of bonito about the bows that day and I thought of how nice it would be to have something fresh for our Christmas dinner. I tried hard to capture one of the fish but they would not rise to my lure.

No particular festivities marked Christmas Day. Big John had kept a bottle of cognac stowed in his bunk all the way from Iquique, which was something of an accomplishment for him. Often, on our way south, as he sat on the edge of his bunk and quietly smoked his long-stemmed pipe, he would suddenly yell 'Christmas!', dive his hand behind him, seize the bottle and wave it aloft while his trap of a mouth fell open to his deafening 'Haw! Haw!' Old Arthur would look at the deck and mutter 'Bloody fool' into his luxuriant moustache. This day the bottle was opened and with much smacking of lips and gestures of appreciation, we all drank to John's and to each other's health but there was no shout from aft of 'Splice the main brace'. Various comments were made about stingy shipmasters.

As it was a Thursday, we had our usual breakfast of haricot beans boiled with molasses but this day the dish was garnished with a slice of fat bacon for each man. At midday we certainly had plum duff but we had duff anyway on Thursdays and of what it was made we never knew but it was a soggy business and this was no exception. We did have one great treat for this meal. The spuds were peeled!

The first of the westerly winds came with the New Year and we bowled along merrily. It was cold in spite of summer and as we sailed further south the cold grew bitter and the seas much larger. We did not as yet take much heavy water aboard but the ship would roll her scuppers under every now and then and the decks were kept wet and slippery. We really had a remarkably fine weather run and we took in no sail, barring one squally night when we stowed the royals, until the 5th of January when we were getting well down to the latitude of Cape Horn. That evening at eight bells all hands took in the mainsail and the royals as the breeze was really beginning to freshen up. It blew hard all through the first watch and before midnight we stowed the fore and mizzen t'ga'nts'ls. Bill and I furled the fore and I had some pardonable pleasure at the improvement in my skill and health and strength. Conditions were not of the best and I suffered from a continual gnawing hunger but I felt that nothing could be too much for me. I sailed into that canvas as if it were possessed of an inimical personality and I felt that it could not get the better of me. I took the weather side and Bill had the lee and we had it snugged up on the yard in quick time.

The wind held steady through the night but there were some heavy squalls in the early morning when the ship lay over and tore along with an acre of white water around her bows. Shortly after dawn we were called to take in the main t'ga'nts'l and as Porteous and I pulled hard on the port clew-line the rusty wire rope carried away and the heavy block came down fairly between us. A matter of inches either way and one of us would have been brained. Then, from the extra strain put upon it, the leech line parted and we ran aloft to smother the sail before it should blow out. It was lashing furiously in the gale and the iron clew flung murderously but we stowed it without mishap. We gloried in the scrap and we knew that real pleasure of pitting our strength and skill against the elemental fury of the gale, but we added more curses to the tally against that cotton sail.

The wind was now piping in good style and we were driving along in a yeasty expanse, now lifted aloft on the great seas and anon down in the trough with our horizon limited to the crest of the next wave. It is not easy for one who has not been in the Southern Ocean to realise the size of those huge seas which roll on unhindered around the world for fourteen thousand miles.

On and on they go, ever growing. From Cape Horn they pass far south of the Cape of Good Hope, on past inhospitable Kerguelen, cover the long leagues between and ring with snowy foam the other sub-Antarctic islands. They gather size south of Australia and New Zealand and sweep majestic-

108

ally across that vast empty tract of the South Pacific till they crash in thunder on the western coasts of Patagonia or take up the tale again to the south of Cape Horn. Sometimes they travel under blue skies before gentle winds in slow and solemn array. At other times the mad gale rips off their tops in flying mist while grey and tattered clouds lower over their dull and foam-streaked slopes and their breaking crests are snowy caps which gleam through the haze of spray and rain. At times the winds oppose them but their progress is too indomitable for them to be checked and only their crests are blown back to form the flowing manes of wild white horses. To see them march on in their might, half a mile from the crest of one wave to the crest of the next, relentless, inexorable, their grey inclines lacy with foam, their broken creamy heads flying away in smoke, while the westering sun gleams through their summits to turn their grim colour to brightest emerald, is a thing to remember.

Now conditions hardened. Our watch again put a frapping on the main topmast backstays in one dog watch and we hove it tight turn by turn with the main deck capstan. As we worked there in the waist of the ship in that heavy weather when big seas broke aboard, we were several times washed half round the decks and thoroughly drenched through our old and worn oilskins. Then we had to go aloft and take in the foresail. Another glorious scrap when hail and rain drove at us and the wind-tormented sail did its best to defeat our efforts.

Thereafter we did many repairs aloft. First it was the leather service which protects the foot of the foresail from chafe on the forestay. 'Sails' repaired it on the yard while I held it for him and cold grim work that was to gather and hold up the sail with numbed fingers. Sailmakers, in common with all good sailormen, take pride in doing a job properly, no matter what the conditions and so we clung there on the yard in the bitter gale and I held the roping and the leather for him while he carefully stitched with a needle that was as brittle as glass in that weather.

He was going on as usual about unappreciative shipowners

109

and I asked him if he wouldn't rather work ashore like many other tradesmen. He sniffed and said that there would be plenty of jobs afloat if only ship-owners would see that sailing ships were better than stinking steamers.

'But', said I, 'it's in sail lofts ashore that fully qualified sailmakers work now, even if they are stitching hatch covers or making covers for winches and other steamers' equipment. Surely that's a better job than being afloat on a sailing ship with all the hardships and short commons that goes with this life? Do you really prefer to turn in to your lonely bunk under the focsle head each night, to being tucked up snugly in bed with your wife at home?'

He looked at me a bit sternly but I concentrated on the job in hand and kept my face blank.

'I've always been at sea, effer since I finished my apprenticeship, indeed,' he said shortly.

'Wouldn't there be plenty of jobs for an experienced man like you in making yacht sails?'

'Yacht sails!' he snorted. 'D'ye think I'd want to earn me living making sails for the idle rich who neffer did a hands turn of honest work intheir lifes whateffer? D'ye think that I could effer sleep sound at nights if I effer did anything to help them indulge their extravagances? 'Twould blacken me soul indeed!'

'There may be something to be said for that but you work for a ship-owner, and if you saw him riding in his carriage, you'd probably think him idle and rich. One has to live and I should think that those people would pay you well for your skills. You could even make a name for yourself.'

'Come on,' he said as he made off the last stitch. 'You make fast that buntline again with a proper backing hitch now. Learn how to be a real sailor young man and leaf me to know best how to spend my life. Down on deck I'll go. You roll up the sail again and make the gasket fast,' and he made his way along the footrope and swung into the rigging.

Then the clewline on that cursed main t'ga'nts'l had to be renewed and new buntlines were rove off for it while the

110

wind whistled about and through us. We came on deck for one watch as the iron sheave in the pennant block on the brace at the fore upper topsail yardarm carried away and flung its fragments down on deck with a rattle like rifle fire. Luckily no one was hurt as the terrific strain on the brace shot the pieces with dangerous force. Doubtless the intense cold had something to do with its breaking. We found how cold it was as we lay out at the yardarm and rigged a gantline to send the damaged block down to the deck for repair. I well remember what a ticklish business it was, for the yardarm of a ship running in a gale with the brace adrift is none too secure a perch, and when everything that one touches is painfully cold, it does not add to one's safety. There must have been a whacking great iceberg floating up the wind.

Next day it was the fore royal gear and a general rapid overhaul with an eye to Cape Horn weather. There was a strand to be put in here, a seizing to be renewed there, this block to replace and that one to secure. So we worked aloft on the swaying spars, examining, testing, and repairing, while there were sails to be stowed or to be set, braces to be hauled and the tricks at the wheel and the lookout to be kept.

We had several days of squally weather when the wind freshened to gale force and died out every twelve hours. Naturally these conditions called for a repeated shortening or of setting sails and we were endlessly hauling on ropes on deck or up aloft furling canvas.

There was one weekend that started with a light air from the nor'east to which we lay close-hauled on the port tack. Gradually it veered to the south and we had to wear ship to be able to lay our course. For the rest of the weekend we sailed gently along with the benison of bright sunshine from clear skies. Except for the perishing cold it was quite enjoyable as at that time of the year in that latitude, there were no more than three hours of night and then it did not grow properly dark.

Then the wind drew aft and freshened to a good spanking breeze. It sent us along at over eight knots while the skies

111

were obscured by flying wrack and there were some slight falls of snow . . . and this was midsummer!

Soon after midday, 13th January, we sighted land close on the port bow. The old Mate hailed it as an old acquaintance. 'Diego Ramirez Islands,' he said. 'It won't be long now before we're round.'

We passed the islands some six miles away at three o'clock. There were three large and several smaller islands and ugly, grey, barren rocks they looked. They rose steeply out of a grey sea into a grey sky and they were outlined in foam as the tireless seas crashed into them. We saw them under fine conditions as we sailed past before a fair wind but many a stout ship's company had seen them suddenly loom out of driving rain or blinding snow, while the towering seas lashed themselves to fury on their iron cliffs . . . and sometimes it had been too late.

Old Arthur told us how, on a ship outward bound from London to Valparaiso, they had sighted these cruel rocks one day in midwinter when beating against a howling westerly gale, with the air full of snow and the ship's gear encased in ice. For weeks they sailed close-hauled now on this tack and now on that as they strove to get to windward against the ceaseless westerly winds. Their galley was washed out and for a whole week they had no hot food. They slept when and how they could and for days on end no man was able to take off his clothes. Then one day, *ten weeks later*, they sighted land on the weather bow . . . Diego Ramirez. It was two weeks more before they got a lucky slant and were able to get away from that terrible region.

'All for some well-fed shipowner,' he said.

Paddy Murphy came out of his shell for once and told us of a barque in which he had sailed in similar circumstances but, when the Skipper found that after a week he had made no progress into the contrary wind, he shouted from the poop, 'Square the main yard!' The ship turned before the wind and sailed away eastward. In fifty-five days she made her port of Valparaiso. She experienced strong west winds

112

all the way south of the Cape of Good Hope, on across the South Indian Ocean, south of Australia and New Zealand and across the South Pacific.

That day we bent a crossjack, which Sails had made up from an old foresail. No sail had been bent on the cro'jack yard for the whole voyage and the opinion was freely passed in the focsle that the sail was not much help to the ship. It certainly made the steering more difficult and she carried more helm.

At four the next morning, Cape Horn stood out clear on our beam, four miles away. I took a good look at it to impress it on my memory, for though countless ships have rounded that stormy headland, few ever sight it. It is most often shrouded in mist, rain, or snow, and many shipmasters give it a wide berth. It is a bleak mountainous island which rises to a solitary peak and far beyond it we could see high, snow-capped ranges. It was a beautifully peaceful morning and the light westerly wind wafted us along at about four knots with scarcely a motion except the gentle lift and descend to the mile long rollers. They were so quiet and steady in their stately progress that we scarcely felt their might. Every sail was set and drawing to the welcome wind.

How differently I had pictured it! I had imagined us storming along under shortened canvas before breaking seas, the air thick with driven rain and spray, the gale shrieking in the taut rigging, sails straining at their sheets and spars groaning their protests. I had visualised the lookout man peering into the murk ahead and the Skipper standing on the poop in streaming oilskins, anxious eyed.

We had only experience of reading weather signs to tell us what to expect, but such scientific progress has been made in fifty years that Captain Cousteau, in his research ship 'Calypso', has been able to forecast the weather accurately in that region from photographs from a man-provided satellite.

113

The *William Mitchell* leaves Melbourne

Big John with his pipe   Bill Porteous

The crew of the *William Mitchell*. I am fourth from the left in the back row

I dress up as the comedy clergyman

Fine weather — N.E. Trades

Bending hard weather sail

White water at her bows

A fair blow — North Atlantic

A good breeze on our quarter

Nitrate lighters alongside in Iquique. The German *Privall* coming to
her buoy

The *Kilmallie* outward bound. We've dropped the pilot

Our quarters — seven men lived in this space

Murphy at the wheel

Jim assists the sailmaker

Snugged down for a bit of a blow in the South Pacific

The albatross resents the camera

I bathe from the jib-boom end

Tom's bike

Heavy weather in the South Pacific

Hands aloft furl the upper topsail

Before a stiff breeze

Meals from the galley with difficulty

Apprentice lads

The hillside picture in Pisco Bay

The island is white with guano   The apprentices rig out a diving board

Loading guano

"Alongside your funny li'l ship"

The big Dorado that didn't get away

CHAPTER X   ON TO FALMOUTH

These conditions did not last long though we passed Staten Island next day in fine clear weather, but a freshening wind gave us six knots. Two days later we passed the Falklands before a steady and strong wind but with calm seas and doing a good nine knots. It was good to be heading up to the north and to warmer latitudes and Sally was more often in my thoughts, but the work now going on aboard was the worst in a sailor's life. It was the custom from time immemorial to clean up the teakwood of rails, charthouse, binnacle, wheel, etc., with sand and canvas and always in the coldest weather. It was always so in these ships and I suppose that it was so for as long as they sailed. 'It is the custom' was a perfectly irrefutable reason for doing many things in windjammers.

To describe the torture; a piece of heavy canvas was folded to a suitable size and held in the hand, wetted in a bucket of salt water and dipped in a bucket of sand. It was then, with the sand adhering, vigorously rubbed on the teakwood to remove the old varnish and to make a clean smooth surface. It may not sound so very bad, but with wet hands in a bitingly cruel wind and cold salt water that *will* run down your sleeves no matter how carefully you lash your oilskins about your wrists, it is sheer misery. All of us had 'sea cuts', those deep, painful cracks on fingers and palms that are caused by constant wetting with salt water and by hauling on wet and harsh ropes, and when the sand and salt water get into these cuts the pain is acute. The job seems futile and senseless and the agony of stiff fingers that have no suppleness left in them and which hit up against corners and scrape their knuckles along sand-covered wood is exasperating. I hated it as everyone did. We went at it because the harder we worked the sooner it would be over but how glad one was to spend two hours of the watch at the kicking wheel even though the cold rain blew under one's sou'wester and wandered down one's back like some horrible creepy-crawly thing with frost-bitten feet.

We could be washed around the deck and bruised and battered as she wallowed in green seas, pull and pull and pull again till every muscle was an aching pain, be wet and cold to the bone and so hungry that we could chew our boots, have finger nails broken and torn in furling a frozen, iron-hard sail. We could take that as part of the game and get a laugh out of it, but ... sand and canvas the brightwork? No. The devil take it.

We saw a number of porpoises, blackfish and cowfish in these latitudes, and one evening as I leaned on the focslehead railings on lookout, I marvelled at the wonderful co-operation displayed by two porpoises that came playing round the bows. They dived at astonishing speed right under the forefoot. Now on this side and now on that, they darted ahead on the bow wave as the ship broke over a swell but always side by side with only a few inches between them and swimming 'fin and fin'. I have often remarked the amazing co-ordination of movement between a pair of these animals and by night in tropic seas, when their trails of phosphoresence have made them appear like twin fiery snakes, I have watched their complete synchronism, spellbound by its perfection.

A few days later, when there was a calm, a number of cowfish which are somewhat larger than porpoises, but with a blunt head, came quite near the bows and we watched some twenty of them from the focsle head. They dived till they were mere grey shadows in the crystal clear water and then came straight up together and as they broke water with their coughing blow, they would stand erect half out of the water in grotesque and wavering balance till they fell over to one side. Some of them rolled over and over or they somersaulted and fooled about like children showing off their tricks.

That particular morning I had been at the wheel as day broke and we passed through water that was discoloured by irregular streaks of what appeared to be muddy water. These streaks stretched to either horizon up and down the wind and I could not make out what caused this strange phenomenon. Darwin observed this when on the cruise of H.M.S. *Beagle*, and he believed it to be composed of countless hordes of those tiny crustacea upon which some whales feed but they did not appear to me to be like those minute shellfish plankton which dust the surface of the ocean with gold. It looked exactly like the dirty water that a clay-banked river will send down in flood time but we were at least six hundred miles from land. I think that Mr Darwin must have been right.

As day followed day the weather improved. The chill went from the strong wind and cheerful sunshine warmed us. The ship sailed on with her sails piled proudly in firm rounded tiers. The gracefully curved triangles of her jibs pointed her course while the sun pencilled the lines of her intricate cordage on them all. Men swung aloft at their work on the towering masts and spreading yards or they crawled like spiders in the network of her rigging.

Then light and uncertain winds were with us for a time but these gradually freshened and aligned themselves till they became the constant south-east Trades, the day after we passed Trinidad. We sighted this island on 12th February and as we drew up on it, its jagged outline showed clearly against the clear blue sky. We stole past it before a gentle wind in the beautiful moonlit night and in the still bright silence, broken only by the whispering chuckles of the parted water, it looked like a fairy place and gave no hint of its ghastly barrenness or of its repulsive land crabs.

All hands now had an energetic time at bending fine-weather sails to save the better sails for hard weather. Then we painted the bulwarks and deckhouses and varnished the brightwork. It is said that half a voyage is spent in making a ship ready for sea and the other half in getting her ready for port. We were busily engaged these fine days in the latter activity. I suppose that skippers had to show their owners how well a ship was maintained.

Everything aloft that was not painted had to be tarred and up we went with pots of stockholm tar and wads of cotton waste and we tarred iron sheets and shackles and chains and wire pennants. We tried, not too successfully, to save the tar from flying about and we stained our hands and forearms black in the process. The tar could not be washed off but at length it wore off and the stained skin peeled in patches and gave to our hands a horribly mottled appearance. Then we painted the masts and yards while the steady Trade wind thrust us surely through the deep blue ocean but spattered the lee clews of the sails with spots of paint.

Sails, with Big John to help him, was overhauling the hard weather sails in preparation for them to be bent again when we had lost the north-east Trades and had to sail in the more violent conditions of the North Atlantic. John and he arranged their benches on the poop at right angles to each other with the sail-locker hatch between them. Sails would chatter on about how sinful we all were and how we should all reform under his instructions, with the hand of God to guide him. John would appear to drink it all in and he would have nothing to say for quite long periods. Then he would suddenly come out with an outrageous comment that would shock Sails to silence. He would hide his face while John gave vent to his shattering guffaw.

They had the help of two apprentices to haul out of the sail locker the carefully labelled sails and to open them out for examination. When the sails had been repaired as necessary by a centre stitching here, a renewal of service there, a chafing cloth to be replaced, or a cringle to be made, the boys would make up the sail and bring another on deck for attention. One of the boys went below to select the sail asked for, and handed it up to the boy on deck.

Sails asked for a forestaysail as I walked along to take my trick at the wheel. The apprentice could see the sail from on deck and he bent over and reached down to seize it and haul it up. It did not come away from its rack as easily as he had expected. He was a fat youngster and his well-rounded bottom rose in the air as he tugged at the clew of the reluctant sail. Big John's expressive face wrinkled in wicked glee and his eyes sparkled as he leaned towards Sails and jerked his thumb at the youngster's figure.

'Py Gott, Sails,' he said, 'Vot a lofly leetle bum! Vouldn't you lake him in your bunk tonight? Vouldn't you yust lake to fok dot poy?' and his clattering laugh split the air at Sails' shocked and horrified expression.

The Trades were with us in earnest now and they bowled us along at a constant six or seven knots while we got on with our painting and made a real job of brightening her up, and took some pride in this. Shrouds and backstays were tarred at the splices and painted down, service was repaired as necessary, and the doublings, where the standing rigging was secured at the deadeyes, were painted a glossy black and the seizings picked out in white. During the passage across the South Pacific we had chipped and scraped all the old paint from the bulwarks and deckhouses and we had painted them for protection with red lead. Now, after every watch on deck had been spent by most of us with paint brush in hand, they shone white. It was quite astonishing what a difference the gleaming paint made to the ship after the sombre colour with which we had become familiar and I firmly believe that all hands brightened as a consequence. In spite of hunger and hard toil, we usually found something to laugh at.

On Sunday, 22nd February, when we were seventy-eight days from Iquique, we crossed the Line and we still had the south-east Trades though they were fading away. We had the

119

good fortune to hold a fair wind through the Doldrums and except for once checking in the yards a couple of points, and again pointing them during the next watch, we did not have any of the pulling and hauling on the braces which is generally associated with these latitudes. A few dorado came swimming around the bows here and we tried hard to catch one of these beautifully coloured fish. We did hook one but our hook was not strong enough and it straightened out when Svensk started to lift the fish from the water. This fish was commonly called a dolphin by seamen, but it is not to be confused with the sea animal of that name. Its correct name is *coryphoena hippuris* and it is possessed of tremendous speed and vigour and is credited with being the fastest fish in the sea. Its colouring in the water is brilliant purple, red and canary yellow with bright red spots along its flanks. Immediately on being taken out it is simply bright yellow with a green shading along its dorsal fin which extends the length of its body. These colours intensify to an amazing degree as the fish dies, but in only a few seconds they are quite gone to leave it a dull grey.

At midday the sun was right overhead and the ship slipped along lazily under a blazing sky. The deck was blistering hot and the pitch bubbled up from the seams so as we were mostly barefooted, we had to be careful where we trod. It was hot and stuffy in the focsle at night and so we slept on deck on the main hatch where we caught a down draught of air from the mainsail. By night we were not disturbed much in our watches on deck and if one had neither wheel nor lookout one could turn in again after muster at eight bells.

The hard hatch was uncomfortable with the movement of the ship and sleep was not very profound. I spent several watches below in making rope yarns up into sennit and with this I fashioned a net hammock which I slung from convenient hooks under the focsle head. Thereafter I enjoyed sound and refreshing sleep. I made a similar hammock in almost every ship in which I served and I know no better way of sleeping well in hot weather than in a net hammock with a

120

blanket flung over it.

On Saturday, 28th February, the first of the north-east Trades came on us with a rush. I was at the wheel from ten till twelve that forenoon and the ship had all sails set to a light wind that barely gave her steerage way. At about six bells I could see a very heavy bank of clouds coming up on our weather beam. Soon we saw the distant wave tops whipped away in smoke and I took a firmer grip of the spokes of the wheel.

It was on us in a few minutes . . . WHOOSH! The sails roared as the wind filled them and the ship heeled over till the lee rail was at the water. Her masts and rigging cracked and groaned at the strain. I eased the helm down, luffed, and spilled the sails to a certain extent and the old ship lay over and flew along like a bird. At once the rain came in torrents that streaked horizontally and stung so that I had to keep my weather eye shut. My lee eye was strained aloft to the taut canvas to keep only the slightest shake on the weather clew of the fore royal. The blow lasted for a lively half hour with the rain driving hard, the ship tearing along in a welter of spray, myself clinging to the wheel, soaked and streaming, delighting in the lively response of the vessel and enjoying every moment of it. I saw the main tack carry away and the watch run to secure it but the preventer had held. Then the main topmast staystail blew out at the head only, but otherwise there was no damage and we lost no canvas.

I have kept a vivid memory of that morning when the storm blew up out of a peaceful sky. I can still recall the fine thrill of the good old ship as she responded to the whistling wind like a live thing as if she were tired of hanging around lazily and she wanted to be up and doing. There's a good feeling in being in control of a ship at such a time. She's at her best then. You watch her with every nerve at the alert; help her a little here; head her off there; perhaps you murmur, 'That's the stuff, old girl!' She seems to know that the grip on the spokes is to help her and she behaves like a lady. You

121

know that she's just a complicated fabric of steel and timber, canvas and rope, but the breath of heaven has put life into her.

William Mitchell was an easy ship to steer on a wind, and close-hauled in the Trades, she would steer herself. Watch after watch went by without the wheel being altered a spoke. With the wind a few points forward to three points abaft the beam, steering her was a pleasure, but when running before the wind with a following sea she was anything but a lady. It was as if, like most of her sex, she could be led but not driven and she would yaw about in the wildest way. Up on the crest of a sea, her stern would swing away and the heavy wheel would kick and jerk to be free of those restraining hands. At times one could only brace oneself and hang on grimly till the awful pressure eased and the helm could be altered to correct her wayward behaviour. Many a time, when running the easting down in the high latitudes, we felt that we eased our shoulders back into their sockets when the trick was over.

We were through the north-east Trades in ten days; ten days of rainless skies and brilliant sunshine; fresh steady winds and blue seas flecked by the gold of the drifting gulf weed.

As the Trades died away and light westerlies sent us further to the north, we unbent the fine-weather sails and sent the hard-weather suit aloft once more. We did the whole job in fourteen hours which was good going for six men and two apprentices which was all the hands available in a watch for one A.B. had to be at the wheel.

A fair wind gradually strengthened and we sailed along before a useful breeze to make eight knots. Hopes ran high for a good run from here to the Channel and the older hands told us of the times they had taken to sight the Lizard from this latitude. We held the wind for a week and made a thousand miles on our course.

One morning a thick squall came up on our quarter and when it had passed there was revealed to everyone's surprise, a big square-rigger just hull down on the horizon. She came up on us hand over fist although we were making good progress before the fresh wind. By one o'clock, two hours after being first sighted, she was plainly visible a couple of miles away. We signalled her and found that she was *Priwall* which had lain close to us in Iquique. She was one of that famous line, all of whose ships' names began with a P, owned by Herr Laeisz of Hamburg and which were known as the 'Flying P Liners'. Old Arthur claimed that he knew that if one of their skippers took more than one hundred days on the passage from the west coast of South America, he was promptly sacked. Big John had sailed on one of those ships and he confirmed that this was so.

Bill and I had been aboard *Priwall* in Iquique and we could see that they were hard-driven ships for they carried a heavy press of canvas and all their standing rigging was doubled to enable them to carry all possible sail. It had been said of them, and it is possibly true, that in strong winds the topsail halliards were padlocked so that no fearful member of the crew could lower the yards without authority and pre-venter sheets were shackled to the clews so that the sheets could not be let go from on deck. When one of them ran ashore under all sail in thick weather close to Dover many years ago, it was claimed by many experienced sailors of that time that sail could not be reduced in time to save her because of these preventer sheets.

Priwall had arrived in Iquique Bay in ballast five days before we left and we learned that she had sailed ten days after us so she made a very quick turn round for those days for those ships. Now here she was, and her graceful lines made a handsome picture as she overhauled us. She could certainly sail for she was abeam before three o'clock and she showed us a clean pair of heels as she was nearly out of sight by five. In 1932, she made a passage of sixty-eight days from Hamburg to the Spencer Gulf in South Australia, a time of which any of the earlier famous clipper ships could have been justly proud.

As I write of this encounter, I am reminded of a yarn I have heard from almost every square-rig sailor that I have met, though in various forms. It is always told of rounding the Horn and the teller was in a ship which was either hove to, or running with fore and main lower topsails only in a howling gale and thick weather when they were passed by a Flying P Liner though sometimes it was a Frenchman or an American, with all sails set, even to royals. The sequel varied. Some said that they came up on the ship a day or two later lying broached to and dismasted and the weather was too bad for them to be able to render any assistance. Some said that the ship was never heard of again. One version was told by a man who had served his time in a very well known ship of her day, *Loch Torridon*. She had a notorious bully of a master who drove his ship and his crew to the limit and who would never admit that any ship could sail faster than his. This man told the tale that when the skipper saw the other ship passing him, he ordered all sail to be set but they did not sight the other vessel again. When they sailed up the Channel and were off Beachy Head, they saw a ship outward bound and the Second Mate said to the Skipper, 'There's the So-and-so, the ship that passed us near the Horn, discharged and outward bound again!' The bully thrust his face close to that of the astonished Mate and bawled, 'If anyone tells me that that is that same ship, I'll . . . KILL HIM!'

That night we ran into a north-easterly gale which held us close-hauled on one tack or the other for four days. We drove into head seas and kept as close to the wind as we could but it was a dead nozzler and we made little progress. Then on the night of the fourth day the wind drew fair and we brought her to her course. That night the mizzen t'ga'nts'l blew out though there was not a great deal of wind at the time. The middle cloth was as ripe as a pear and it split from head to foot. We stowed it and the royal and another sail was bent the next day. This was the first time that we had shortened sail since we had been in the South Pacific. For seventy-two days we had carried all sail. It must have been quite a record,

124

in spite of the story above, to have rounded old Cape Stiff, come up through the strong westerlies of the South Atlantic to the Trades, through the usually violent squalls of the Doldrums, and to be nearly up to the Azores, before we needed to stow even the royals.

We held a fair wind for a couple of days and though it blew hard with a heavy sea running, the Old Man carried on and we made good going at nine knots. If her bottom had had less weed growing on it we could have made much better speed. The breeze lasted no longer but left us to roll in its swell for two or three days before it came up on our quarter to send us along for the Azores. We sighted the island of Fayal on 27th March. The Azores had always impressed me as being particularly romantic places. I thought that they must be rather delightful spots, all alone in mid-ocean, in a latitude sufficiently near the sun never to be really cold, far enough from the Equator to be free from oppressive heat, and remote enough from the great land masses to be uninfluenced by them to cause great differences in summer and winter temperatures. I imagined them smiling in continual spring sunshine. Perhaps they do. We happened to pass them on spring's day off, for only a small part of this island was visible and the rest of it and all the other islands were lost in misty rain. All we saw of Fayal was a line of inhospitable cliffs, punctuated by little sheltered inlets, a fort on a headland, and beyond and above that a white streak that marked a torrent that tumbled down the hillside.

We were now one hundred and sixteen days at sea and glad of the fair wind that was sending us along for the Channel for we were all getting a little fed up. The unbroken monotony of watch-and-watch, the unrelenting hard work, the constant and closest association of but a handful of men, all helped to make us feel that we should be glad of a change of scene.

The wind held steady and strong and the speed that we were making cheered everybody. It became evident that there was a north-east gale somewhere ahead for a very heavy swell was running from that direction and we were plunging into it heavily. Quite an unusual experience for a square-rigged sailing ship for they do not lie close enough to the wind when beating into a head-on breeze to have the waves running directly at them.

On the night of 31st March, the wind freshened to half a gale and we took in the royals, cro'jack, and mainsail. She was going ahead in fine style and as I paced the focsle head on lookout, she was pitching hard into the oncoming seas. I was drenched with driving rain and flying spray but I sang with joy with the prospect of soon making port and meeting my love. Even when the ship buried her head and shipped a green sea, I laughed as I clung to the after railings, knee deep in rushing water.

Suddenly out of the murk a steamer's lights appeared close on the bow. The Skipper was out and he had a paraffin flare lit on the poop and he sent an apprentice forward with another. Either the steamer's people thought that we were in distress, or they wanted to have a good look at us, for she rounded to and slowed abreast of us, no great distance away. We must have looked quite a picture to her as we forged along before the strong wind, spray flying over us, and the bright flares showing up the shining oilskin-clad figures on our streaming decks and lighting up the white sails against the inky night.

Shortly after this encounter we met the foretold north-easterly. The wind drew ahead and we had some very wet work at the braces as we brought her close-hauled to the unfavourable wind. Some of the high spirits were washed out of us and we went squelching and disconsolate to our bunks at the end of the watch. The wind grew stronger and the next night it carried away the main t'gallant sheet and that cotton sail blew out with a noise like thunder, before we could get aloft to stow it, all the lee side was in tatters and ragged sheets of canvas were carried away on the wind. None of us was sorry to see it go and if head winds, hunger, stress, and cruelly hard work had not contributed to general misery, we could have cheered. Gladly we went aloft in spite of cumbersome seaboots and oilskin suits and we laid out on the yard and leaned over to grasp the hard canvas. We took firm hold and braced our bodies and straightened our backs to bring in the sail, or what was left of it, up on to the yard. We held it there with chests and upper arms while we reached forward to grasp another fold. Bit by bit we spilled the wind from it, lifted it over the jackstay, banged it down with fist and forearm, passed the gaskets and made all fast. Then, to balance the sail arrangement, we stowed the fore and mizzen t'ga'nts'ls and this was another exhausting job for it was now blowing to beat everything.

Next day the gale had eased but high seas were still running and we bent another main t'ga'nts'l. It was a difficult job to handle the long sausage of sail on the wet and slippery deck. Then as the sail was hauled aloft, the ship rolled so heavily that the sail swung about wildly and it wanted to take charge. Then there was another hard struggle to stretch it out along the swaying yard as the spars described wide arcs across the heavens and the man astride each yardarm who was hauling out the head ear-rings was one minute high above the deck and the next, he was low over the sea. It was not long, however, before the sail was set again and we hove to to wait for a favourable change.

The bending of this t'ga'nts'l was not such a very strenuous job as these tasks go on a windjammer, but it caused me to think how, in the logs of these ships, one may read bald entries that a topsail or a t'ga'nts'l has carried away and under the date of the same day or of the next, that a new one has been bent. How many stories of courage, determination and of herculean effort under impossible conditions lie behind these matter-of-fact entries? Down in the wild west winds of the roaring forties, or in the region of Cape Horn, the gale driving hail, rain, or snow, men toiled who had reached the limit of human endurance and who had fought cruel weather for weeks, but still carried on.

That evening we sighted a small tramp steamer and signalled

127

her with the international flags 'XN' (Will you tell me your Greenwich time?). She obligingly altered course and, rounding to half a cable's length away, she gave a short toot on her whistle and then hung out the time on a blackboard from the wing of her bridge.

As the day died the wind came fair so we set all sail but it faded away altogether before dawn and throughout the day we rolled and rolled on an oily swell. A fair breeze came with the night and this time it freshened and blew. We had to stow the royals in the middle watch and the old hooker snored along with a bone in her teeth. 'The girls have got hold of the tow-rope now, lads,' said the fat old bos'n with a naughty chuckle and we all felt sure that the next time we went aloft to hand canvas would be on coming to our anchorage and everyone was sniffing for the land.

It didn't work out like that because fog came with the morning and as we were nearing the dense traffic of the English Channel, the Skipper had us shorten sail down to five topsails and the main t'ga'nts'l to check her speed while an apprentice ground away at the foghorn to sound its mournful note from the focsle head. There was a lot of grumbling at this and the men told of how, in the last windbag they were in, the Old Man "ad carried on everything in thicker'n this. An' 'ow can yer 'andle a ship wi' no way on 'er? Annyway, the 'aze ain't so thick an' this'll keep us out o' port fer another day.'

'Yus,' said Old Arthur. 'There wus a Skipper wot done that back in '82 an' 'e thort 'e wus 'arf way acrost the Atlantic, w'en orl od a sudden like, 'e piles up on the bleedin' Bishops!'

At the change of the watch at midday the fog cleared and all hands set to and hauled away on sheets and tacks, halliards and braces, and set all sail again. Naturally the grumblers said, 'There y'are! Told yer so!'

Now the wind fell light and all that day we rode along slowly and steadily over an easy swell in the beautiful April weather. The sky was clear and the sun shone warmly but

128

there was a healthy nip in the air that made us feel glad to be alive. All around us the sea was dotted by the rich brown sails of fishing boats and by smoky-looking drifters and our ship stood on among them like a tall and stately lady.

When I went to the wheel at six the next morning, Lands End was barely in sight, broad on the port bow. While the Mate and the rest of the watch were busy taking the lashing off the anchors on the focsle head, I held the ship on her course with no difficulty as she pushed along at four and a half knots and I kept my eye lifting for the many small craft about and on that little streak of land on the port bow. As I glanced at the compass, I saw that we were apparently four points off our course! I looked about. The sails were still full. The wind still came on our quarter. That Brixham trawler still bore three points on the starboard bow. The slip of land had not changed its bearing, and again I looked at the compass. As I stared at the card it swung slowly and completely round!

Doubtless we had passed over a wreck, probably sunk there during the recent war and as I steered on I wondered what manner of ship it was whose bones lay there. Was she some tall ship like ours, homeward bound from around the Horn, and who, after the stormy stress of the voyage, had sighted the shores of England only to be sent to her end by a cowardly act? Perhaps her men had been allowed to take to the boats or she may have been mined or torpedoed without warning, her watch below drowned like rats in a trap. Had she been some tramp, laden with food for England and her armies or a destroyer engaged in protecting her shores and shipping? Or perhaps it was a U-boat sent to her deserved end, her poor devils of men to die slowly and horribly.

We sighted the Lizard before noon and at three we were abreast and signalled. The station had no orders for us so we stood on for Falmouth. At 3.30 p.m. a trim little sailing cutter put the pilot aboard and all hands were called. A tug came and offered assistance but the Skipper ignored him.

Why would we need a tug when we had a fair wind and a master who knew his ship and his capable crew? The apprentices hauled up the royals and went aloft to stow them and then from four till six, we laboured at the sails and gear.

First we stowed the mainsail to a succession of orders from the Mate.

'Haul away clew garnet! Slack tack and sheet! Outer buntlines ...! Inner buntlines. ..! Leechlines ...! Up aloft and hand it!'

Up on the yard someone sings out 'Up wi' the bunt me boys! Come on now. Up on the yard wi' it! Now ... out to the clew! Make a real harbour stow of it an' show 'em we know how. No loose ends. No Irish pennants. No canvas hanging below the jackstay!'

We are no sooner down on deck again when sharp commands are given from the poop. Blocks and gear chatter smartly as three t'ga'nts'ls come in together.

Up we go again. Out on the yard we clutch the canvas. 'Get those clews well up! Never mind how heavy the chain sheet is, get it well up!' And up it goes. The sails lie neatly along the yards with no lumps or bumps and no gaskets hanging loose.

Now we have a spell as the ship steals up to her anchorage. We wait expectantly. Another order comes from the poop and there is a cluster of men at the masts and rigging. Commands are given and six tops'ls come in to rapid orders. 'Slack away sheets and halliards! Haul away downhauls, clewlines, spilling lines, buntlines!' Down come the yards and up go the sails in their gear. 'Up smartly lads! Get way off the ship! stow 'em well. There's no more after this!' Again we jump into the rigging and run aloft. Then, with a mighty splash and a roar of chain the anchor goes down, the ship swings to the wind and tide and we have arrived.

One hundred and twenty-three days from Iquique to Falmouth. Not a good passage but not a particularly bad one. *Priwall* had passed three days before so she had held her lead on us as one might have thought after having seen

130

her walk away from us ten days before. The little *Glenard* d
not arrive till ten days later.

CHAPTER XI   UP CHANNEL

The ship lay at Falmouth for a whole week awaiting orders. She was anchored in Carrick Roads, just inside the harbour entrance and of course we could not go ashore. We could see the masts and funnels of the steamers in the port and the tall tapering spars of *Cutty Sark* which had recently been purchased from the Portuguese. They had sailed her for years, rigged down to a barquentine, now old Captain Woodget had rigged her again as she was when in her prime. We watched as *Anitra*, a trim little Scandinavian barque was towed out to set sail for her port of discharge and as she went, the four-masted barque *Myoti*, flying the flag of the free port of Dantzig, sailed in and came to anchor near us. Otherwise we remained aloof from the many vessels that sailed or steamed past us.

The bumboat did a good trade and Bill and I must have consumed about two dozen fresh eggs and several tins of condensed milk during that week. We would slip into the focsle when the Mate or the Bos'n was out of sight, break a couple of eggs into our big enamel mugs, add sugar and milk and a little water, whip them up and gulp them down and smack our lips and grin. The mixture tasted fine and it did us good after months of salted and dried food and never enough of that. A tailor came aboard and fitted out a few of the hands with all the clothes they needed at what seemed to me to be mighty stiff prices but they did not handle the money and it was easy to sign it away.

The suspense was lifted and various rumours quashed when we received orders on Easter Saturday to sail for Rotterdam to discharge but bad and adverse weather kept us swinging at anchor till the Monday evening at 5 p.m. when the call came, 'Man the windlass!'

Round and round we walked the deck of the focsle head and hove at the capstan bars while Old Arthur expressed the feelings of most of us as he cried, 'Come on boys! 'Eave an' pawl! Dig yet bleedin' toes in! Fink yer in the whoreshop an' git yer toes in 'er garters an' SHOVE! It's on'y a anchor an' it's fer the larst time on this 'ooker!'

As soon as the anchor came in sight a tug made fast and off we went while the crane tackle was hooked on. As we hove up on this, the cheek of the lower block split and half of it fell away. The fall would not stay on the sheave so the Mate sent me down to ride up on the anchor and to keep the fall of the tackle in place with a capstan bar.

We went up Channel during the night before a fair breeze and with the dawn, the green hills of England gladdened our eyes as they smiled in the Spring sunshine. The second day, off Beachy Head, we sighted *Magdalen Vinnen*, the German auxiliary barque with which we had been in company in Iquique. She was outward bound once more and plugging along against the wind under her engine and with only her spanker set.

We signalled Dungeness for a Rotterdam pilot at 6 p.m. but none was available and we could not wait about there. We got a message that a pilot and a tugboat would meet us at the lightship off the Hook of Holland. We stood on before a freshening wind which showed promise of blowing hard. It continued to increase and at eight o'clock, in the darkness and cold rain, all hands were called to take in the royals and t'ga'nts'ls. I remember that Bill and I were together on the

134

foremast furling the t'ga'nts'l when we sighted a tug on the bow and she ranged alongside. A voice from a megaphone offered to tow us.

'How much to Rotterdam?' bawled our Skipper.

'Three hundred pounds!' came the answer.

Our Skipper did not deign to answer, or if he did we couldn't hear him above the noise of the wind and the rain and the tug soon dropped astern. We drove on and passed Dover at good speed but the weather came in thick in the middle watch and we took in the three upper tops'ls and hove to. More fighting with wet hard canvas we had. More punching and clutching and passing of gaskets in driving rain and then at dawn we set them again with the main t'ga'nts'l. We carried on all day before a strong breeze and by sunset we reckoned to be near our destination.

It was getting misty and visibility was very poor as we took in the foresail and the main t'ga'nts'l to take way off the ship. We had no longer stowed the sails when the lookout reported the lightship on the starboard bow. There it was only a cable's length away, clearly to be seen in spite of the writhing mists but there was no sign of the pilot boat or of a tug. Here we were, right on our rendezvous, and no one to meet us. If only the pilot had been there we could, with this favourable wind, have sailed into the mouth of the Maas without the help of a tug and have got to a safe anchorage and saved all the anxiety we had to come. What a let down!

'Vot do ve expec' from a lot of fokkin' Dutchmen?' said Big John and to the accompaniment of equally lurid and emphatic language we set the foresail again, took in the three upper tops'ls and hove to.

It was miserable at the wheel that night. We had to stand there with the wheel amidships, with no exercise to keep ourselves warm while the rain and hail pelted down and freezing water ran all the way down our backs into our sea boots. Anxiously the man on look-out forward and the man at the wheel and the Mate aft, peered around for the sight of the welcome white and red lights that would denote the

135

pilot boat but none showed. We lay hove to all night and half the next day in half a gale under a dirty sky that poured a soaking rain on us and we wore ship in the evening to lie on the other tack. Still no sign of the longed-for tug.

Some time during the morning Old Arthur came into the focsle for a crafty smoke, where we, the watch below, were resting. He saw me awake and spoke to me in a hoarse whisper.

'Paddy sez there's a bleedin' airship or sumfink over'ead. Dunno wot 'e's torkin' erbaht.'

I slipped out on deck. At intervals, through gaps in the ragged clouds and at no great height, I could see a long dirigible. As I peered through the sunless gloom at it, I saw that the bow appeared to be damaged and I mentioned this to Paddy. He answered, 'Now what wud 'e be doin' to be goin' out over the North Sea wid a damage to 'is nose? Wait till 'e comes to view agen an' ye'll see that ye're wrong.'

It didn't come to view again so I didn't see, but we learned later that the British airship R34 had broken away from her mooring mast in a gale and had been blown over to the Continent that day.

All through another night we drifted at the mercy of wind and tide. The yards were braced up as far as they would go and the helm held hard down. Mournfully the chill wind whined aloft. Ever hopefully we strained our eyes into the blackness but no gleam of light showed. We must have drifted miles from the lightship but no observations had been possible and our position was uncertain but before the south-westerly we must have got well to the north and east.

Next morning the wind drew to the north and lost its strength and we stood back in the direction of the pilot station before a light breeze. We had been hove to for thirty-six hours in thick weather and in such conditions it is impossible to determine with accuracy how far a ship may drift under the influence of wind and tide. There was no such thing as a Decca Navigator in those days. The Skipper could not be at all sure of our exact position and clouds obscured the sun and mists lay low on the horizon. We hove to again at the beginning of the forenoon watch and a look-out was kept all the time from the focsle head. At eleven o'clock the mists lifted a little and land was reported to the southward.

We altered course at midday and bore away for the south and east and by half past twelve the land was plainly visible. Now the wind drew more to the west and the yards were hauled round and the ship headed as close to it as she would lie. The wind was light and we could make little headway while, because of the leeway we were making we were being steadily and surely forced down towards the shore to leeward. At times the wind freshened for a few minutes and foam curled away from the forefoot and the wake straightened but hope soon faded. The wind fell lighter than before. The stem only gurgled through the pale green water. The wake trailed off at an angle. Eddies along the weather side showed how she drifted as much sideways as she sailed ahead.

At three o'clock we could plainly see houses above a sandy beach and a church spire pointed from behind some trees. The Skipper paced the poop with short impatient steps. Five miles to the south he could see the mouth of our harbour but the ship's head would barely point up to it. Very surely the distance between us and the beach was lessening. Suddenly he rapped out, 'Mister Mate! Call all hands to wear ship, and then, make sure for'ard that the anchors are clear!'

We sprang to it sharply and we ran the braces along the deck as we hauled the yards round on the other tack for we were all very conscious of the situation in which we lay but the manoeuvre lost us valuable offing. As the ship took up her new course, we could see the seas breaking on the sands.

I went with the Mate on to the focsle head to see that all was clear to let go the hook and I couldn't help an anxious eye from lifting to see how we were heading up on the new tack. We did not appear to be any better off and I looked out to seaward in hope of a catspaw and then back to the light-house at the river mouth. I looked again. I thought that the

137

outline of the steamer heading our way was typical. The Mate said to me, 'Come on, look what you're bloody well doing!', but I forgot the feeble wind and the imminent shore and said to him, 'Isn't that our tug, Mister?'

The grim old sea-dog made no answer but he wheeled and strode to the break of the focsle head and yelled through cupped hands, 'Tug away on the port quarter, Captain!'

All hands lined the rail to watch as she came up on us, the foam piling round her straight bows. The big Dutch sea-going tugboat stopped her engines when close alongside and her master called in accentless English, 'We've been looking for you, Skipper. Must have missed you in the thick weather!'

There was a moment's silence broken by Big John's derisive 'Haw . . . Haw!'

Our Captain asked, 'How much to tow us in?'

'A hundred pounds, Skipper.'

'A bit steep, isn't it?'

The Dutchman put his hand to his engine room telegraph and rang, 'Stand by', and called, 'Well, Skipper, I haven't time to argue.'

Neither had we. Our Skipper called, 'All right. Give us your wire!'

What else could he do?

Before we could take her hawser we had to haul the yards round to point them into the wind on our new course and so spill the sails. The decks resounded to the stamp of seabooted feet as we walked the braces in and blocks rattled cheerily as the long yards swung. The tug's great towing line came aboard, of wire as thick as a strong man's arm but as pliable as manila. No sooner was it fast to the bitts than we jumped to the gear to take in all sail.

Never had we gone to the job more cheerfully and willingly. After this there would be no more pulling and hauling on those damned ropes; no more sweating at sheets and halliards; no more hauling, waist deep in water at stubborn braces; no more of up aloft in tearing rain, groping for that gasket which should have been there. That we might each of us be doing such things in some other ship in a matter of weeks was of no consequence.

We came down from the trimmed yards as the ship entered the river mouth and we slipped smartly along in the wake of the tug. We cleared the decks and hauled the mooring lines from their long stowage in the fore 'tween decks in readiness for the last job of making her fast. It was my turn to take the wheel at eight o'clock and I was proud to be the last man to steer her to the end of her voyage. She slid quietly into her berth liked a tired traveller, glad to rest awhile after her long journeyings. We made her fast with lines fore and aft and with springs to save her from surging about and it was a quarter to midnight when the Mate concluded our contract with the historic words, 'That'll do, everybody.' The traditional phrase that has ended so many voyages.

I stood at the rail for a few minutes to watch the lights of Rotterdam and I wondered what the future held for me. I was glad of the experience of the voyage, for though I had known discomfort, pain, and hunger to spare, I had also met with courage, high endeavour, and true comradeship. A neighbouring clock struck twelve as I turned into the focsle, shed my outer clothes and climbed into my bunk.

I lay there in pleasant weariness and I took in the familiar features of that part of our quarters that had been wholly mine. There at the foot was the rude shelf that I had knocked up, with its few treasures. The Ingoldsby Legends, The Rubaiyat, Longfellow, Read's Seamanship, Norie's Epitome and Tables, and a novel or two. There hung my palm and needle, and the marlinspike that Bill had given me, with the fancy lanyard that I had made for it of square sennit, fixed by a diamond knot. An odd array of clothing swung on a cord stretched from end to end of the bunk, hung there for convenience as I had taken them off. I looked up at the deckhead, its once white paint now a dirty grey from the smoke of many pipes and of the oil lamp, stained where a seam leaked, and marked where the water had dripped through

139

and run athwart the planking as the ship rolled. There was the piece of tin that I had tacked up where the leak was worst, to take the water that came through and to mingle it with that condensed on the steel bulkhead. And there, the photograph of Sally smiled at me from the middle of a Finnish ship's biscuit.

Here I had spent my leisure hours for ten months, slept the sleep of deep exhaustion while the gales shrieked without and the crashing seas thundered. Here I had tossed and perspired when the blazing sun made an oven of the place. Here I had breathed the sweet air of the Trade winds as they blew in at the open port. I had read and studied and pondered and written here, and here the fiendish fleas had sucked my blood.

I realised that I had grown attached to this grubby corner and it was with a vague regret, lost in pleasurable anticipation of the morrow, that I pulled my old pea jacket, which I used as an extra blanket, closer round my shoulders and dropped off to sleep there for the last time.

CHAPTER XII   LONDON

We had expected to be paid off the next day and we all trooped along to the Shipping Office in the morning. Here the Skipper told us that the necessary money had not arrived but we were given five pounds each and told to return on Monday afternoon to collect our pay and our passage to London.

Bill and I secured clean and comfortable lodgings for ourselves and we spent the weekend exploring Rotterdam and in eating great quantities of delectable food. This was a very real pleasure after the tedious monotony and paucity of our shipboard fare and our appetites were insatiable.

Monday came and we were paid off in the late afternoon and passages were arranged for us in the overnight boat for Gravesend. As we steamed down the Maas in the failing light I stood at the rail and watched the variety of shipping and I thought that it could not now be long before I saw Sally. It was a lovely thought that after this long voyaging I should look again in her dear eyes and hear her sweet voice. We should share the sights of London and of the Exhibition and then there would be no more wanderings. We would go back to New Zealand together.

Bill and I were up with the dawn to see the life of the

141

Thames Estuary. The red-brown sails of the spritty barges were dwarfed by the big passenger liners from Tilbury. Towards Thameshaven, long deep-laden tankers passed and were passed and little tugs fussed about. All the business of the river held our interest and let me forget for a while the urgency of my need to get to London.

The disembarking, the Customs procedure, the wait for the train to start, were unbelievably slow. The train crawled to Victoria. We went by tube to Aldgate and so to the Sailors' Home.

Bill and I booked a cubicle each, dumped our gear and went downstairs to collect our letters. As we waited for these we looked at the bulletin of shipping. Steamships for everywhere were arriving and sailing. In Liverpool, the barque *Kilmallie* was nearly loaded for Australia and wanted a crew.

We each had a packet of letters and we went to our cubicles to read them. There was none for me from Sally. There was one from her mother. She and I had always been the best of friends and I admired her immensely. She wrote me such a pleasant letter that nearly broke my heart. She told me that they had decided not to come to England. Sally was preparing for a new life. She was sure that Sally would be very happy for she had always loved the open country and she and her husband were going to live on their sheep station.

I sat on the edge of my bed with the letter held loosely in my fingers, and I thought that I might as well have had a bit of fun with that lass in Iquique after all when Bill burst in.

'Frank,' he said grinning all over his face, 'I've had an invitation from my relatives in the Shetlands to come up and spend as long as I like and to bring a shipmate if I wish. Let's have a week or two in London and then go up there together.'

'Sorry, Bill,' I answered. 'Tomorrow I'm going to Liverpool to join *Kilmallie*.'

142

CHAPTER XIII   *TO SEA AGAIN WITH* KILMALLIE

Kilmallie's spike jibboom poked over the quay from a corner of Salthouse Dock in Liverpool. Alongside her, a float with a donkey engine was fussily engaged in loading her with red lumps of rock salt. I stepped aboard to find the decks in the usual disorder of a ship in port. The Mate was lounging by the break of the poop and I walked up to him with my discharge book and asked if he wanted a seaman.

'We won't be signin' on yet. Not fer six weeks or so,' he said in good Cockney. 'But, lemme see yer book. Huh! *William Mitchell*, ten months eh? An now yer want ter sign on another windbag? Well, there's no accountin' fer tastes. Orl right, come an' see me later. We're goin' ter Sydney. No. I don't want anyone workin' by. Yus. In about a month. Good-day.'

Now I had some time on my hands. That suited me. I should have that walking tour in Devon which was something I had long wanted to do.

By highway and byway and along windblown moorland path, by sandy cove or rocky shore, I enjoyed the quiet beauty of that lovely county.

Three weeks later I returned to Liverpool when most of my money was gone but I had enough to pay for a month's

143

rent of a cubicle at the Sailors' Home. There were numerous delays before *Kilmallie* completed her loading and I spent a very lonely and poverty-stricken four weeks till she was ready to sign on her crew. I could have got a berth on a steamer but I needed to put in twelve months in a sailing ship in order to qualify for a square-rig ticket. Most of the days I would be prowling round the docks or I would tire of the waterfront and go through the town and into the country. I crossed the river and explored the Wirral Peninsular. Always walking. There was little else to do and I had scarcely enough money to get enough to eat and none for entertainment.

I managed somehow and I wasn't the only hungry one. I met an American sailor who was also 'on the beach' and he told me, 'Say, Bud. There's a place along Scotland Road where y' kin git a bunch o' goldfish an' a loaf o' bread f' *five cents*.' I found the place from his sailing directions and discovered that I could, for threepence, buy two tiny bloaters and a roll.

There was a trim little barquentine across the dock from *Kilmallie*, and I visited her several times. She was the one-time *Lady of Avenel*, then renamed *Island*. She had been bought by a British Columbian named Algarsson for an attempt to be the first to fly over the North Pole. Her Captain was Commander Frank Worsley, D.S.O., another New Zealander, and he offered me a berth aboard. I would have liked to have sailed under that famous Skipper and in that handsome little ship but my time in her would not count as sea time as she was not a commercially engaged vessel but, officially, a yacht. Moreover, there would be no pay for me if the venture were unsuccessful. It would have been an interesting experience to have sailed in this 114-ton craft which had sailed the Atlantic for over fifty years and had at one time actually beaten its way round Cape Horn, but there was no future in it for me. I stifled my more adventurous yearnings for the practicality of completing my square-rig time. In the event, the project was unsuccessful.

144

At long length, I signed on *Kilmallie* for her voyage. I took a month's advance of nine pounds ten shillings, vast wealth to me then, and I went and sought an Irishman with whom I had shared some of my poverty. We went to a restaurant where we had a good meal. With hunger satisfied, but far from replete, he helped me to get my gear aboard and we spent the rest of the day enjoying ourselves by attempting to satisfy appetites that had been sharpened by weeks of inadequate food.

For the next few days some of the crew were busily engaged in reeving off new ropes, bending sails, and generally getting the ship ready for sea. She had been dismasted in the Bay of Biscay at the end of her previous voyage and she had lain idle in the river at Bordeaux for four years. New masts had been stepped and yards crossed, and with the exception of the mizzen, the standing rigging had been renewed throughout. As could be expected the running rigging was pretty ripe and we rove off new braces, halliards, sheets, and other important ropes. The few more conscientious ones or, like me, those who had no other place to sleep except the barque's focsle, did all of this work. Most of the hands were spending their advance in the time honoured fashion of deep water sailormen and we did not see them aboard till the morning when we were casting off to leave the dock. They were somewhat the worse for wear. A couple of ordinary seamen and one A.B. failed to turn up and the Skipper was forced to take whom he could at the last minute and we shipped a couple of 'pierhead jumpers' as they were called.

We started at six that morning when the ship was moved to a position just inside the dock gates. There she waited till the tide was high enough to enable the dock gates to be opened and to let her out. This took place at ten o'clock and our voyage began. A tug took us slowly down the Mersey against a strong wind and we said farewell to Liverpool landmarks as we set off on our first leg of some 15,000 miles to Sydney.

Early in the afternoon the Pilot was dropped near Formby

Light and we set the fore-and-afters as the vessel curtseyed to the first of the open-sea rollers. That first gentle rise and dip exhilarated me as it always does and I lifted my head and filled my lungs with the clean sea air. The fresh wind whipped the tops off the dark green waves and the sun shone brightly from a deep blue sky over which a few white clouds scudded and I thought of Masefield's words:

. . . . . a windy day and the white clouds flying.

The barque followed the wake of the tug through the afternoon and most of the night, while the crew had an easy time of it. They slept off their sins and were only required to relieve the man at the wheel at two hourly intervals until 2 a.m. when we were off Holyhead. All hands were then called out, the tug cast off and we set all sail.

It was a dark night and the sky was heavily overcast. Men with sore heads and sad with alcoholic remorse groped about the decks and fumbled for the ropes on unaccustomed pins. It was very quiet, and the wind, which had fallen considerably, made only a subdued murmur in the rigging, and little waves made low chuckles and splashes along our sides. There was not much talking and none of the laughter and chaffering that goes on when men are better acquainted with the ship and each other. We tailed out on the halliards and hoisted the yards. It was a real effort for the gear was stiff with disuse and our muscles were flabby from the same reason but we knew that this was only the beginning. Those yards would have to go aloft time and time again before we reached British waters once more. We groaned and put our backs into it and all sail was set and drawing by three o'clock when watches were set.

Kilmallie was stump t'gallant rig, i.e. she carried no royals, but big double t'ga'nts'ls and they *were* big. The upper t'gallant yards were each sixty-two feet long and weighed over a ton. It was a heavy pull to raise these the twenty-five feet necessary to set the sails, for, as usual, the only power available was the strength of our bodies. The topsail yards

146

were of steel and they weighed two and a half tons each. They had to be lifted some thirty-five feet. We were glad that she was square-rigged on two masts only and so there were just four yards to be hoisted when all sail had to be set. The mizzenmast carried one big leg-o'-mutton sail, or Bermudan, you'd call it nowadays, and it was secured to a jackstay up the mast and was simply hauled out along the boom to set it and brailed into the mast to be stowed.

I was in the starboard, the Second Mate's watch, who were the lucky ones, for after clearing decks and coiling all ropes down, we went below at 4 a.m. There was then a light but fair breeze on our starboard beam. When we came on deck at eight, there was no wind at all. The midsummer sun shone clear and warm and the sea was calm. The coast of Ireland lay to the west and away to port, a hazy blue outline suggested the Welsh hills. As I stood at the wheel and whistled for a wind I saw that the water ahead was violently agitated and soon we passed over the disturbance. The sea boiled and bubbled and gurgled about us and volumes of water rose to the surface. It was quite weird in that flat calm and it was probably due to the meeting or change of tidal currents though it may have been because of a steep and sudden alteration in soundings and its effect upon the tidal flow.

We were busily occupied in overhauling everything aloft and especially things on which our lives depended. The ship had been lying untended for so long and we did not know in what condition the gear had been left. Footropes, ratlines, and the rigging on the upper masts received our particular care. There were blocks to be overhauled and re-stropped, seizings galore to be renewed, eyesplices on the wire ropes of clewlines and downhauls to be parcelled and served. We were kept busy aloft for many days with marlin spike and serving board, tar, spun-yarn, and slush can.

The younger members of the crew and all the apprentices had not been in sail before and going aloft was a new and terrifying adventure for them. It was amusing to watch some of them struggling up, heavily breathing and with teeth

147

clenched, their bodies pressed hard against the rigging, their hands gripping the swifters with a strangling grasp and their feet fumbling desperately for the ratlines. On arrival at the top, the futtock shrouds, which project out from the mast to the edge of the top, were too much for all of them at first and they squeezed themselves uncomfortably and awkwardly through the lubber's hole. This is an opening in the decking of the top which is scorned by experienced seamen and indeed by any lad who had been any good in the gym at school. Once they were out on the yard, their one thought was to hold on to anything and everything available, rather than to get on with the job to be done. However, with the calm weather the ship was stable and they soon got over their nervous fears. After a week or two, they were running aloft and swinging about in the rigging like monkeys.

Apparently the watches had been picked with the idea of separating youth from age, for the First Mate's, the port watch, was composed of hardened shellbacks, while we, with one exception were all young men. We would gladly have had our oldest member in the other watch. Never had I known a more dirty, stupid, or ignorant fellow. He claimed to have been in sail before but he didn't know a halliard from a brace. He smelt, and he would declaim the most amazing balderdash about any subject with the greatest assurance. Such as that Drake sailed round the world and came back to report to Queen Victoria, or that King John was the first king of England and that Charles the third was the second. When questioned, he would declare that he had read of it though he must have been fully aware that we knew that he could neither read nor write. We nicknamed him Horace in a spirit of facetiousness.

There was a Welshman who had been a ship's fireman, had been in the Army and claimed to be a blacksmith and to have other accomplishments. He did not give the impression of being sufficiently intelligent to be a master of that trade and he did not know appreciably more of sailoring on the day he left the ship than on the day he joined, but he was

148

willing and cheerful.

There were two more A.B.s besides myself and we were all under thirty and had had other experience of sailing ships. Jim was short, active and as hard as nails. He had put in a lot of square-rig time, knew his job inside out and was a really good shipmate.

Bill Harle was tall and spare and he had made two voyages in that fine old ship *Terpsichore* where he had had as shipmate Old Arthur who had been with me in *William Mitchell*. Also he had been in the barque *Garth Garry* when she had been dismasted off the Horn and had completed her voyage to Queenstown (now named Cobh) under jury rig. She had not lost her sticks in the very bad weather which she had got through safely but had rolled them out of her in the confused and heavy swell in the following calm. Bill was a very good sort and, like me, he was serving his time 'before the stick'. We used to have many long and interesting discussions for he was prone to philosophise on any subject.

Two young ordinary seamen made up the watch. Len, a clergyman's son, had much of the world, the flesh, and the devil about him. Paddy from Howth was a strong well-built youngster who was very religious and he was filled with conscious virtue. He was a good lad and was very keen to improve his seamanship. One could not wish for a better man to be with on any job that called for courage and determination.

The port watch lived in the other half of the deckhouse which was divided by a fore-and-aft bulkhead so we did not get to know them so well. I shall always remember Fred Ulring, the big powerful and good-natured Norwegian and Charlie Brimblecombe from Brixham. There was Ned who had been in many sailing ships, and 'Cockney' who had had all sorts of jobs in ships but never in sail, and a little under-sized shrimp of a man from the back streets of Liverpool. The others do not stick in my mind as personalities except Old Tom who was an experienced sailor but not very bright.

During that first weekend at sea a deal of time was spent at

149

the braces as we hauled the yards round to every wayward puff of wind for the breezes were light and erratic. We would trim sails to a gentle air which bade fair to freshen but in no time it would die away, the sails would hang slack or they'd shake in an air from another quarter and we turned out to pull and haul some more. Then, on Monday came a light northerly which took us right across the Bay of Biscay. For five splendid days the barque pushed along before fair winds, the summer sun shone from a cloudless sky, the gentle breeze kept all sail drawing by day and night. The Bay forgot its reputation and was all smiles for us till we were off the coast of Portugal. The wind now shifted to the north-east and the sky became flecked with the little fleecy clouds that invariably accompany the Trade winds. This wind was what old sailormen called the Portuguese Trades, and they are in fact the beginning of the north-east Trades which are felt far north in summer. We had picked up the Trade winds when but a week out from Liverpool which was a great help to an outward-bound ship.

About this time Horace brought his violin to light. We had noticed it when he came aboard and I had said to Bill, 'Good-oh. We'll be able to have some music,' but we were doomed to shattering disillusion. He sat on the edge of his bunk and removed the instrument from its case with loving care. He tucked it under his chin, squinted along the bow, then drew it along the strings which emitted weird and disjointed noises while his ape-like face was wreathed in rapturous smiles. Bill raised his eyebrows and said, 'You know, Frank, I think that there's nothing more delightful than the sweet tones of a violin.' I did not know what to answer and Horace beamed with delight and kept up his ghastly scratching and squawking.

It was all very amusing for a time but later it was only a respect for other people's property that kept me from pitching the wretched fiddle over the side and I had no doubt that my shipmates had similar feelings. Sometimes in the dog watches when it got too awful, all hands would set up in

150

opposition. We bashed tin cans as we sat around the fore hatch and we sang as lustily as we could all the songs we knew. There was a donkey engine lashed there and this was our big drum. It gave out a deep hollow boom when struck by a belaying pin . . . not always in time. Horace was quite undeterred and he fiddled on.

In common with all the latter day windjammers, food was none too plentiful and our Old Man was as mean as any limejuicer could be. He was an ancient mariner nearing seventy and he had spent nearly all his seafaring life in sail. He still had a voice that could be heard above a Cape Horn buster but parsimony was a religion with him. He even remarked to me one day when I was at the wheel, anent the ship's cat, 'Our Jerry's a good cat. He doesn't each much.'

The steward was not a bad old chap for a steward and one day what should appear for breakfast but tripe and onions! There was powerful little of it but it was tasty and welcome and with thankful hearts for something succulent and out of the ordinary, we lapped it up. We thought with gratitude that we were going to be well fed on this ship. Somehow the Skipper got to know of it as skippers know eventually everything that is done or said on their ships. Shortly after our watch came on deck we heard a great roaring and stamping from the poop. Our Old Man used to wear fur-lined clogs that came half way up his calves and they had wooden soles an inch and a half thick and he stamped on the deck with these and yelled.

'Come up here stooard!'

The steward went up the ladder to the poop chewing his moustache which was the only sign of emotion that I ever saw him display. When he had still a step to go, the Skipper thrust his face close to his and he shouted:

'DID YOU GIVE THE SAILORS TRIPE!?'

The steward was very slow of speech and he drawled, 'Why, yes. I only . . .'

'Tripe for SAILORS!' and the Old Man jumped and banged down with both feet. 'Tripe for SAILORS! Never heard of

151

such a thing in all my days at sea! And DON'T ever let me hear of it AGAIN!'

'Well,' remarked the steward meekly, 'I thought that the men would like something different for a change,' but the Old Man snorted with rage.

'TRIPE? for focsle hands! Never heard of it! IMPOSSIBLE!'

We saw no more tripe. Our breakfasts thereafter consisted of the usual so-called 'curry' and rice on Mondays and Wednesdays, porridge on Tuesdays and Saturdays, beans boiled in molasses and water on Thursdays and Sundays and salted dried fish on Fridays. We smelt the latter coming on Thursdays and it was quite uneatable. It was even unacceptable to Paddy's insatiable hunger. The meals told the days of the week.

The Trades took us along well and we held them to 14° north when we ran into the Doldrums, just three weeks out. The whole Trade wind system moves north in the northern summer for a few degrees and to the south in the winter, but in such a hot summer as 1925, it moves further than is usual. Here we had periods of calm interspersed with strong westerlies. We'd hold a good stray wind for perhaps eight hours, then have an hour or two of baffling airs which would die away to a steady calm. That might last for an hour or even a day and be followed by any kind of weather. Mostly it was thunderstorms and rain. And what rain!

New standing rigging was aboard for the mizzen mast and we took advantage of the calm spells to set it up. I was rattling down on a day of blazing sunshine and flat calm when a steamer was sighted coming up on our quarter. She was the *Highland Rover* of London and she slowed and circled round close to us. Doubtless to give the passengers a treat and they lined the rail with cameras at the ready. There were a number of young ladies who smiled and waved and called to us.

Bill grinned as he said, 'They're all smiles and friendliness when there's a cable's length of sea between us, but if they saw what a scruffy lot we look close to . . .'

I said, 'There's some stunners among them, I wouldn't mind getting a bit closer.'

'They all look beautiful after a few weeks at sea,' he said.

Later we had a wet night and a brisk squall and we had to stow the mainsail and the fore upper t'ga'nts'l and it was awkward in the darkness and wind and pouring rain with lads who had not handled canvas before. No-one knew why, but of course there were not enough gaskets on the yards. It was just one of those things that happen at the start of a voyage.

Here Horace showed another facet of his unpleasant nature. He had no idea of furling sail, couldn't make a gasket fast properly, and he cursed and swore at everyone and everything in the filthiest language. When he came into the focsle he sat on the edge of his bunk, said, 'Wot a dirty fuckin' ship,' hawked and spat on the floor. We reckoned to be able to go barefooted in the focsle and this was a bit much. I stood and grabbed the front of his clothes and pulled him to his feet.

'You may be able to do that at home, but you don't do it here,' I said.

'I'll do wot I fuckin' well like,' he said. I brought up the heel of my right as hard as I could under his jaw and let it slide up to shove his nose up to his eyebrows and followed with a left hook to the side of his jaw which knocked him down. I stepped back with my shoulders against an upper bunk and wondered what to expect. I half expected him to come up with his sheath knife out or to attempt some dirty trick but he only scowled at me and muttered, 'Ye didn' 'ave to do that.'

'Somebody has to teach you manners,' I answered. 'Next time, you spit over the lee side or in the scuppers. We have to live here too.'

Out on deck Jim said to me, 'You were a bit hard on him, weren't you, Frank?'

'Maybe I was,' I countered, 'but I don't think you could reason with such a bloody horrible man. One thing, he won't spit in there again.'

153

A couple of evenings later I went to take my trick at the wheel at eight o'clock. It had been a day of light and contrary winds and there were heavy rain clouds all around us. Their lower edges seemed no higher than our mastheads but half a moon showed where they towered away up to the high heavens. The barque was close hauled on the starboard tack and was heading east nor' east. I had not been a quarter of an hour at the wheel when it fell to a complete calm and then, a few minutes later the wind sprang up on the port quarter. This was a fair wind and the Second Mate shouted to his watch, 'Square the main yard!'

I had just got the vessel steady on her new course to the south when it started to rain. And did it rain! It poured down in streams as thick as a pencil till a few minutes before ten o'clock when I was relieved. During that time the other members of the watch had been filling our fresh water casks. There were two wine tuns lashed abaft the foremast and they each held 252 gallons. These were filled bung-full from the water that ran off the deckhouse in those two hours. It was not rain. It was a solid downpour. The house was thirty feet long and fifteen feet wide and only a proportion of the water that fell on it was caught. Some was lost at first in scrubbing it down to wash the dried salt away and a lot slopped over with the roll of the ship while our method of collecting it with buckets from the downpipes was crude and wasteful. We were able to bath in reckless quantities of fresh warm water, and did we enjoy it! Not Horace. He said it was unhealthy. Only a very limited quantity of fresh water was carried on those ships and only in times like this were baths possible.

It rained heavily again in the middle watch and the covers were taken off the ship's boats. The next day we took advantage of the fact that they were half full, to scrub them out with the fresh water that we could not otherwise have spared. It had rained over ten inches in three hours.

The continual tuneless strumming from Horace's violin was getting on everyone's nerves and we tried to think of some way to put him off. He had a skin like a rhino and even when someone told him bluntly to 'Stop that bloody awful row and when you get back to Liverpool, spend your payday in taking lessons. Then you might know the scales.' He only muttered profanely that we had no appreciation of music and he scraped on. Len said that it was a pity that the humid weather did not affect the thing in some way and this gave us an idea. While our 'musician' was at the wheel, we ran a piece of tallow over the strings of the bow, wiped off the surplus grease and put the instrument of torture back in its case.

In the dog watch, he sat on the edge of his bunk and said gruffly, 'Let's 'ave a bit o' bluddy music,' and he drew the fiddle from its case. He made a pretence of tuning it and tucked it under his chin as he squinted along the bow. He grinned in anticipation as he drew the bow over the strings. Not the slightest sound came and a look of utter dismay spready over his ugly features.

'It's gone fuckin' well deaf!' he howled.

He fiddled about with it for some time in an atmosphere of foul profanity while we made helpful suggestions and expressed our sorrow at its 'deafness'. We tried to persuade him that the damp air had affected it, and that if he would put it away till we reached Australia, the dry air there would put it right, but he seemed to doubt our sincerity. Eventually he threw it down with disgust and we slipped out on deck one by one and silently gripped one anothers' hands.

I was beside young Paddy as we sat on the fore hatch and congratulated each other and I offered him a cigarette. He refused it saying, ''Tis a sinful lust of the flesh.' He was always hungry like any growing lad and anway weren't we all? If he could manage it he would get more than his share of any food going for which no one blamed him. We had plum duff from the galley on Sundays and Thursdays and it was a soggy business and indigestible to most of us so Paddy had at least half of it. I asked him if he ever thought of the sinful way he lusted after the plum duff.

'Oh, well. That's different,' he said.

155

CHAPTER XIV SOUTHWARD

After ten days of rain and variable winds, the weather cleared. An apprentice and I were working aloft one morning when the sun blazed down on a sapphire sea and a light breeze blew that bade fair to be the first of the south-east Trades. The ship heeled gently, every sail drawing. Her forefoot easily parted the clear water and only occasionally, as she put her nose into a slight swell, did any white water appear at her bows and foam drift lazily along her sides to be lost in the eddies astern.

'Ooh! Those are whoppers, aren't they?' he asked as he pointed out some big fish that were playing about the bows.

'Certainly are,' I answered. 'I'll see if I can catch one as soon as we go off watch and have had some grub. They're albacore, or tuna, or tunny, whichever way that you prefer to call them and they'll give you more sport than most fish.'

I had wanted to capture one of these fish ever since I had first read of them in my early application to books of the sea and the life of it. I have always been a keen fisherman and especially so when the prey have been big and fierce fighters. I had got myself some strong hooks in Liverpool and with rope yarns I had made a fishing line of sennit with a trace of seizing wire. The hook was wrapped round with a piece of

157

white rag in the way that Big John of *William Mitchell* had shown me.

After our midday meal I went out to the end of the jib-boom and I dangled my bait over the waves in the hope that one of the big ones would take it for a flying fish, but they would not rise to it. Try as I could, I could not deceive them. They would come close to it, give it a cold stare and quietly slide down to the depths. I thought that perhaps later in the day, at dusk, they would not see my line which could be putting them off. I gave it up for the time and went inboard and turned in.

Towards sunset I had another try and I had not been long at it when there was a mighty rush from under the bow and my line came taut. With my heart pounding I hung on to the stout line with both hands, caught my legs firmly round the boom guys, and prepared for a fight. The fish took one vigorous run but my line brought him up sharply and nearly dislodged me in the process, whereat he sounded, but the next moment he shot right out of the water. His great body, six feet long if an inch, leapt almost to the height where I clung and fell back with a resounding splash. With that mighty effort, my line fell slack, all the fish swam away and sadly I recovered my tackle. Another fish story.

The short twilight had passed and it was now quite dark. I went into the focsle to find Horace drying his bow carefully over the lamp and muttering blasphemously to himself as he alternatively held the bow over the flame and wiped it with a piece of rag. After continued efforts he succeeded in making some sort of noise, more like that of a saw striking a nail than the notes of a violin. Of my charity I hoped that it was sweetest melody to him.

The light breeze steadied to the pleasant Trades and we crossed the Line on Thursday 23rd July, thirty-five days from Liverpool. The old barky sailed along in her best style as we steered her full and by on the port tack and her bluff bows sent a vast area of white water ahead of her. She had no very fine lines and when there was anything of a breeze she pushed the ocean ahead of her rather than cut through it.

As we got well into the Trade winds we found them unusually squally and strong and one evening we were called to take in the fore upper t'ga'nts'l, the mainsail and the spanker. The barque lay over and snored along and she gave us the feeling that she was carrying all the sail that she needed.

The next morning the foresail gave us a picnic. It was an old fair weather sail and it had split in one place and a seam had come adrift. We clewed it up and Sails went aloft to repair it. He was a Swede and a nice old chap with a very generous waistline and he was asthmatic to boot. He puffed and blew like a grampus as he leaned over the yard and stitched away. He mended the sail and we pulled down the clew and were hauling the sheet aft when another seam went. We hauled it up in the buntlines and old Sails gasped as he stitched at it. At length he called, 'All ri' dis time! Slack avay de buntlines!' and we came from our several jobs to set the sail. We were getting the sheet aft again when a third seam went, from head to foot.

Sails's language was anything but polite and he roared curses as we pulled it up once more and he said that he 'hoped de dam' t'ing blow ri' avay dis time. Den I not be boddered vit de bogger any more,' but the next time it was set without further mishap.

The wind died away towards evening and we set the fore t'ga'nts'l again together with the mainsail and spanker. I noticed that each time that we set sail the yards went aloft more easily. Doubtless the gear was getting over its stiffness by use but equally our muscles were strengthening and hardening with the fresh air and exercise and the fine healthy life and in spite of the failure of the catering to satisfy our hunger.

Now came the calm area of the 'horse latitudes' where the air was warm and the sun hot. The ship drifted in dead calm or she lazily pushed forward before variable and light airs for which we were endlessly hauling on braces to trim the sails to every change of direction.

I stood on the focsle head one Sunday forenoon towards the end of my watch below at midday and I watched the bluff bows as they forged slowly ahead. The hot sun beat down on my back and the water looked cool and tempting. I took the coil of the jib sheet from its pin and went out to the boom end with it. I let down a bight to the water and I made it fast when the loop was just clear of the sea as the barque rose on a swell. Then I stripped off what little I wore, went down the rope and had a glorious dip. I sat in the bight of the rope and as the ship lifted on the seas I was hoisted out of the water and swung forward to be dumped in the next wave as she came down in the trough. The water was cool enough to be refreshing without being cold and as I swung and splashed about, I whooped for joy like a child on a swing.

I heard a shout from the deck above and Cockney of the other watch called.

'Hi, Frank! . . . Blimey! What the bleedin' 'ell d'yer fink ye're doin'? It's yer wheel in five minits. Crikey! Tork erbaht the daring actions of British Sailors. Cor, I wouldn' want ter do that!'

I answered, 'I'll be right up. Don't for God's sake tell the Old Man or he'll have a bloody fit!'

I climbed up and coiled up the sheet and put on my clothes and as eight bells struck I went aft to take my trick. Then I realised just how daring I had been for swimming about the stern was a tiger shark. It was some seven or eight feet long and I asked my relief how long it had been there.

'Oh, 'bout an hour or so,' he said. I gave heartfelt thanks that it had not been interested in the other end of the ship.

The Mates and a couple of apprentices tried to catch him but he was too wary. A pilot fish swam over his head. An active little fish that one of the boys described as 'wearing a football jersey' because of his gay stripes. These little fish are very often seen to accompany sharks in the deep sea. They swim over the shark's head, in my belief, because it is the

160

safest place for them. Old sailors say that they are the shark's little friends and only if they approve of food will the shark eat it. I believe that they are only hangers-on after unconsidered trifles. Something like the little birds that will pick the teeth of crocodiles and which live on the fragments which they gain precariously from the crocs' mouths.

I have often observed that when a lump of salt pork has been dropped overboard to tempt Mr Shark, the pilot fish will dart forward to inspect, take a bite at it and quickly return to its position over the big fellow's nose. The shark then swims over the morsel and gulps it down. When the piece of pork contains a large hook, he will, after it has been inspected and nibbled by the pilot either ignore it or merely hold it in his mouth. A pull on the line fails to hook him for he promptly opens his mouth and lets the bait go. The sea scavenger *appears* to wait for this inspection by the pilot fish but I believe that the shark is slower in his reactions than the pilot fish. The latter is lively enough to get there first but he knows that it is unwise to linger in a vulnerable position and he has not time to do more than take a quick bite at the bait before prudence compels him to return to his safe place. The subsequent action of the shark in swallowing the food or in ignoring the baited hook is due to his own observation and caution.

While these attempts to capture the brute were in progress, four big whales came alongside the now becalmed ship and rubbed themselves against her sides like so many great cats. The Old Man said that they did this to rid themselves of barnacles and other parasites. There were a lot of whales about in these latitudes and one near the barque was diving deep and then coming straight up to shoot out of the water as far as his big dorsal fin, hang in an upright position for quite an appreciable time and then fall over with a reverberating crash that sent the spray fifty feet in the air.

Fresher breezes came out of the south-west and we made preparations for the wild weather of the roaring forties. The fine weather sails were sent down and the hard weather suit hoisted aloft and bent on to the yards. We looked to lashings on all gear, passed a heavy rope round the boats to reinforce the gripes, led the main braces on to the poop and the fore braces to a spar lashed to the fore part of the deckhouse out of the waist and the heavier seas. We passed a mooring line across and across the main hatch and everywhere made provision for heavy weather and not least to our seaboots and oilskin suits and their lashings.

On the day we left the latitude of South Trinidad (20° 45′S) we saw the first Cape Pigeon, sure sign of approaching hard weather. They are pretty little birds of the albatross family, but they do not approach the size of the mollymawk or the king albatross. They have black bars on their wings above, which are speckled with black spots, and their breasts and the undersides of their wings are snow white.

The wind held its direction and the barque remained on the port tack to the 27th parallel of latitude when the wind gradually worked round to the north-west and we laid the yards square. She pushed on to the south and east for a week before a light wind that became variable in direction and caused the usual business of pulling on braces and gear and which disturbed our rest when we tried to sneak a sleep when on watch at night.

We had had a wonderful run of undisturbed night watches and except for the squally weather when we had stowed the t'ga'nts'ls and once or twice for brief periods to trim the yards to a change of wind, we had not been called out by the Mate's two whistles or the 'policeman's' nudge for nine whole weeks. When I had a 'farmer' in the middle watch, I would turn out for muster at eight bells at the last minute, stumble aft for line up and keep my eyes closed as much as possible so that I should not properly wake. As soon as the Mate called, 'All right the watch . . . Relieve the wheel and lookout!' I would slip back to the focsle and turn in and be asleep in a moment, secure in the thought that my watch on deck would be one of peaceful sleep.

Now there was an end to all this for the serious business of the voyage was commencing. We got out our heavier clothing for we knew that we would soon have to turn out for our watches on deck well lashed up in seaboots and oilskins and prepared for the worst that the elements could offer. We regretfully said farewell to the period of comparative ease that we had enjoyed.

The first of the strong westerlies greeted us early one morning and the barque sailed before the fresh wind and did a good seven knots. As day broke we saw a big stump t'gallant four masted barque hull down ahead of us and only a point on the bow. Jim had a good pair of binoculars that he had picked up from the skylight as he went to take his place in one of the boats of a ship that had been torpedoed in the recent war and we trained these on the vessel ahead. From the cut of her I was sure that she was *Pommern* that I had last seen in Iquique. She was making the same course as ourselves and she must have passed quite close to us in the night, but following the usual custom of the ships of her particular owner, who ran his ships on a shoe-string, she showed no lights in these unfrequented parts of the ocean. She was below the horizon by midday.

Now the seas began to run and a few dollops came aboard to show us what to expect. Bill looked ruefully at me and said, 'Crikey, we're in a wet ship. If this bit of a sea comes over the rail, what shall we get later?' However, there was not much of it and we did not bother to shut our focsle door. The weather was fairly mild and the wind steady, so the 'farmers' could still chance to lie in their bunks in their watches on deck at nights.

I came from the wheel at four bells of the middle watch and slipped into the focsle for a smoke. I sat talking quietly to Len, who had come off lookout, while the others slept. We heard a big sea come growling along the rail. As it came opposite our deckhouse it broke aboard and a cataract of green water came slap in at the door. Jim's bunk was in line with the irruption and he woke with a yell.

'What the fuckin' 'ell!' and as I dashed to slam it to, 'Oi!

163

Can't ye shut the bloody door *afore* the ocean comes in?'

A foot of water sloshed across the deck and seamen looked over the edges of their bunks and grumbled as they rubbed sleep from their eyes. Grumbled as they swung barefeet into the swirling cold. Grumbled as they wrung out socks and emptied boots, baled, and mopped the focsle dry. Fortunately, no-one's bunk was seriously wetted.

The wind now freshened day by day. The seas got up to the size one expects in these latitudes and the weather grew cold and damp. Hail and rain squalls alternated with bright periods but the skies were almost always heavily overcast. Solid water broke aboard as we pulled on braces. We were knocked into the scuppers by the green seas and we climbed aloft to the swaying yards in tearing rain to fist madly slatting sails.

It was on 18th August, two months out from Liverpool, that we had our first hard blow. It started that morning with a strong wind and a green tinge in the sky to windward which told of more to come. We took in both fore t'ga'nts'ls without a great deal of difficulty and all day long the barque tore ahead, up and over the rolling hills of water to do her best speed, about nine knots. I stood right forward at the knight-heads and I could see her dripping forefoot as the seas lifted her and then she buried her blunt bows and pushed white water ahead of her beyond the end of her jib-boom.

With sunset the wind gradually increased its force and soon after ten, we were called to stand by main t'gallant halliards. We stood by for half an hour or more, huddled under the lee of the deckhouse as she stormed along and the seas cascaded aboard. With a scream in the rigging the wind came in a fierce gust and the Old Man's deep voice rang out, 'Upper t'ga'nts'l!'

The yard came down with a run and we soon had the sail up in its gear. Some of us jumped into the rigging and squelched aloft. She rolled so heavily that one moment we were clinging like flies to look up at the overhanging mast and the next we were crawling up almost on our hands and knees. Out on the yard we found that the weather buntlines

164

were not up or they had not been properly belayed and the sail was bellying out, full of the gale and as wet and as hard as a board. By punching at it and grabbing the folds so made we hove it up on the yard, got it stowed and secured. We had shouted to the deck to haul away on the slack ropes but our yells could have been heard only a long way down the wind. By the time we were down on deck again it was almost eight bells when all hands clewed up the lower t'ga'nts'l. While we clumped wearily to our focsle, the port watch went aloft to furl it.

We sat on seachests or on the edges of our bunks and were peeling off soaked oilskins and dragging our feet out of wet seaboots when the door was thrust open and the Second Mate's head appeared.

'All hands. Fore upper tops'l!'

Of course we cursed as sailors do, the weather, the rain, the sea, the Second Mate for calling us out, the Mate for telling him to do so, and the other watch for not being able to take in the thrice accursed tops'l by themselves. But, we got back into our oilskins as fast as we could, or went without, and got out on deck to the job.

We had the yard down and the sail up in its gear and were going aloft to furl before the port watch were down from the main, but they were on the yard as soon as we were and with so many hands the sail came up quickly. Jim and I were out at the yardarm and we feelingly cursed this speed for, as we followed the others into the rigging, we found that our less experienced shipmates had bundled up the sail any old how and the gaskets were slack and in one case not made fast at all. In short time the sail would have blown out again, so we two had to get it up on the yard, furl it properly and make it fast. By the time we got down, half our watch below had gone. We told them about it in no uncertain terms. Horace had been next to us inboard and he should have seen how things were if he had been anything at all of a sailor and he got some picturesque Liverpool language from Jim.

I turned out with the watch at 4 a.m. and took my trick

at the wheel and I had a busy time there. A fair sea was running and the barque yawed wildly as her stern lifted and the wind and sea caught her under the counter. There were sudden wild squalls accompanied by freezing, stinging rain and hail but there was a glorious dawn.

We were sailing nearly due east into the prospect of sunrise and the eastern sky was paling. Gold and scarlet edged the torn shreds of clouds. Before the sun rose there was a sharp flurry of hail and then the wrack cleared rapidly to show white cirrus clouds high above which the sun already saw and away to the south-west mighty cumulus reared column on column which frothed in huge piles and heaps of wondrous colour. Down at the horizon they were indigo and dove grey. They shaded gradually through rose to delicate pink, up to daintiest orange, to gold and lemon yellow which grew more brilliant to where the sun shone in dazzling splendour on the snowy whiteness of their billowing crests. The great seas kept their ceaseless march. Though deepest blue close alongside, ahead their tops showed emerald where the first light of day shone through them and aft their breaking crests were stained with the reflected glory of the masses of cloud.

All that day she plunged along before the gale. Green seas curled over the rail and sometimes caught us unawares as we made our way about the decks, bowled us off our feet into the lee scuppers and found weak spots in oilskins and sea-boots. I had a job in the afternoon to put tarred hemp preventer sheets on the lower topsails and while the wind howled in my ears and a bitter rain stung, I clung to the yardarm in constant apprehension. It was grey now. Sea and sky were neutral tones and colour seemed drained from the world. The rain came. Not bright and sparkling but dull and harsh and cold it spattered on grey canvas or splashed on drab brown spars. It flung out of the slaty sky and the drops pitted the grey-green sea from which the violent wind blew the caps in murky mist. Sometimes in the gusts the wind thundered in the sail and jerked the yard in rapid motion as if to try to rid itself of the chilly human who passed a secure seizing with stiff fingers. Wildly the vessel heeled and ran as the gale thrust at her sails.

In the evening the wind died and all sail was set once more. Within an hour there was only a gentle breeze and the barque wallowed drunkenly in a heavy swell while we pulled with soft wet hands on hard stiff ropes and staggered and slid about slippery decks.

In the first dog watch I was at the wheel again when we had a sudden shower. As it passed ahead the sky cleared and the sun came out brightly just above the horizon. A rainbow formed above the barque and under its arch she sailed. In brilliant contrast the sun showed her up against the dark rain cloud ahead and she lost her homely looks for she was transformed into a faery ship. Every spar gleamed gold. Her soaked canvas was pearl and opal and every dripping rope a string of jewels.

Next day dawned fine with a fair wind that sent her along at a good eight knots and I slept soundly through our forenoon watch below with the singing wind and the rushing seas for a lullaby. When we came on deck at midday a gale was brewing and all hands took in the mainsail. The wind continued to increase and we spent the watch shortening sail. No sooner had we stowed the two t'ga'nts'ls on the foremast than we clewed up and furled those on the main. Then, with the crescendo shrieks of the gale and the roar of the ocean in our ears, we stowed the fore-and-afters and then had a great fight with the fore upper topsail.

All this took time and the watch was drawing to a close when the Second Mate told us to stand by for all hands to take in the main upper topsail at eight bells. It had rained hard and we had shipped a few green ones during the watch. My oilskin coat was soggy and cold so I peeled off the comfortless things and put on my long oilskin coat which normally I used for wheel and lookout only. I lashed it about me with a couple of rope-yarns. Bill took off his waterlogged seaboots, rolled up his trousers and went barefooted to the job. At the end of the watch it was blowing heavens hard.

'Stow the main upper topsail!' shouted the Mate.

As the yard was lowered and we pulled at clewlines and buntlines, the sail tugged at the gear like a thing possessed. The ropes were hauled as tight as possible to quieten it and then all hands went aloft to furl. Strung out along the yard, men fought and punched at the hard canvas and had it almost smothered and a gasket passed here and there when, with a prolonged roll of thunder, a terrific squall struck the barque. Hail came pelting on the wind in jagged lumps as big as sparrows' eggs. The sail tore itself free of restraining hands and banged about with a frightful din. The yard jerked fiercely and we could do nothing but hang on for dear life, fearful of being flung off by its violent motion. The hail cut Bill's bare calves till they bled and it blew up under my long coat and half filled my seaboots with icy water. We were more than grateful when the height of the storm was soon passed and we were able to smother the fury of the still maddened sail, pass the gaskets about it and make all secure.

We no sooner came down from the mainmast than we had to clap on to the foresail gear and force our aching limbs and stinging hands to clew it up. We dragged weary bodies up the swinging rigging, squelched out along the yard and thumped and pounded with ragged knuckles to fold the canvas, lift it on to the yard and make it fast. This was a new sail made of the heaviest canvas and soaked with rain and coated with ice it was as hard as a harlot's heart. Many of us showed broken and bleeding finger nails as a result of the battle we had had with it up on the pitching yard.

Kilmallie drove on through the night under two topsails and she rolled heavily with a nasty jerky motion that threw one about. The masts and spars creaked and complained. The mighty seas rolled on. Their white crests gleamed weirdly in the dark. They hissed along the rail or they crashed aboard to go roaring and gurgling through washport and scupper back whence they came.

Thus we passed the meridian of Greenwich.

168

CHAPTER XV   THE ROARING FORTIES

With the next week the wind slowly died away and one by one we set the sails again. The seas still ran high and the old barque wallowed on and made less and less headway as the wind fell and she rolled more sickeningly than ever. Too great a proportion of the cargo had been stowed in the lower hold and this made her too stiff to take these seas easily. A cargo of rock salt was only a glorified ballast and it didn't earn much of a freight.

Horace showed his colours as a confirmed grouser this weather and with low and unpicturesque language he cursed the sea, the officers, the food, the ship, and everything and everyone came in for obscene abuse. Certainly it was not all it might have been and we were always hungry. Rations were meagre and the cooking vile but it was wiser to make the best of it than to grumble continuously. We thought it better to ignore him.

A frequent dish at tea-time was sloppy hash. This was composed largely of water thickened with something which we presumed to be flour. In it scraps of tough salt beef or pork floated greasily among odds and ends of alleged vegetables and broken ships' biscuits. We found it neither digestible nor nourishing but we could get no other and it served to fill a gap.

One day when the weather was comparatively calm and the decks clear of water, the Second Mate got Jim and me to open part of the fore hatch and to break out and open one of the barrels of salt beef that were stowed there in the 'tween decks. There were elaborate seals on the head of the cask and rusty tin labels confirmed that the meat had been laid down in Her Majesty's Shipyard at Portsmouth in 1875! When Jim read these he exploded.

'Well . . . Fuck me for fourpence! Trust these lousy blasted belly-robbing barstuds of shipowners! I bet they got this at a dockyard auction of useless stores for next to nothing!'

When we knocked in the head of the cask, we revealed large irregular lumps of meat of a dirty pink colour. They swam in thick brine of a grubby grey and crystals of salt as big as broad beans fringed the margin.

A lump of this beef would be taken from the barrel and soaked in sea water for twenty-four hours in the 'harness cask'. This was a peculiarly shaped cask in that it was wider at the top than at the bottom. It was specially made for the purpose of reducing the brine content of the beef which sailors said was from the flesh of horses which had died from old age and decrepitude. Then the cook simmered it for a further twenty-four hours. After this, when cut into very thin slices, it neither tasted nor chewed differently from a piece of red flannel. It didn't look very different either.

Our 'cook' was an elderly little crippled Swede who had a quite unimaginative way of dealing with such food as was aboard our ship. There were the traditional dishes of porridge, uneatable salt fish, haricot beans boiled in molasses and water, hash in dry or sloppy form, 'apple daddy' made of soggy pastry and dried apples, unappetising dishes concocted with salt beef or pork which was invariably a bit whiffy, and the inevitable lump of sodden plum duff on Thursdays and Sundays. None of it was interesting in appearance or flavour and we had no choice but to accept the tasteless messes. It was no wonder that the quiet, slow-spoken steward did all the cooking for the afterguard.

170

It is perhaps worth while to anticipate here and to tell that later in the voyage the cook fell ill and for two days his duties were taken over by the steward. For those two days the food was well prepared and tasty dishes were made from it. No comments were made for I am sure that my shipmates and I were too ashamed to express our thoughts on the cook's recovery.

A few days later we came on deck in the forenoon to find the skies clear and the sun shining while all around us the sky was filled with birds. Countless thousands of snow birds flew with stormy petrels and Cape pigeons and a sprinkling of mollymawks, skua gulls and albatross. I had a job aloft and even from the upper t'gallant yard, 110 feet from the deck, I could see no end to this great flight of birds. They were mostly snow birds, a pretty little tern about the size of a dove, with an erratic flight. Each flap of their wings sent them off on a slightly varying course. They were all heading south and their white breasts glinted in the sun as they flew but a few feet above the surface of the sea.

At the beginning of September we were at Long. 21°20′ East and Lat. 40°46′ South and holding a good fair breeze. It was variable both in force and direction and over the weeks we had plenty of work aloft in stowing and setting the t'ga'nts'ls for our Old Man was not one to carry on. He said to me as I fought with the wheel one breezy morning while the watch were furling the upper t'ga'nts'ls, and I flatter myself if I thought that he may have sensed that I doubted if it were really necessary, 'I've known what it was to storm along here with everything set and the spray wetting the upper tops'ls, but it doesn't do these days. We can't afford to lose canvas and we don't get the experienced crews who could stow sails in quick time in the first of a squall.'

The latter part of his statement was true enough but one couldn't help noticing that now the sails were taken in much more quickly and they were better handed and secured. The greenhorns were growing more used to working aloft and they worried less about their personal safety. The old Skipper

171

did not appreciate their efforts. One dull and dirty evening we strained at the weather main braces till our muscles cracked as we strove with every nerve and sinew to check in the heavy yards and the gale-filled sails. He gave us a new version of the saying of old timers that 'at one time there were wooden ships and iron men, but now there are iron ships and wooden men'. He made quite a picture as he stood there at the break of the poop, his oilskin coat flying, his legs braced to the motion of the ship. He was bare headed and his white hair blew around his weather-beaten face. His hands gripped the rail as he watched us straining, up to our waists in water, getting only an inch at a time on the stubborn braces. In a tone of utter disgust he yelled down at us.

'Pull . . .! Blast you! I never saw such a crew! When *I* first came to sea there were wooden ships and IRON men . . . but now there are steel ships and PUTTY . . . BLOODY . . . MEN!'

It was about this time that 'Chips' the carpenter noticed a sag in the fore lower t'gallant yard and he went aloft to examine. He found that the wood was rotten at the truss and he drove in some wedges to tighten it up. A day later we found the wedges sunk deep in the rotted timber and that a spike would go six inches deep into the yard before it met with sound wood. The Old Man had the upper t'ga'nts'l unbent and the lower yard lashed to the upper. We were all rather relieved when this was done for the stress on a 68-foot spar slung 100 feet above the deck by its middle is something to reckon with. It was not very comforting to know as you worked below it, or were out on the yard, that its point of suspension was unreliable. It was awkward to have to crawl round the lashings to furl the lower sail and especially at night, but it was a deal safer.

The waves grew and grew in size and the winds became wilder and wilder as we drove on before them. Day after day, week after week, the barque sailed on, thrust by the roaring gales and the mountainous seas. Always the decks were wet and in the waist long green weeds grew which made the deck slippery and perilous to walk on. Time and again we tried to scrub them away with the help of ashes from the galley fire, but as soon as we started with our brooms, a great wave would come crashing in emerald and snow about us, washed the ashes through the scupper holes and bashed us against the bulwarks, or some of us clung to the lifelines or in the lower rigging and jeered at our less fortunate shipmates. It was hopeless to try to remove it so the marine growth was left in slimy peace to be dealt with under more favourable conditions.

Sometimes the wind held in the south-west for a day or so and it was cold but the wind was steady and strong. All sail could be set and we made good progress. We knew that it would soon fail, to leave us rolling wildly in the swell it left. Then a little wind would come out of the north and freshen, draw to the north-west and blow hard while we toiled at sodden ropes and rigid canvas to shorten sail. The wind would back to the south and west and hold. All sail could be set again and good progress made.

I remember one evening when the wind was growing to a gale, that I went up the mainmast with an apprentice to stow the upper t'ga'nts'l. I went out to the weather yardarm and was surprised to find myself alone there. I looked in towards the mast to see the boy hung over the yard with his hands to his head. I slipped along the footrope and grasped his shoulder.

'What's wrong?' I shouted.

'My head,' he muttered.

'Can you get down?'

'Yes. I . . . I think so,' he mumbled, and he looked up at me in a dazed way.

'Well, GO!' I cried. 'Get the hell out of this!'

'I . . . I'll be all right.'

'No you won't! If you're sure you can get down, get there as quickly as you can. If not I'll take you down. The devil take the sail.'

'I . . . I'll be all right,' he breathed vaguely.

I seized him by the collar of his jacket and swung him into

173

the rigging where he hung on. He started to make his way down while I got ahead with the sail when I saw that he could manage. I had a hearty scrap single-handed and after a struggle I had all securely fast. The boy never again complained of vertigo and he was a fine healthy lad, always with a grin and a cheerful word in the worst of conditions, willing and eager to learn, and apt to pick up the details of a sailor's business.

So it went on. Rain came, and hail, and howling wind, and troubled seas. We were so often up to our necks in water to shorten sail or working our guts out to set it again. Sometimes it would be an audibly increasing gale from the northwest or a steady strong wind from the southward but always the mighty marching seas.

I stood one evening under the focsle head in the dog watch with Cockney of the port watch and we were seeing how the troubled horizon appeared to rear itself over the poop as a sea ran from under her bows. The crest of the next wave was over a quarter of a mile away and the Londoner said, his voice hushed with awe, 'Blimey, Frank, if yer was ter tell 'em of this at 'ome, they'd say as yer was a flamin' liar.'

One can never forget those great seas that towered above our tops'l yards when we were down in the trough and as we rose to the crest, we looked back down to a green valley laced with white and on and up an advancing hillside to a crown of thundering, tumbling, snowy foam which ever threatened to engulf us. One felt very small.

We fought our way across the stormy ocean with hands that were raw and sore with grazes and sea cuts, muscles that ached, and joints that cracked from the strains that we put upon them, bellies that grumbled with hunger, and bodies that were always cold and wet, and yet we could get a laugh out of it.

One night of strife when all hands were out and we were hauling with dogged determination at the weather braces, the barque rolled a huge sea aboard. As she recovered and the water poured over the rail, Tom was lifted off his feet and started to go with it. He was next in front of big Fred Ulring who was fortunate that he was able to hook his leg round a convenient stanchion. Fred grabbed old Tom by the collar of his oilskin jacket, brought him back aboard with a mighty heave and yelled in his ear.

'No you don't! You can't get out of it as easily as all that! Clap on to the brace and pull y'r weight!'

'Orright. I couldn' 'elp it,' Tom grumbled and he looked quite crestfallen as if caught in some guilty act. Some of the others shouted, 'No good tryin' ter jump ship 'ere, Tom!', or, 'Yer carn't git ter Australia that way!'

Tom was a simple soul. He came from Park Lane in Liverpool and in those days that street was nothing like the Park Lane of the capital. To him Australia was a wonderful land of promise. He had been there many times and the waterfronts of Melbourne, Sydney and Newcastle held no secrets for him. He believed that the interior flowed with milk and honey and that one had only to dig to find gold. This time, when the barque reached Sydney, he was going to leave her and he was going to leave the sea. He was going into the bush and he was going to dig for gold. Some day he would return to Liverpool, buy up all the shipping companies and he would give all the poor sailormen £20 per month and plenty to eat and no work.

Some of us, with the help of Chips, built him a 'bike'. For the wheels we used the ends of a wooden drum on which had been coiled a wire rope. Odds and ends of timber made the frame. We hung it about with everything we could think of that he might require. A shovel, a lantern, a pick, a frying pan, a coil of rope, a broom, and sundry other objects adorned it. When it was completed we presented it to him so that he could travel at ease in Australia. He was as pleased as punch and he sat astride it with his two feet on the deck and he trundled it around with the greatest glee.

There were solemn moments too. One night after twenty-four hours of battling with the elements and as the wind was falling, the watch took the fore topsail halliards to the main-deck capstan and walked wearily round it to hoist the yard and set the sail. It had risen above five feet when there was a terrifying bang from aloft and a jar which shook the whole fabric of the ship. The fall of the tackle had parted and the yard crashed to the cap of the lower mast. The apprentice whose job it was to overhaul the buntlines was usually on the yard for this but by good fortune he had stayed in the rigging and he caught his leg around the shroud for greater safety. This saved him from being flung off to almost certain death. My mind went back to a similar happening in *William Mitchell* and to thoughts of shipowners who couldn't afford to renew important ropes.

The upper block was stopped to a backstay, a long splice was made in the rope and it was 'end for ended' and rove off again. There was not enough suitable rope in the sparsely-stocked rope locker to reeve off a new rope. In the meantime the watch had gone aloft and furled the sail. It was nearly eight bells when it was ready to set again and so it was made a job for all hands.

I remember that night so well. I was at the wheel and so I escaped the long hard pull. It was pitch dark and the wind had fallen but a long swell was running which growled and gurgled along the rail, and this, with the creaking of spars and rigging were the only sounds. The two Mates had gone forward to supervise the setting of the sail and I had the poop to myself. Above that great silence I could hear their voices.

The Mate's voice:

'Up aloft there! Overhaul those buntlines!'

A thin boyish answer came wailing down:

'Ay . . . ay . . . Sir!'

Old Sails's deep tones:

'Come on lads! Tail on and stretch it out!'

Here there was a murmur of voices and a shuffling of sea-booted feet. Then came the high tenor of old Charlie Brimblecombe of Brixham:

'As I was a-walking down Paradise Street!'

Then the rousing chorus accompanied by the rattle of

176

sheaves in the blocks and the voice of the sea:

'To me way . . . HEY . . . Blow the man DOWN!'

'A saucy young p'liceman I chanced for to meet!'

'Oh . . . ho . . . GIVE me some time to BLOW the man down!'

It is a memory that I treasure. I can hear again the whispering ocean, the rustle of canvas and cordage, the hearty old shanty that has sent God knows how many yards aloft, led by a splendid old shellback and followed by many young and old voices and strong muscles working in harmony to the age-old accompaniment of the song and of chattering blocks and straining hemp.

The weather no longer allowed us to spend the dog watches on the main hatch or under the focsle head but the watches would visit each other in their respective focsles and swap yarns of places and of happenings. Cockney of the port watch had apparently had a wonderful variety of experiences and he was ever ready to tell of them. He once told us a far-fetched tale of what he said was the best job he had ever had.

'I've 'ad some good jobs in me time but I carn't stick 'em fer long. Too bleedin' restless I am. I 'member I 'ad a fine job one time. A flamin' fine job it were, but at larst it broke me 'eart. Fair broke me bleedin' 'eart it did. You know Ned,' and here he pointed his short pipe at a shipmate, 'them ferry boats wot ran 'tween Gryvesend an' Tilbury? Well, I 'ad a job on one o' them. Not arf fine it were just poppin' acrost the river an' back. Not too much ter do an' the best o' grub. The pay wasn' too bad an' yer could alwys make a bit 'umpin' passengers' luggage.

'One day a passenger comes aboard . . . an' Gorblime, 'e weren't arf a dude! A bleedin' swell 'e were. 'E 'ad a trunk erbaht as big as this 'ere deck'ouse. I makes 'im aht fer a good fing an' w'en we gits acrost, I goes up ter 'im an' touches me lid an' ses, "This yore trunk, Sir?" "Oh yes," 'e ses, "You may carry that, Sailor." I picks 'im be the tone of 'is voice ter be a real toff, so I works the trunk ter the edge o'

177

the 'atch coaming, an' wiv a 'ard struggle I manages ter 'eave it on ter me back, an' orf I starts.

'There wus erbaht a dozen blighters wanted ter giv me a 'and but I chased 'em orl orf. Greedy yer know. I reckined there wus at least a five bob piece ter come orf 'im an' I didn' want ter share it aht. You remember Ned, that wharf at Tilbury in them days? Erbaht two miles long it were, an' I struggles along wiv the sweat just porin' orf of me. At larst I gits ter the stashun an', arter chasin' erbaht a 'undred porters away, I gits ter me passenger's train. I'm that egg'austed that w'en I goes ter put this 'ere bleedin' trunk dahn, I collapses an' we reaches the grahnd tergevver! Well, I wipes the sweat aht o' me eyes an' I looks rahnd fer me passenger an' sure enuff, 'ere 'e comes in a minit or so. 'E's lookin' like 'e owns the 'ole bleedin' show.

' "'Ere yer are, Sir," I ses. "Trunk's orl right an nuffin' broke," an' I watches 'im diggin' 'is 'and inter 'is pocket. Then . . . wot d'yer fink 'e done? Wot d'yer fink that bleeder 'ad the bleedin' owdacity ter say ter me?

' "Ow, thenk you, sailor," 'e ses, "an' I'm sorry thet I 'ave no money, but, I'll give you three 'earty cheers. Three 'earty cheers fer a British sailor. Hurrah! Hurrah! and Hurrah!"

'It were altogever too much fer me overwrought system an' I on'y 'member me legs givin' way under me an' nex' I know I wus back on the boat, a layin' on the 'atch an' they wus frowin' worter over me. Yus, but it wus a good job.'

Week after week it went on. Toil and wet and cold and hunger; wind and rain and great seas; continually wet and slippery decks; sodden clothes and blankets; muddy coffee and biscuit hash; these were our portion. We got so tired that we flopped into our damp bunks and slept like logs in our watches below and drove ourselves by force of will and the knowledge of the work's necessity in our watches on deck.

One night there was a fearful banging and slamming going on aloft but I was so sleepy that I was only dimly conscious of it till Bill turned out of his bunk next to mine and said, 'Something big has carried away, Frank. Don't you think

178

that we'll have to turn out for a job for all hands?'

I thought that it was the topsail and said so but I was so bone weary that I didn't care if the masts were all gone and the ship was sinking so long as no one worried me about it or woke me up. I turned over and was at once asleep.

When we came on deck for our watch on duty we found that it was only the fore topmast staysail which had blown out and it was the loose canvas in the gale that had made all the noise. We might have known that in spite of all the din it couldn't have been the topsail, or anything serious, for in such case it would have been 'All hands on deck!' for certain.

Many times our watch was called out in our watch below to shorten sail and we wearily cursed as we hastened into our clothes and out on deck, for 'growl you may but go you must' was true at sea. As I've said our Old Man wasn't one to drive his ship and if he thought there was going to be a bit of a blow, he would have the sails in before it started. Naturally there were the usual remarks about the Skipper of the last ship and of how he had carried on all sail 'and got the ship there in 'alf the time without wearin' the sailors' soul cases out forever fightin' fuckin' canvas.' And of how our watch was always the one to be called out and the port watch never.

One night we were called out to take in the foresail and this was a hard weather sail and was stowed only if we were going to be under two lower topsails and probably about to heave to. When we got on deck, hurriedly and inadequately clothed for that weather, we found that the port watch had clewed up the port side of the sail and were aloft and furling it. They had left the starboard side set. We clewed up the starboard side of the sail and left it to those aloft to furl and we coiled up all the ropes and went below. It did not seem to us to be blowing so very hard and there was a lot of justifiable muttering and grumbling. I rather think that we had to suffer because of personal feelings between the two mates.

We passed the meridian of Cape Leeuwin, the westernmost point of Australia on 3rd October before a good breeze. In spite of its reputation for gales, only variable winds took us

179

across the Great Australian Bight, but the huge seas still ran and we were for ever setting some sails or stowing them or dragging at braces while waves flopped aboard and drenched us and the green weeds grew ever longer in the waist. It was at dawn on 12th October that we sighted land near Cape Otway. The first land that we had sighted since June 20th, nearly four months ago, had that familiar Australian skyline of low rounded hills topped by the skeletons of bare trees.

The next day Wilson's Promontory was dimly visible on the port bow while ahead was the thickly wooded cone of Sugarloaf and the barren dome of Skull Island. A strong freshening breeze sent us bowling along and for once the Old Man carried on all sail. His lined old face had an anxious expression for, like many old deep water men, he hated to be close to the land. We passed the Promontory before midday and here we got a bit of a puff and we had to get moving to stow the t'ga'nts'ls and soon after we braced the yards as the course was altered to head up towards the east coast.

The breeze held all the afternoon, fell light during the night, but it freshened with the dawn and by nine o'clock we were abreast of Cape Howe, with only three hundred miles to go.

It was a bright morning of sunshine and clear skies and the old hooker pushed her blunt bows through the blue ocean before a pleasant but not very strong wind. It seemed too fine to last but no one believed that the wind would not hold. The watch below washed and brushed their go-ashore clothes, darned socks and polished the mould off shoes.

To disappoint the optimists the wind died away with the sunset. All through the following night we sat in calm in sight of Gabo Island light which scarcely altered its bearing. It was pleasant and warm but after so long at sea we thought only of getting to port and the only weather we were prepared to appreciate would carry with it a strong fair breeze. We sat upright and still all next day. The warm sun shone but upon us no wind blew. Until 4 p.m. we were painfully conscious of Gabo's supercilious tower sneering down on us.

A wind came in the first dog watch, but from the north. We braced the yards sharp up and stood away from the land. For the rest of the week we sailed off and on. Now on this tack and now on that, we beat against a wind that grew in force but kept its unfriendly direction. By the Saturday we were down to lower topsails and we rode out a hard blow. That afternoon the wind moderated and drew fair so that we were able to lay our course but still close-hauled. As if the Old Man wanted to stay at sea, he had only the lee side of the foresail set. Here we were, with a useful fair wind and looking as if were were under jury rig, but before midnight the wind was in the south and we were going with square yards, hell-bent for Sydney.

The elements were only teasing us for by eight o'clock on Sunday morning all sails were set and the barque was sailing close hauled again to a light northerly breeze while a hot sun blazed down from a cloudless sky. Hundreds of birds were flying around us and numerous whales disported themselves on all sides, but we weren't interested. We could think only of the delights of port, of friendships renewed, of no more watch-and-watch, no more seaboots and oilskins, and all night in.

For the next two days we made a series of short tacks against the exasperating northerly. At every change of watch, we hauled at braces, sheets, and tacks to put the ship about and on the Tuesday we were ninety miles from Sydney and we had made good only seventeen miles in the previous twenty-four hours.

To be within sight of the land but to have to fight every mile of the way promised to go on indefinitely and we became almost resigned to be blown about the Tasman Sea for years. We could imagine that in years to come there would be an old rusty barque sailing there, manned by octogenarians with long flowing beards, her sails patched and patched and patched again. The old men fished overside to augment their failing rations or they scrounged from passing steamers. They stumbled about feebly as they tacked ship against a continually foul wind and they hitched a handy billy to each brace to aid their failing strength.

Our watch came on deck at midnight to find a fine fair wind and the ship going along at a good seven knots. I was at the wheel from two till four that morning and it was great to have the good wind and the calm sea instead of those big rolling waves shoving the stern around, so she was a pleasure to handle. Perhaps the old girl wanted to get to port and to have a quiet rest for she steered like a yacht. On that calm sea she needed only a gentle touch to the wheel now and again, a check here and a help there and she responded without any wild yawing.

When our watch came on deck again at 8 a.m. Sydney Heads were in sight, the barque was under three tops'ls and fores'l and the wind was freshening. At 10 a.m. it came on to blow hard with fierce squalls and we stowed the main upper tops'l and the fores'l. We were cheered that for once the other watch were called out in their watch below for this job, the first time in the voyage, though our watch had been out many a time and oft. Then the order came, 'Lee fore brace!' and we knew that it could only mean that we would heave the barque to.

It was a despondent crew that hauled on the lee braces, glowered aft with mutinous scowls and who muttered among themselves about panic-stricken skippers who were scared of the sight of land. They grumbled bitterly about ''avin ter spend another bloody night at sea in this 'ere God-forgotten barge an' keepin' fuckin' watch w'en we should ought ter be tight in our bunks at a safe anchorage.'

I will never know if the two Mates expressed similar feelings at our being within a few miles of harbour with a wind fair to take us in, but the Old Man came on to the poop and shouted, 'Square the main yard!'

We sprang to it with an involuntary cheer. A fair sea had got up and we had a ducking at the fore braces but we didn't care then if it snowed. A tug picked us up at two and we entered the Heads at three, one hundred and twenty-five days from Liverpool.

It was a bleak grey day as we passed up the harbour to Double Bay and dropped anchor. 120 fathoms were slacked away on the cable, the other bow anchor splashed in, and then we walked round and round the capstan and hove in 60 fathoms of chain on the former and slacked off correspondingly on the latter.

This secure mooring was made because the barque was expected to lie here for some time before she could get a berth. We learned that British seamen in port were on strike in protest against a reduction of pay of ten shillings a month and many ships from the Home Country were laid up. These ships were at anchor in the harbour and there were a lot of rebellious seamen ashore that were more than ready to make trouble for any sailorman who was not ready to join them. I had every sympathy for their case for indeed we were all in the same boat, but a strike could not possibly succeed.

We had all agreed to a special clause in the Articles, which we had signed on joining the ship, that stated that if there should be a reduction or increase of pay during the time of the Articles, such would operate from the date of the alteration notwithstanding the rate of pay ruling when the Articles were signed, or words to that effect. The clause was always brought to the notice of men when a crew signed on. They had agreed to it because they had no choice, and now they were kicking when it operated against them. Incidentally, it' never did operate in their favour. A year or so later there was an increase in the rate of overtime granted to the crews of ships which signed on *after a certain date*. If a ship had signed on its crew only a day before, possibly for two or three years, the men did not get the benefit of the increase. Overtime in *our* ship was something that we worked but for which we had not the remotest hope of being paid.

When we had been granted pratique, we were boarded by several newspaper reporters and photographers and the next day the local papers had a write up about 'the last of Britain's fine old windjammers', 'real sailormen', etc., with views of

183

the barque at anchor and a group of the crew. We perused them with mixed feelings.

It turned out a beautiful evening and I leaned on the rail of the focsle head and I looked out over the calm water to the houses and trees and green growing things. I thought of the people who lived their secure lives there and I envied them not. The wild places of the world for me, and the road that leads over a hill.

CHAPTER XVI   SYDNEY AND NEWCASTLE

Next morning, to the surprise of all forward, the Mate called, 'All hands! Man the windlass!' and we were told that we were to go alongside at Woolloomoolloo at once.

We leaned against the capstan bars and dug our toes into the deck as we hove in on the port cable and slacked away on the starboard till we had the former's 60 fathoms aboard. Then we hove in 120 fathoms on the latter. One hundred and eighty fathoms of chain we brought into the lockers that morning by the strength of our backs and the thrust of our bodies. It took us four hours of stamping and heaving and trudging and pushing, the capstan bars hard against our chests. Our heads bowed, our backs and legs braced and thrusting, we walked the windlass round and round and round. Yet it was four hours of rousing singing. The harbour rang with every capstan shanty we knew and some we did not. When we had sung them all we sang them over again or old Charlie Brimblecombe, who led most of them, improvised verses that poured scorn on the ship and her food or told of men and women and drink.

We must have shocked the boys and girls that sailed their yachts near us and hove to to photograph us, when they heard some of the verses.

A favourite was the song about the maid from Amsterdam who was mistress of her trade. This always started politely about how 'I took this fair maid for a walk, that we might have a private talk'. Then, I think that most people know the chorus that goes on about going no more a-roving 'cos roving's been my ruin, largely through the sea shanties sung by that popular group on TV, The Spinners. Further verses give various reactions by the maid to where the soloist puts his hand and they get less and less polite. Thus:

I put my hand upon her arm, said she, young man that
    does no harm.
I put my hand around her waist, said she, young man
    you're in great haste.
I put my hand upon her thigh, said she, young man you're
    rather high.
I put my hand upon her heart, said she, young man you'll
    make me fart.
I put my hand upon her breast, and the wind from her arse
    blew sou-sou-west.

and so on. There are endless varieties on the theme.

We were towed to the wharf and as we made fast, quite a crowd of curious and interested people were there to watch. They didn't have a lot to do with us forward but the apprentices were in their element as they showed the visitors and reporters round and spun yarns of hair-raising adventures. I heard the young rascals inventing the details of some particularly lurid 'experience' which they planned to tell, each contributor going one better than the last.

I noticed one young man who stood aloof from the crowd as he appraised the vessel. He was well groomed and he had that indefinable air of prosperity. He cut a very different figure from when I had last seen him. I went up to him and held out my hand.

'So', I said, 'you've returned to the fold. I'll warrant that you sleep better between sheets than you did in the focsle of *E.R. Sterling.*'

He recognised me at once. We shook hands.

'Do you know,' he answered, 'I'm not so sure that I do,' and we laughed.

We recalled Iquique Bay, the clear sky and the ceaseless roll of the Pacific where the square-riggers lay at their moorings and the winches rattled the nitrate aboard. We spoke of the drab and barren land and the sailors who left their ships to work on the nitrate mines, only to return to Iquique and to ship on another hungry windjammer. *E.R. Sterling* had brought him back to Australia and the family business had claimed him.

Farmers came with drays and wagons and collected their requirements from the two thousand of our three thousand tons of rock salt which was dumped on the wharf. The remainder was kept aboard as ballast.

Bill introduced me to friends of his who lived at Manly and we spent many delightful weekends swimming in the Bay or surfing from the outer beach. Here I met Max Stanton, an old shipmate of Bill's and also of the Second Mate of the tanker *Orowaiti*. He was an outstanding personality.

Often in the evenings we went to the Seamens' Mission and we made friends there. There was to be a concert at the Mission and some of our lads persuaded the Padre that we had an accomplished violinist aboard, who would like to contribute an item. Back aboard, they told Horace that the Padre had sent him an invitation to come and give a performance on his fiddle at the Mission concert. Horace beamed all over his ugly face and with suitable smirks of modest reluctance, he consented to give a selection from his repertoire. By this time he had, in an atmosphere of perspiring profanity, removed all traces of grease from the strings and the bow and he often scorched our souls with his vile attempts at music.

The great day arrived and he spent all the time after he had knocked off work in polishing his fiddle and in dressing himself up. He even borrowed a collar and tie to put on his

187

shirt which I'm sure had never seen one before. He got to the Mission much too early and he was shepherded along and introduced to the Padre who was suitably impressed. He was billed for half-way through the programme and he sat at the back of the crowded little hall in sweating apprehension till his call came.

The Padre came forward and announced that he had a great treat for his audience. He felt sure that a crew member of that fine old sailing ship *Kilmallie* who would not in the least mind being called a shellback, would give them real pleasure as he played on his old violin which had been his constant companion in a life of stress and toil on the Seven Seas. (Cheers.)

While we could not expect to hear music of the modern style with its jazz influence and dance rhythm, he felt sure that we would hear music that would appeal to real he-men and which would carry with it the tang of the sea. (Prolonged applause.)

During this introduction, Horace had been standing in the middle of the platform with a sickly grin on his face. As the Padre retired, he drew up a chair and sat down. A young lady with an armful of music appeared and offered to accompany him on the piano, but he gruffly refused saying,

'I don' need any bl——, I don' need any help.'

He produced a large red handkerchief, carefully dusted his instrument, squinted along the bow, and tucked the bandanna into his collar. With his big hand grasping the end of his fiddle as if he would strangle it, he thrust it under his chin and commenced to 'play' with his usual disregard of any tune, time or air.

People looked at one another with puzzled expressions. Others gazed hopefully and wondered when he was really going to start. Some tried to read a meaning into the ghastly scraping. Then somebody tittered and in a moment the hall was in fits which ended when some brawny sailor stood and led a proportion of the audience in 'counting him out'. Not till then did Horace realise that his effort was unpopular. He rose as the laughter turned to jeers, glared at the company and bawled, 'None of yer carn't bluddy well unnerstan' music!'

I'm afraid that no one wasted any sympathy on him and the incident made no impression on his thick skin. Evenings in the focsle continued to be marred by the howls of the tormented instrument which said much for the tolerance of his shipmates.

In Sydney a second-hand lower t'gallant yard was towed alongside and we lowered the rotten one and sent the replacement aloft and crossed it on the foremast. The old spar was soft for more than halfway through at the truss and we were relieved to have a sound one in its place.

Also we painted the ship overside and removed what we could of the generous growth of sea grasses and goose barnacles from her bilges. I worked at this with the big Norwegian, Fred Ulring, from the port watch. He was a splendid figure of a man. He stood over six feet tall and he had broad shoulders, and arms that were as big round as my thighs but he had a most gentle and charming nature and he was kind-hearted to a fault. He told me that he had a Norwegian Officer's Certificate but that he preferred to sail in British ships. When I ventured to ask him why, he told me as we sat on the stage and painted away, of his 'Dora' who lived in Liverpool and whom he obviously adored. He told me in his slow quiet way of how he had come to meet and marry her.

She had been cold and hungry and in great distress. It was during that previous war and Fred had tried to help and comfort her. At length she told him how a soldier had taken her and had gone away and left her and in some months' time she would have a child. She was homeless and friendless and Fred got lodgings for her. As soon as he could he married her and he made arrangements for her to have an allotment from his pay.

I could picture her as Fred described her to me. She was tall and dark and splendidly built and eternally grateful to her big gentle sailor who loved her with all his kindly nature.

He knew that she was not always faithful to him while he was away, often for years, but with his wealth of understanding, he forgave her because of her loneliness and her vitality and her love of life. He was proud of her little son, almost as proud as if he had been his own. He said to me as our legs swung and the rippling water chuckled along the ship's sides, 'Some day Frank, I go back home and get a good shore job an' we settle down an' be ever so happy.' An almost childlike smile spread over his fair face and his clear blue eyes were very bright.

Poor great-hearted Fred. He couldn't know that his dreams would never come true.

We were some seven weeks in Sydney. Then, one evening a tug came alongside and made fast and at midnight we cast off and left Wooloomooloo and were towed the seventy miles to Newcastle, and arrived the following forenoon after a fine weather uneventful passage.

Such of our cargo as had been discharged in Sydney had been taken from under the main hatch and in this space we took on a thousand tons of coal as stiffening. The remainder of our rock salt was discharged on to the wharf for the farmers to collect, as in Sydney.

A couple of days after our arrival I woke early on a calm clear morning. I lay in my bunk and listened to the musical lap of the water along the side as the tide ran. I gazed half sleepily at the blue circle of sunlit sky that the porthole showed. As I rested there in pleasant idleness, I was surprised and delighted to see Max Stanton's face appear and to hear his deep voice.

'Tumble out and come along and see me Brookie. We're tied up just astern of you.'

I got up, slipped into my clothes and strolled along the wharf to where his ship lay. He was Second Mate of this little coasting steamer which was on a regular trade between Sydney and Newcastle. While her crew were busy discharging her cargo we stood yarning of our lives and prospects and of ships and the sea. All her cargo was handled by her crew, and as I idly watched them shoving bales and cases ashore, I recognised one slightly-built youngster and called,

'By Jove Gatty, What the devil are you doing there?'

Gatty grinned and answered, 'Doing pretty well.'

They were busy but with Max's agreement we were able to have a word or two together. When I had last seen him he was Third Mate of my first ship, the oil tanker *Orowaiti* and I was astonished to find him working as a deck hand on an Australian coasting steamer. His story was interesting.

He had been trained as a naval cadet but, rather than join the Australian Navy as a middy, he had passed his examination for Second Mate and had gone into the Merchant Service. When we had been together on the tanker, we had often yarned during the night watches when I had been at the wheel. Then soon after I had left her, *Orowaiti* piled up on a reef off the coast of California and his job was gone. He decided to give up the sea and he went into the import and export business in Tasmania, his native land.

He was doing well when a shipping strike in Western Australia held up some machinery he was importing for a customer. There was a time/penalty clause in the contract with the consignees and he was involved in litigation for failure to deliver on time. Although he had been helpless to do anything to collect the goods, he lost the case. The costs and the heavy fine inflicted took all his available capital and he was obliged to give up his business. After several vicissitudes he had obtained this job and he told me that he was better off than when he had been on the bridge. Though the work was hard and the hours long, he earned about £40 per month which was very much more than he had earned as an officer and with all found, was a reasonable income in 1925. I heard later from Stanton that Gatty had got the job as Second Mate when Max had left to take command of a schooner trading in New Guinea waters. Thereafter I lost sight of him for some years till I heard that he had established a school of navigation in San Francisco. Then quite suddenly, he made himself quite

191

famous by flying round the world in eight days with the American Wiley Post. Together they wrote a very interesting book about it.

I did not hear again of Max for some years till I went to London Dock to meet my pal Bill Porteous, home on the old *Discovery* from Sir Douglas Mawson's expedition to Antarctica. To my surprise and pleasure I found that Max was Mate of the ship, for her last voyage.

The first Friday in port we were able to draw some money against our pay and I went ashore with Fred Ulring and Old Charlie Brimblecombe for a drink. We took a shortcut across some unfenced railway sidings to the nearest pub. I paid for a round and then said that I must beat it as I wanted to get back aboard for some food before it all went and that I had some shopping to do. The two wanted me to stay but I was determined not to get into a drinking session and I left. I ate my tea and went ashore again, bought myself some seaboots and oilskins which I needed badly, some soap and matches, and I returned aboard.

About ten o'clock, as I lay in my bunk smoking my pipe and reading, Cockney stepped into our focsle and said, 'Freddy's been killed.'

I sat up and said, 'Rot! He can't be. I had a drink with him not so long ago!'

'Well, 'e's dead nah, an' pore old Charlie's 'ad bofe legs cut orf. They wus takin' the shortcut acrost the sidings in the dark an' a shunted waggon caught 'em. They've just taken 'em away in a ambulance.'

I sat and stared at Cockney in horror, unable to believe my ears. I could not accept it. Fred of the powerful body and the gentle nature to be dead? It was not possible. It could not be. I went out on deck and I leaned on the rail and looked out over the dark calm water to the lights across the river and tried to take it in. I had looked on Fred as my pal. He was a very quiet man and though he had been in the other watch, he had talked with me more than anyone else on board. I could not for the life of me realise that he would

192

never talk with me again. I leaned there and sucked on a dead pipe and stared with unseeing eyes into the night. I tried to understand why these things happen. It seemed so devilish senseless and futile to me and I felt as bitter as hell. Then a strange thing occurred. I don't pretend to be psychic but I thought that I heard Fred's calm slow voice saying, 'It doesn't matter Frank. I'm all right and quite happy.' With the words a peacefulness came to me. I went into the focsle, turned in to my bunk and was soon fast asleep.

Next day Jim and I went to see Charlie in hospital. The doctors had operated and removed the poor mangled shreds of his legs and he lay there in agony but he knew us and spoke to us. I tried to cheer him and I lied to him and said that he would soon be all right again. I saw a doctor in the ward and I went to him and asked what hopes there were.

'He's goosed,' he answered. 'He can't possibly last more than a few hours.'

I went back to Charlie and took his hands that were so yellow and wasted, and as I did so he died.

Poor old Charlie. As fine a shipmate as ever trod a plank. 'Black Charlie' they called him in Liverpool, because they said that while he was ashore he never washed. When on the beach he would drink anything to raw methylated spirits, but afloat on a sailing ship where he belonged, he was a real sailor and a splendid shipmate. He laughed at difficulties, never grumbled at the worst of conditions, was ever the first at a rope or to jump aloft though he went before those young enough to be his grandchildren and he knew his craft as few afloat know it now. He used to say as he stepped out of the focsle to take his watch on deck. 'Here I am. The little shiny shilling in the mawnin'.'

When all the rock salt had been discharged, we were towed across the river to Stockton where we lay for some time as we waited for our turn to load a cargo of coal for Pisco in Peru. I renewed my acquaintance with the Rev. Vickery of the Seamens' Mission there and I improved my friendships with the charming young ladies who assisted him to entertain

193

the sailor lads.

While there we smartened up the barque by painting all the masts and spars, but in truth, no amount of fresh paint could make her tubby lines graceful or give any stateliness to her stumpy rig. She was of that breed of sailing vessels which were built towards the end of the era of sail. They were designed to carry the maximum of cargo, the minimum of men and to make only average passages. Sailors said that they were built by the mile, cut off at suitable lengths and the ends pinched together. It was thought that they could be operated economically enough to compete with steamers but the day of the sailing ship was fast passing into history.

By the time that we had completed our loading and were moored to the farewell buoy in the stream, the number of our focsle hands was sadly depleted. Chips had been the first to go. He had an idea that someone was sleeping with his wife while he was away and he packed up his tools and gear and quietly slipped ashore. He intended to turn up announced like Byron's Beppo. Then Bill got paid off on medical grounds though he was extraordinarily healthy. Those hands who had taken a pierhead jump in Liverpool discovered that they had not in fact signed the Articles, for which the Old Man must have kicked himself, and they were paid off on this technicality and were glad to go. Murphy, an old sailorman of the port watch, left without telling the Skipper after Fred and Charlie were killed because he swore that the barque was cursed and she'd go to sea and never be heard of again. Jim got himself paid off also on medical grounds, though like Bill, it was hard to see what they could have been, and he got himself a job on the pilot boat.

There were four of us left in our watch and only one in the port watch and the Old Man was finding it difficult to make up his crew. Australian ships were then paying able seamen £16 per month and overtime. They were fed on the best of food and they worked only eight hours a day. They were not willing to ship aboard a hungry limejuicer for £9 per month, twelve hours a day of the hardest work and twenty-

194

four hours a day of probable cold and wet and of certain misery. How could we expect to get real sailors? I would have cleared out myself but I wanted to complete my time in square-rig and to get a clean discharge. Moreover I wasn't going to let hardships get me down. I think that the Old Man was astonished that I was still aboard the ship.

Eventually, after lying at the buoy for ten days, we got our complement and what a crew they were!

There were two experienced sailors among them. Jock, from Aberdeen, was anxious to get back to Britain, and Peter, the Norwegian, wanted to get back to Norway. Peter had broken his arm when at sea years before and it had not been set properly so that he had one permanently bent wing. I never knew it to stop him from doing his job ably and well. Jock had sailed in Geordie brigs around the British coast and he had also crossed the Atlantic in small sailing ships in the logwood trade to the islands of the West Indies.

Tom was a lad from Birkenhead who, though he had never been in sail before, was interested and quick to learn. He was big and strong and we soon became fast friends. As for the others, there were two who had been farming in Australia, were fed up with that and wanted to get back to Britain. There was an old derelict sailor, at least he claimed to be but he wasn't much more use than the two farm boys, and a poor little knock-kneed undersized rat of a man who signed on as carpenter but who had a minimal knowledge of the trade.

Two apprentices also joined the ship here. One was an Australian lad and the other was a scion of a very old English family, full of irresponsible charm but not very helpful as a practical seaman. We hoped for the best and that the lubbers would prove adaptable, but hopes are not always realised.

December was half over when the Customs Officers came in their launch to give us clearance. Their dismay when they found that the seal on the lazarette was broken was equalled only by the Old Man's fury when he discovered that the 'medical comforts', two bottles of brandy, had disappeared. Now he understood the sometimes peculiar behaviour of his steward. In a tearing rage he rushed to his cabin and, much to the amusement of the Customs men, returned to brandish a huge .45 Colt revolver of ancient pattern which he thrust in the steward's face.

'You —— you —— VILLAIN!' he raved. 'You've broken the seal and stolen the stores! I'll —— I'll —— SHOOT YOU!'

The steward stood and chewed his wispy moustache and he didn't bat an eyelid. In his slow, almost laboured diction, he said, 'Oh, go away. You're always bothering me.'

CHAPTER XVII   ON TO PISCO

As the sun rose on 17th December, 1925, a beautiful summer morning, a tug towed us over the bar and out to sea. The air was fresh, dew-washed and invigorating. Little fair-weather clouds floated over the very blue sky before a light southerly wind and girls were waving towels to us from bedroom windows. When we dropped the pilot, Jim was at the long steering oar of his boat. That first lift of the bows to the swell filled me with gladness. I forgot all the events of the past few weeks, the people I had met and the good shipmates I had lost, in the sheer joy of being at sea again. We were towed twenty miles off shore and we set all sail to the light wind.

Variable, but fair and fresh winds were our portion for the first few days and we kept making to the southward. We had a squall or two which was nothing to worry about though I remember being called out in our watch below one afternoon to take in t'ga'nts'ls, as if the watch on deck couldn't do it without help. We had not been below for long and we had heard the port watch hauling up the mainsail, so we were scarcely taken by surprise. As there was no rain when we looked out and the job was regarded as urgent, we did not stop to don oilskins. We quickly had the sail up in its gear.

197

As I jumped into the rigging to go aloft to furl, I felt unaccountably certain that the approaching storm would hit us hard and that lightning would strike us. As we reached the futtock shrouds, the squall smote us. The rain came in torrents and we climbed up through its lashing fury while lightning flashed and thunder rolled about us. We had strung out along the tossing yard and were about to grasp the sail when there came one blinding flash which stabbed down to the t'gallant stay and ran down it in quivering brilliance to the boom end. The thunder deafened us in one violent explosion as we clung blinded to the jackstay and it was some seconds before we could see to move and to stow the sail. No one was hurt and on deck they did not even know that the barque had been struck.

By Christmas we had had some dirty weather and some heavy sail drill in taking in tops'ls in hard winds and the work was made harder by the clumsy efforts of the greenhorns. They did not take kindly to handling mad canvas on a pitching yard and we more experienced ones had much more to do and we had to check their work. The Tasman Sea lived up to its notorious reputation and the barque rolled heavily in the seas. I recall one occasion when I was on the poop and five big seas came aboard in succession. We could see only the masts sticking up out of the ocean, the tops of the bulwarks at bow and stern, the focsle head and the tops of the deckhouses, and nothing of the decks and the hatches. The old hooker wallowed out of it. She may not have been anything to look at but she was well and strongly built. In spite of secured doors, our quarters were well wetted by King Neptune as he squirted water in round the edges and we had quite a bit of mopping up to do.

Christmas Eve was fine though cold and a big swell was running. There were several albatrosses swimming at the stern and I got a hook and line and I scrounged a lump of salt pork fat from the cook. I asked one of the apprentices if he would go on the poop and see if he could catch one. The idea is that the bird takes the floated bait and the hook catches in the curve of his beak. So long as one keeps a strain on the line, the prey is secure for the stupid bird pulls against the crook of the hook and tries to fly backwards. If it only knew enough to fly with the pull it would gain sufficient with one flap of its powerful wings to be free. I wanted to capture one of the birds and to photograph it but I could not attract one to the fore part of the ship and the poop is sacred to officers while apprentices are suffered there.

The Old Man caught one later and he kindly sent for me to bring my camera. Two of the boys stretched out his wings while I got his picture. He was a splendid specimen but unfortunately the light was poor by then and hardly favourable for a picture to do him justice. His head and breast and the undersides of his spread wings were positively snow white and the topsides of his long narrow pinions were beautifully speckled with jet black. They measured 11 feet 8 inches from tip to tip. Left to himself he could get about the deck only with difficulty. His legs gave way under him as if his bones were of rubber and in a few minutes he was very seasick. In the days before the introduction of rubber seaboots, sailors would catch albatross in order to obtain this regurgitation for it was the best-known preservative and waterproofing for their leather seaboots.

He was something of a handful to put back in the ocean for his body was much bigger than a full-grown goose and his fiercely hooked beak was something of a menace. A bolder one among us caught his head and wrapped an arm about him before he could spread his wings, carried him to the rail and shoved him off. He flopped ungracefully into the water and favoured us with a highly indignant stare as he floated away.

Christmas Day was peaceful and calm and we had no sail drill. Indeed in the afternoon there was absolutely no wind and during my trick at the wheel I simply leaned there and did not move a spoke. The barque lay like a log while the masts and spars creaked and the sails flapped as she swayed gently in the long easy swell. Our celebrations were mild. We did get an awning of pastry spread over our usual dish of stewed bully beef, and we had a plum duff which was no different from the regular soggy lump. My mother had made me a perfectly gorgeous cake which she had sent to me at Newcastle and which I had saved for this occasion. It was now produced from its large biscuit tin and it was cut with all due pomp and ceremony. All voted it delicious as her cakes always were. We were in the latitude of my home town of Invercargill, but 500 miles to the west of it.

The weather broke in the early hours of Boxing Day and we had a hard time of it for the next week with heavy gales and great seas. As we made around the south of Stewart Island we were continually hauling on braces and halliards, setting or stowing sail, up to our necks in water on the wildly rolling decks and generally getting a good taste of what the South Pacific could do.

One morning we had furled the main t'ga'nts'l as the gale freshened and were down from aloft and were walking forward along the weather side. That was always the safer side to go because if one was caught by a sea coming aboard, one had a chance of grabbing something before the water took one over the lee side as it poured overboard. Tom was ahead of me as we passed the deckhouse focsle and he was looking out over the rail to the sea. I saw it coming as the ship made a particularly severe roll and I seized him by the only thing that offered, the collar of his oilskin jacket. He gasped as I jerked him back on to his seat with a thud and the freshwater cask blundered across the deck, just missed his toes and fetched up against the bulwarks with a crash. It did not break but fortunately it tipped on to its end.

'Grab it!' I yelled and I flung the end of a buntline off its pin, swung a bight of the rope round the cask and caught a turn on a belaying pin before the ship rolled the other way. Thus I held it close up to the rail. There was no time for me to apologise to Tom for mishandling him or for him to thank me. I shouted to him to throw an opposing turn round the tun from the fife rail. He quickly did so and the others lent their weight. As the barque rolled to leeward, I slacked off and he hauled in while Paddy, Horace and Peter hove mightily with their shoulders to keep the barrel on end. Gradually we worked it back near to its chocks while one got a watch tackle from forward. With this aid we tipped it on to the shaped blocks which normally held it. Frantic moments ensued as we replaced the broken lashings turn by turn. When the decks rolled to an awful angle we held the cask with handspikes for breathless seconds before the ropes were secured. We made all fast, saw that the other tun was safe, went forard to the shelter of the focsle head and from sheer relief we laughed and laughed as if we had been having the greatest fun instead of having risked being crushed and mangled by a tun full of freshwater that weighed over a ton.

That afternoon the fore upper topsail sheet carried away and we had an awkward and dangerous job as we clung like flies to the swinging yard and the clew with a few links of heavy chain flapped in the wind. Somehow we quieted it and put in a split link to replace the broken one. Then in the evening we were all washed about the deck when the fore upper topsail was taken in and while we floundered and gasped the seas filled the decks rail high. Late the same night the whole watch was nearly washed overboard and drowned at the weather braces while checking in the yards. The decks had filled from a big wave that had broken aboard and as she rolled to windward, it spilled over like a waterfall. Only the presence of mind of the last man on the rope who caught a turn on a spare belaying pin and held on, saved them as they grasped desperately on the brace, half over the rail. They were able to scramble back aboard as the vessel righted.

So it went on as the old hooker drove ever eastward.

Kilmallie crossed the 180th meridian on New Year's Eve and the next day was also New Year's Eve as we were now in West longitude. The last job in the Old Year was to take in the fore upper topsail and we saw the year out as windjammer sailors might be expected to do, up aloft in a tearing gale in a tussle with wind-whipped canvas.

We were down on deck for the end of the watch at midnight

201

and the traditional sixteen bells were struck aft and repeated forward then the lookout man rang the bell like mad while someone knocked blazes out of the old donkey boiler whose sides boomed under the belabouring of an iron bar. I don't know what there was to be happy about, but we all gave each other good wishes with smiling faces though we were cold and wet and weary and our stomachs were empty. The brandy which the steward had surreptitiously consumed had not been replaced so there was no cry from aft of 'Splice the main brace!'

We lay hove to all that night and all the next day to a hard gale that blew great guns from the south. The shrieking wind blew the tops off the waves and sent them flying in the misty rain that enveloped us. It was impossible to see more than a quarter of a mile from the ship. The next day it moderated and drew to the sou'-west, the yards were laid almost square and she ran before it. It was blowing mighty hard and a big sea was running which kept the decks full of water. The barque yawed wildly as the seas ran up under her quarter. She made it hard work to steer but we took up the challenge and we felt that we had control of something alive and capricious which was trying to play us tricks all the time. In baffling and forestalling her there was something exhilarating which made us forget, while we were at the wheel, the cold and hunger and sticky dampness. In our watch there were only three of us whom the Old Man would allow to steer. We three had more than our share of tricks on the poop to fight the kicking wheel.

In twenty-four hours the wind settled to a steady strength and the seas went down. It was not long before all sail was set again and we pushed on at a fair speed under blue skies. Breezes freshened and died away. We reduced the spread of sails or we set them again. Sometimes the sun shone but more often the heavens sent rain and hail upon us and always it was cold.

One evening the horizon was obscured by rain and the sky was covered by masses of dense black clouds which put us in a late twilight though the sun had not yet set. Only for a short arc of the horizon in the west the lowering sun touched the edges of the clouds with saffron and rose but this soon disappeared in a squall of heavy rain. It was an awe-inspiring spectacle. There was only a light air which gradually drew ahead and the barque could no longer lay her course. We put her about and then stowed the four t'ga'nts'ls in a truly terrific downpour of rain. When this had passed there was no more than a breath of wind. The sun had set and it was pitchy dark and an ominous quiet lay on our world. Everything was so deathly still that we were almost constrained to speak in whispers. The gurgle and wash of the wavelets alongside and the slatting of the sails as the vessel rolled only accentuated the unearthly hush. The dense clouds pressed down to the very mastheads. We could have expected almost anything to happen but nothing further developed save a further downpour of rain that was followed by a light breeze. It was quite disappointing. We slipped quietly through the night under our shortened sail and with the dawn the sky cleared to leave only some torn shreds of cloud.

On we went. Sailing ever eastward; now with comparatively fine weather, now before a howling gale; forever taking in or setting sail; hauling at braces, tacks and sheets; wallowing in water; in soggy oilskins and leaky seaboots; chilly in wet clothes and blankets; suffering rain and gale and cold and the ever present hunger.

By the end of January we started to head up to the northward to finer weather as we were around 90° west. Soon after, we picked up the gentle and constant southerly which accompanies the Peruvian Current. Now the scene changed to clear skies and bright sunshine. Calm seas and peaceful times followed and all hands were glad to dry out their sodden gear. We had a good run north under these pleasant conditions but at no great speed for we averaged only a little over 120 miles per day.

At dawn on 6th February, the lookout reported land ahead and we could make out two grey smudges on the dim horizon to the north. As the sun rose and the slight mistiness cleared we could see the islands of San Felix and San Ambrosia and what appeared to be a barque off the former island but which turned out to be Peterborough Cathedral Rock. This rock is a very peculiar formation for from one aspect it looks exactly like a barque under single t'ga'nts'ls but from the sou-west it gives the appearance of a cathedral with twin towers.

We passed close to San Felix at nine o'clock and very barren and deserted it looked. I could see no sign of water or of vegetation of any kind and it looked more like a giant's ash heap than anything else. San Ambrosia's high plateau towered far to the east and if it were more habitable it could not be discerned from that distance. Many beautiful little white petrels and terns with big cormorants and gannets flew over and around our mastheads and some bonito sported at our bows but there was no other sign of life. I made an attempt to catch one of the bonito but without success. A few days later I landed my first dorado.

It was my watch below that afternoon, the wind was light and the sun hot and I could not sleep. I strolled out with my pipe and I climbed to the focsle head. I leaned on the rail and fell to thinking. As I pondered and gazed into the clear water only gently parted by the slow-moving barque, I saw the beautifully coloured outline of a dorado that came swimming lazily from under the forefoot. Suddenly brought to action, I ran to the focsle, grabbed my line which always hung ready, and I was shortly seated at the jibboom end with my feet safely caught about the eyes of the boom guys. I dangled my lure over the dancing waves. Soon the fish, which I could see some twenty fathoms away to leeward, made a wild rush and my heart leaped as I felt him take the hook and his rush was checked. Anyone who has known the first run of a salmon who has taken his fly, will know how I felt. I had him securely hooked and he tore about and leapt from the sea but to no avail. I feared that he might shake himself free with his violent action so as my tackle was strong, I hauled him up

204

while he was still madly struggling. With one hand I held the line close up to the hook and with the other about the small of his tail, I tried to hold him across my knees. It was as much as I could do for he bent his body with all the strength of a steel spring this way and that while I could do nothing but hang on and I dared not make any attempt to move. I yelled for help and one of the hands of the port watch who was working under the focsle head, put his head through the hawse-hole. He knew at once what to do, and he came out to me with a sack into which we stowed the catch and brought him aboard. He was a beauty of four feet in length and he provided all hands with something tasty for tea. The scales of these fish are too dense and firmly attached to be scraped off and the fish has to be skinned. The flesh is white and firm and excellently flavoured.

The barque held on her way but the breeze fell lighter as she got further north and she now made scarce fifty or sixty miles a day. It was delightful to be pushing along quietly in this lovely weather with a cool breeze to mellow the heat of the blazing sun. Save for the customary daily 'sweat-up' on braces and sheets we did not have any of the pulling and hauling that went with variable winds. All sail was set and drawing. There was no clambering aloft in pitch darkness to claw with stinging hands at hell-born sails and we were no longer lashed up and marled down in oilskins and heavy seaboots. Even our hunger did not seem so bad in the balmy weather.

There was, as always, a fly in the ointment. Those horrible, flat-backed, bloodsucking insects, bugs, had appeared in the ship. Only a few of them had been noticed on the outward passage and there had been a slight increase in their numbers in Australia. Since then, the cold weather had apparently kept them quiet. With these warmer conditions they appeared in hundreds and we found their repulsive bodies in every nook and cranny. The beastly things were between bunk boards, in the junctions of the planks of wooden bulkheads, in old nail holes, under our mattresses and even between the leaves and under the spines of books.

These fiendish creatures and their irritating bites kept me awake at nights, till, disgusted at squashing their filthily swollen bodies, I would leave the focsle with a single blanket, go forward under the focsle head, roll myself in the blanket and sleep soundly and undisturbed on the unyielding deck. The nights were cold and I had not slung my hammock. Even now, the very thought of those hateful things makes my skin creep. I couldn't understand how my shipmates could sleep. Perhaps their skins were tougher. Horace said that they didn't bother him. He said that he believed in 'live and let live'. I suspected that he had been brought up with them. Paddy, Tom, and I made constant war against them and we spent a vast amount of energy in trying to stamp them out. Though we slew thousands of them in bloody stinking carnage, their numbers were undiminished.

We were getting near to our destination and at daybreak on Sunday 14th February, land was in sight on the starboard bow. It was a large island with low-lying land beyond, while far in the distance could be seen the outline of the mighty Andes. The Old Man had foresail, mainsail and all t'ga'nts'ls stowed for it is a lengthy and laborious task for a sailing ship to make to the southward on that coast and he was filled with nervous fears that he could overrun his port. Then, only by standing out to sea for a couple of hundred miles or so and getting into the Trade Winds could he make southing and then he would have to make easting and a landfall well to the weather of his port, as I explained when writing of *William Mitchell* and her time in these waters. There is an unvarying combination of wind and current from the south along that coast and the wind is too light for a square-rigged vessel to beat against it successfully even without the adverse current.

We had made a good landfall for the island was the largest of the Chincha Group which lies off Pisco Bay. At 8 a.m. the courses were spread to the light wind which sent her slowly north and more towards the shore. By eleven, she was abreast of the island and had brought the other guano-covered islets into view. T'ga'nts'ls were then set, yards braced sharp on the starboard tack and she stood into the bay. The breeze drove her in towards the land and the current set her to the north. So she came past the sterns of two Peruvian men-of-war that lay at anchor there and our hook was dropped just inside and ahead of them, fifty-six days from Newcastle. It was shoal water for a long way off shore and we had only three fathoms under our keel though we were over a mile out.

We had to jump to take in all sail as she came to her anchorage and there was a hectic time. The greenhorns in the crew were as helpless now as in stormy weather. They followed me about the deck and did what I did. If I took hold of a rope to haul, they tailed on and lent their weight and I'm sure that they had no idea why. If I picked up a rope and started to coil it down, they fell over each other to coil down any other rope that was lying around. When I went to the heads they even followed me there.

They had never gone through the whole operation of furling all the sails from the outer jib to the spanker, squaring all the yards, coiling up all the many ropes and stowing them all out of the way in preparation for the business of unloading. It must have been rather bewildering to people who were not particularly interested.

The warships took no notice of us and we disregarded them. The Old Man did not pay them the compliment of having the ensign dipped and I think that he condemned all South Americans as 'hombres', which was about the extent of his Spanish. From the way he used the word, I imagined that he believed the term to be subtly derogatory.

No-one in the town, which we could scarcely see, seemed to care about the new arrival and no boat put off for us. Neither Pilot, harbour authorities, Doctor, Customs, nor Agent was sufficiently interested to break his Sabbath rest. We were in the land of mañana and it was Sunday.

There was little to see. A line of breakers broke along the

beach. A jetty poked out from the shore where there were a few buildings and a mile or so inland we could see a scattered town dominated by a church tower. A mile down the coast a few huts huddled and the many small boats drawn up proclaimed the fisherfolk. Beyond and to the south the great Atacama Desert sloped for miles upward to barren, jagged, rocky hills and mountains. To the north, the course of the Pisco River could be traced by a line of green and beyond it lay the bare brown hills. A deeper shade to the blue heaven suggested the higher land but by some peculiarity of the atmosphere, the outline of the main chain of the Andes was visible only at sunset and at dawn. There were no small boats to come alongside and offer to take any of us ashore as in Iquique, and no opportunity to take some French leave.

CHAPTER XVIII   COAL OUT AND GUANO IN

Next morning a launch brought out the Agent and the port Doctor. We were granted a clean bill of health and they took the Old Man ashore. The day was spent in unbending the sails, labelling them and stowing them away in the sail locker. The hatches were uncovered and cargo gear rigged.

In the evening the Old Man returned and a batch of letters was sent forward. There was not much conversation that night for each man either lay in his bunk reading and re-reading his mail or he scanned the illustrated papers sent him. Some leaned alone at the rail, their eyes on the horizon, their thoughts half across the world.

For weeks following, seamen became ordinary labourers as we proceeded with the business of the discharge of the coal. This was hard going as every pound of the coal had to be put into sacks. When in *William Mitchell* we had worked out coal in Iquique, the cargo had been discharged in bulk. It had all been shovelled into huge baskets and once down on to the floor, the coal could be made to fall into the basket. Now, every shovelful had to be lifted to the mouth of a sack. We worked in gangs of three. One shovelled, one held the mouth of the bag, and one sewed up the bag and made up the sling, and we took turns at each job. Eight bags made a sling and there was one gang at each corner of the hatch. One may imagine that it was hard work to keep pace so that each gang had a sling ready when the cargo hook from the winch on deck came round to its corner. There was no time for a spell.

The ancient donkey engine kept puffing away. It must have been good for it wheezed on manfully in spite of the fact that the engineering knowledge aboard was about nil. It kept us busy down in the heat of the hold as we toiled and sweated. We were only 14° South of the Line and the sun was right overhead at that time of the year. We often prayed that the old engine would break down and give us a rest but it coughed and spluttered on. The first four days were the worst. Men came up from the hold at midday and in the evening and laid out flat on the deck, too exhausted to move for a few minutes. All they wanted was to get an equal strain on all parts.

Day after dirty day we toiled in the dust and the heat. All hands became irritated with the work and conditions for there was little relaxation. Our Skipper was one of the old school who did not believe in letting sailors draw any money and go ashore. Minor frictions got out of proportion amongst these few men who were cooped up in a small space with little or no opportunity for recreation and Horace's violin was only a further irritation. Feelings flared up at times and there were some fights. None was serious and they rather served to clear the air. On the whole we got on fairly well together.

On Saturday afternoons and Sundays some of us spent a deal of time in the water. We rigged out a plank from one of the wash ports as a diving board and had plenty of fun but because of the current all the way from Cape Horn, the water was cold. Also the bay would be invaded from time to time by enormous jellyfish. These were fifteen to eighteen inches across and they had fathoms of trailers and stings attached. These produced a painful rash akin to nettle stings which disappeared after twelve hours or so and nobody suffered very much.

Only twice were we allowed ashore, one watch at a time. The Old Man gave us an advance of £1 each as if he were the very soul of generosity and no amount of persuasion could prevail upon him to increase the sum. The ship's boat put us ashore in the morning and it called for us in the evening.

Tom and I set off together and we walked for the best part of a mile to get to the town, along a road ankle-deep in fine white dust. The town was built around a central cobbled plaza, and dominated by the cathedral that I understood had the reputation of being the largest adobe building in the world. We thought that we would explore and we decided that we would walk north to the river. We bought some bread rolls and fruit and we plodded for miles along another dusty road until we came to the stream. I had imagined a crystal clear river whose waters had been filtered through miles of desert sand and gravel and that we could rest on grassy banks under the shade of trees where we could eat our pancitos and fruit. The river ran in many streams over a shingle bed and the water was the colour and consistency of cafe-au-lait. Not a blade of grass grew anywhere and there were only some coarse and stunted scrubby shrubs.

In the stream, men, women, and children were wading and scraping through the gravel two-gallon kerosene tins with many small holes in the bottoms and sides. They lifted out the tins and took from them wriggling crayfish which they stowed in another tin. They looked good fat healthy creatures from six to ten inches long. We watched the fishers for a while but we were thirsty from our long dusty walk and, contrary to our expectations, we did not feel thirsty enough to drink the muddy river water. We thought that the best thing to do was to return to the town to get some liquid refreshment to wash down our food.

We had gone scarcely a hundred yards on our way when we heard shouts behind us. We looked round to see a little portly man running to us and calling.

'Señores! Señores! Uno momento! Son Frances? Son

211

Alemanes? Son Ingleses?'

We stopped and as he came up to us I said, 'Si, señor. Somos Ingleses.'

'Ah. Then will you please join us? We are having a picnic. Perhaps you would like to eat some of the crayfish that we have caught from the river?'

'Thank you very much indeed,' I answered. 'Here is my friend Tom. I am Frank.'

'My name is Garcia. Garcia Vargas.'

We were introduced to Garcia and his friends and their wives and children as Tomaso and Francisco and we sat with them around the remains of a fire on which they had cooked a large tin of crayfish and they invited us to share their food and wine. The fish was delicious and the dry vino refreshing. We shared our pancitos and fruit and ate our fill.

Then we shared in a custom of the country. Bottles of pisco, the local brandy, were produced and the men's glasses were filled with the clear liquid while the ladies had wine. Garcia started by holding his glass to me. 'Salud!' he said, and we drank to each other. Then he explained that I must do the same to another member of the party. I guessed Isabella's age at seventeen and she was quite beautiful. Her big dark eyes smiled shyly at me. I raised my glass to her and called, 'Salud!' to general merriment. So the drinks went round and as one was required to empty the glass each time one's health was called, it could be quite inebriating. Especially as the hospitable Peruvians felt it incumbent upon them to call frequent 'Saluds' to each of us.

It did not go on for long fortunately and we entered into a lively discussion about the Chilian possession of the provinces of Tacna and Arica, which the Peruvians claimed were their own. Garcia acted as interpreter, for my knowledge of Spanish was too limited for me to join in and they talked too quickly for me. Garcia told us that they had been arguing the rights of the Peruvian claim for many years, and today they still are.

Our host had been educated in the University of Lima and

212

he had learned his excellent English from a Scotsman there. He was an exporter, largely of cotton of which much was grown in the district. We sat yarning far into the afternoon and they would not hear of us walking back to Pisco. We all crowded into two big cars and were soon back in the town when these kindly people insisted that they motored us back to the wharf. We were very grateful for an interesting and pleasant day.

The week's work was a round of shovelling and sweating in the murky heat of the hold with the gritty coal dust in every pore. A hateful unintelligent occupation which was only relieved by a daily swim that I was never too tired to enjoy. The weather was perfect and the mornings were particularly delightful. It was always a flat calm at sunrise and it was the one time of the day, with the exception of some evenings, when the outline of the majestic backbone of South America could be seen. Before the sun rose over its peaks, which here towered to 20,000 feet or more, they were silhouetted in clear detail against the dawn-lit sky. Though they were many miles inland, the sun was well in the heavens before it burst in splendour above their eternal snows. As it did so, their forms blended into the distance. If one looked out to sea, the western sky showed the most delicate tints of rose pink and yellow and the sea was of palest shimmering green.

Sometimes when the evenings were clear, the colours of the desert were marvellous. The Andes stood in purple grandeur, their snows stained pink to bright gleaming orange which faded to startling white. The nearer rugged hills and barren rocks which rose from the all-enveloping sand were painted in blotches and streaks of many hues. Brilliant orange and red and blue, green and grey and sudden white, the vast plains and rocky outcrops glowed in the dying light in all shades from white to pearl to deepest black.

I drank in the these beauteous things and they were balm to my soul, for the rest of the life there was brutalising. Nothing but dirty work, poor food, and filthy blasted bugs

213

were our portion. The pests were a never ending subject of discussion and profanity. In that heat they multiplied amazingly and they sucked our blood thirstily . . . Ugh!

I determined to do something about it and the next time we went ashore to the town, which was the last, I purchased with the help of Garcia, a large bottle of cattle dip which he assured me would put an end to the loathsome things. It certainly smelt strong enough. We focsle hands spent the next Sunday in taking all our gear out on the hatch and we turned it all over and slew the beasts therein. We washed out the focsle in a strong solution of the dip and when we found large families of the bugs stowed away in the cracks in the wooden bulkheads, I poured the pure juice on them and in wicked glee I watched them writhe. As a final precaution for my personal protection I painted my bunk around with the last of the undiluted liquid and though the fumes from it were pungent, I turned in that night in the knowledge of peace and no horrible creatures crawled over my naked body.

The next morning I turned out at the usual early call and I stood up to stretch myself. To my horror, my knees gave way under me and I felt an awful tearing pain in my head. I just saved myself from falling and I struggled out to the deck and to fresh air. I could scarcely stand and I could eat no food nor do any work that day. In getting rid of the bugs I had poisoned myself with the fumes from the cattle dip. I think that, if it had not been for the open port at my bunk, the result could have been more serious.

By the next day I was quite well again but so were the bugs for by Tuesday evening they were as plentiful and hungrier than ever. That was as far as we ever got in our ceaseless war against the disgusting vermin. Regularly we turned out our quarters during the weekend and usually we had two nights of undisturbed rest. For the remainder of the week they crawled about everywhere on their filthy bellies and their revolting bodies stank when they were crushed. I remember that the boys amused themselves when they saw one creeping up a bulkhead, by holding a lighted match

214

under it and watching it swell till it burst.

In time, about two-thirds of our cargo was discharged and the vessel was high out of the water and in need of stiffening. This was always a most serious expense in the operation of a sailing ship. At times this would consist of sand, gravel, or anything available. This was carried purely as ballast and would rarely have any commercial value in its port of discharge. Valuable time was lost by it and the cost of loading and of unloading yielded no return by way of freight while it could make a considerable hole in the profits of a voyage. Therefore, one fine morning before the sea breeze had wrinkled the bay's calm, we manned the windlass, and hove up the anchor. A diesel-engined launch made fast to us. In company with a couple of lighters and a villainous-looking crew, we were towed south to the head of the bay. In spite of our light draft, the tug found it heavy going for the prevailing wind soon got up and against the windage of all our spars and rigging, it panted and coughed along at a bare two knots. In the early afternoon we anchored in a little cove where there was a beach of deep fine shingle. This was to be our ballast. The lighters were beached so that they could be loaded at low water and when the rising tide floated them, they would be rowed with long sweeps the short distance to the barque.

We spent that day and all the next in cleaning the remainder of the coal from under the main hatch and we rigged shifting boards in the hold to make a big box to contain the shingle. Then we fixed a stage over the rail to the hatchway upon which big baskets would be landed. The following day loaded lighters were alongside early and steam was up on the donkey engine. It puffed and snorted to heave up the ballast which was tipped into the square of planks we had built down below. The best part of a thousand tons of stiffening was taken aboard during the ten days that we were there.

Close to our little cove there was a deep indentation in the coast and up this arm of the bay was anchored a big Norwegian whale-oil 'factory'. I call her that because she was better thus

215

described than as a ship. She mothered a fleet of small whale hunters. These were sturdy, trawler-like vessels that were distinguished by the harpoon gun on their focsle heads. Every evening we would see some of them come in from the day's hunting with one or two whales made fast alongside and occasionally one would return with as many as four 'fish'. Their people took no notice of us and no politenesses were exchanged between the two ships.

When we had entered Pisco Bay, I had seen on the hillside close to where we now lay, a great picture marked. It was in the form of a stylised or decorative tree planted in a square tub and it had branches at right-angles to the massive trunk. These again turned up at right-angles parallel to the main trunk and then branched out to a formal leaf pattern. The whole things was so vast and yet so symmetrical that I was determined to visit it and to see how it was formed.

We spent Easter here and as there was no work required of us on Good Friday, Tom and I managed to get ourselves put ashore by the ship's boat and we walked on around the coast. The land was of volcanic origin but it appeared to be rotten with age. The outcropping granite crumbled to the touch and we could break off quite large fragments with our hands. There seemed to be every kind of rock imaginable and I partly understood the reason for the wonderful colouring in the desert. Nothing grew there and the ground was mostly sand but one walked over chunks of flint and of rotten granite and of quartz. Yellow calcite grew in mushroom formations that were six feet wide and from the undersides of these depended crystals that were several inches long. These strange growths were three or four feet high and they sprouted from many-hued lava that presented an unlimited range of colour. It was streaked and veined with scarlet and blue and green and every shade of colour between. Pieces of clear crystal were imbedded in it and where it met the sea it was twisted and bubbled into the weirdest shapes. It must have been unbelievably old for in places it was overlaid with a stratum of sandstone many feet thick and over this was more lava.

On one beach I picked up a handful of sand which was a pool of beauty. Every little grain was a particle of glowing light. Some were like bright rubies. Some were as blue as sapphire. Some were clear and some honey yellow while amongst them were tiny bright pieces which may have been tin, mica, pyrites . . . or gold.

From this beach the coast formed rugged cliffs so we climbed up and followed their tops for I wanted to get a photograph of the hillside picture. Up here was nothing but sand and multicoloured stones and out-cropping rock. There were numerous animal tracks that I took to be those of coyotes but we saw no living things save lizards. They were about two feet long, of a pleasing greenish grey colour, and as they moved their scales rustled with a faint whispering. I caught one, though with some difficulty for they could run and dodge with some speed. It opened its mouth and hissed at me. The effect was startling for the interior of its mouth was scarlet in contrast with its neutral outer covering. I put the juicy end of the stem of my pipe in its mouth which effectively stopped his wriggling and I was able to examine him. Later, I caught a much larger one by dropping my linen hat on him as he dodged between my legs and I reached under the hat and grabbed his tail. I lifted the hat and as I did so he shed his tail and scuttled under a rock. I was left with a foot of lizard in my hand. I felt such a fool.

We walked over the hot dry landscape under a blazing sun which beat down unmercifully and after a long trudge we reached our objective. The tree picture was simply dug out of the sand and stone of the desert. I could not make out how long it had been there or of how it had been made. We could find no traces of tools or of signs of man. In that calm and rainless land it could have kept its form for centuries. The main trunk was as wide as any road and 250 yards from base to top. The lower and widest branches made a span of 100 yards. The photograph I took was necessarily foreshortened but the hill was steep and the tree is seen as if upright from out in the bay. I could not conjecture what purpose it served or what it signified but some considerable care must have been taken in laying it out. Though with the passage of time the ridges had become rounded, the lines were true and precisely laid.

I stood and pondered what manner of man had put in the labour required to depict this peculiar tree and why they had put it there in that hopelessly barren and God-forgotten land. Tom had seen it before from the sea for he had been on this coast in a P.S.N.C. Co's steamer and he said that he had heard it spoken of and pointed out as an Inca relic.

Years later, I was suffering under a dentist's hands and I saw that he had a carpet that had a vaguely similar outline as its decoration. My mind flew back to that barren hillside and I told him of it. I asked him if he knew the origin of his carpet. He told me that it came from China and I thought of the tales that were told of the latter days of the China tea clippers. Sometimes when these ships had made poor passages to Foochow and had missed the season's picking, they would ship a number of Chinese coolies and take them across the Pacific. On the Chincha Islands and on the barren headlands along that coast, the coolies were set to dig out the valuable deposits of guano and to load the ships with this unsavoury cargo. It consisted of the droppings of the countless birds which inhabit these islands and which live on the fish which abound there. Their excretions had accumulated there for centuries in that arid climate and it formed a highly concentrated fertiliser. The value of this had only then been realised and thousands of tons of the stuff had been collected and shipped to Europe and America in a few years.

When the ships were loaded, the more unscrupulous masters often left the coolies to their fate and sailed away. Many had died of thirst and of starvation and I wondered if they had dug that picture in that unkindly land and if it held some peculiarly Chinese significance. A warning to future Chinese, or a form of offering to their Gods?

Later still, I learned that there were many such pictures cut into the earth of Peru. Some were of huge birds and some

218

of intricate straight line patterns. Students of the subject believe that they were carved by the Incas, or possibly by an earlier civilisation of which there is evidence in Peru, but their purpose is still a mystery.

We went on a further mile or so but there was nothing more than the barren vari-coloured desert and the tracks of the coyotes. We found a place where we could scramble down the low cliffs to the sea edge and here on flat rocks we saw numbers of crabs brilliantly coloured in blue and red which rattled their way into the sea on our approach. We returned to the cove where *Kilmallie* lay by climbing around the base of the cliffs and struggling over the piles of rocks that had fallen from them. We came to a cave and started to enter but we staggered back in fright when there came a great roaring from within and a sea lion came flopping and bellowing out and dived into the sea. We also caught a fleeting glimpse of a sea otter as it scampered from beneath a boulder and swam away.

Back aboard the barque the weekend was spent in the usual washing and disinfecting our focsle and belongings in our endless fight against the horrible bugs. Then we found that we were expected to work on Easter Monday. We referred to the copy of the Articles we had signed and which were posted under the focsle head, and we verified our belief that we were correct in regarding it as a holiday. Tom and I thought that we would like to have another day in the desert but we didn't see any sense in asking the Skipper for permission. We knew that the cove in which the barque was anchored was on an isthmus and that the deep indentation in which the whaler lay was at the narrowest part and it was our intention to cross the peninsula and to have a look at the coast where it faced south to the Humboldt Current.

Early on Monday the lancheros came alongside with their loaded vessel and as they cast off the empty lighter that had lain by us over the weekend, we slipped down a rope to her and were taken ashore. The men complained that it should have been a time of holiday and Grande Fiesta for them.

219

They were picturesquely abusive in their remarks about the men who should have come to take them to Pisco for jollifications. They told us that their unfriendly companions who were sons of whores and pricks of the devil who were enjoying themselves and had no thought for their mates, should at least have brought them the food which was now due. They were out of provisions and while the men who should have brought them were celebrating, the lancheros could starve for all that they cared. All this in much more graphic language than I could translate. They rubbed their empty bellies and looked sorrowful and they showed us a large and revolting looking octopus that they had caught and were about to cook. They also offered us cooked limpets which they described as 'bueno', but to us, one may as well chew a piece of fishy-tasting car tyre. We sympathised and suggested that they ask the Capitano of the ship for some food though I couldn't think that our parsimonious skipper would help them to any great extent.

We struck due south over the hills of flint and sand. It was a completely sterile desert but by no means flat. Some of the hills, I can hardly call them dunes, were hundreds of feet high. We crested one to look down into a vast basin from which the rounded hills rose on all sides. The ground was all of loose, very coarse sand and the tracks of coyotes crossed and recrossed it in an intricate network. Down in the middle of the basin, about three quarters of a mile away, was a small dark object on which many of the animal tracks converged. We made additional tracks to it in order to investigate.

We discovered it to be an unexploded high calibre shell of a very old pattern for it had copper studs along its sides instead of the rifling band used on shells of more modern design. We saw many more of these later, and we presumed that they had landed there during operations in the Chile-Peruvian war of the early eighties of last century.

Up to this time the skies had been overcast but now the clouds dissolved and the sun beat down pitilessly as we toiled on up sandy hill and down arid flint-strewn slope. We marvelled at the colours of the desert and of the far-distant rocky hills. Over the brow of a long ridge of sandhills we came out on a wide and nearly level plain. I saw a buzzard wheeling overhead and we scanned the clear skies for condors. We could see none but I remembered that I had read of the remarkable way that they appeared when prey was in sight.

We lay on our backs on the hot sand and we stared at the sky that was such a deep and beautiful blue. Minutes passed and the heat of the sun slammed at us.

Tom said, 'There's no future in this. Let's get on.'

I answered, 'Wait a bit yet.'

Soon after we saw a tiny speck overhead which quickly grew clearer. Another and another appeared and dropped out of the sky till we could see the clear outline of their widespread pinions. Still more came as we watched in fascination. One landed on an outcrop over a hundred yards away and soon more wheeled over us and landed in various directions. A few minutes more and there was a wide circle of birds that made no sound and started to close in on us. It gave us the creeps, and almost together we said, 'Let's get out o' this.'

We were hardly on our feet before all the condors were a-wing and they flew off rapidly and rose and rose till they were out of sight.

We walked on and on. Although the country was sterile in the extreme, the way was full of interest. We never knew what was to be found over the next ridge and to try to follow the tracks of a single coyote gave us considerable amusement and confusion. From their sign, I thought them to be carnivorous, but it puzzled us to think what they lived on in that wasteland unless they managed on lizards or were of cannibal habits.

Towards midday we began to smell the sea in the wind and sometimes we found a few tufts of coarse brown grass on the southern slopes of the sandhills but it was well over an hour later that we had our first glimpse of the ocean. As we topped a rise we saw a low two-humped hill far ahead. On the higher hump was planted a tall cross. To the right of this the land fell away and beyond it the calm sea stretched to its far horizon. The desert sloped gradually up to our right to high hills while the sandy plain on our left rose steadily for mile on mile to where the first rocky hills shimmered blue in the heat.

We made the cross-surmounted hill our objective and trudged on through the sand. Now the going was ever so slightly downhill and there was more of the tough dry grass. Another half mile and we came out on a little sheltered inlet across which was the hill with its cross. We were perhaps three hundred yards from the water's edge where a dead seal had drifted ashore and it was surrounded by a group of condors. I thought that these vultures might be so engrossed in their meal that here would be an opportunity for a close-up photograph. I held my camera at the ready, and there being no cover of any sort, I walked slowly straight towards them. They seemed loth to leave their prey but they would not stay long enough for me to get a picture. In spite of their size and fearsome appearance, they struck me as being cowardly creatures and far from aggressive. I got to nearly fifty yards of them and I thought that at least I would be able to snap them as they flew up but they rose suddenly and flew away at such speed that my reactions were not rapid enough to photograph them. We saw that they were ugly birds and they belied their majestic flight and symmetrical form when airborne.

The shores of this little bay were covered with a green mossy growth which was most refreshing to eyes tired of the brazen sun and the glaring sand. The sight of cool water brought a sudden realisation that we were thirsty and that our throats were like parchment. At the head of this inlet a little sailing boat was drawn up and beside it stooped a *pescador*.

We greeted the lone fisherman with a 'buenas tardes' and he did not appear at all surprised at meeting us there or when we told him that we had walked from the English sailing ship in Pisco Bay. Perhaps he was too polite to show surprise but he seemed to regard it as quite a matter of course and the most natural thing in the world that two sailors should walk across fifteen miles of empty desert with no obvious objective and for no apparent reason. He readily assented when we asked for water and he offered us a small wooden bareca from which to drink. We drank the sweetest nectar from the bunghole of that little keg.

We exchanged mutual expressions of goodwill and Tom and I walked on to the hill with the cross. As we approached it we saw that, with its neighbour, it formed a high and narrow spit of land between us and the sea. As we crested the saddle between the two I smelt the unmistakable sickly odour of dead and rotten meat. As we rose over the shoulder of the higher hill and looked out to the open sea we saw a weird and wonderful sight. The little bay at our feet faced due south and the prevailing winds and currents swept into it. There were rocky capes that jutted in ragged heaps far into the sea on either hand and the rocks were of a sombre black. It was still and silent save for the gentle wind and the soft splash of the waves on the beach. But that beach was composed of bones and the smell of dead flesh hung over it like something tangible. We stood and gazed at one of Nature's charnel-houses. The complete skeletons of three whales were there. Though fairly recent arrivals, for their bones had not become scattered, they were picked clean. Like ghastly prehistoric monsters their frames reared from an osseous heap that must have been many feet deep. Ribs and limbs and skulls of all sizes and shapes, from those of whales thirty feet long to tiny slender things of an inch or so were scattered with vertebrae from pea-sized sections to those like great branched logs.

For how many countless centuries had the Humboldt Current and its accompanying breezes washed the carcases of all things that had died along that coast into this quiet little bay? Its spreading capes formed a natural trap for any drifting things that came up on that current that sweeps the thousands of miles of the South Pacific seaboard. We walked across the mass which cracked and scrunched where we trod and we looked out to the black rocks where the silence hung. The little waves that broke on the shore rattled the bones in a gruesome cachinnation.

The Bay of the Dead.

We climbed to the top of the hill where there was a cairn that supported the tall black cross. No marking or inscription marred its severe simplicity. Was it a sign placed there by some devout fisherman to sanctify the graveyard at its feet?

We descended from there and came upon the most amazing contrast and the most beautiful bay imaginable. The crystal clear waves washed sweetly with tinkling music up a beach of purest white sand. Mossy green weed draped the grey rocks and if beauteous mermaids had sat there combing out their long tresses, they would not have been any surprise. Tom said, when I said as much, 'You're just being bloody romantic.'

Across the bay the coast continued south in a line of towering cliffs of astonishing colour. One cape stood out in dazzling whitest marble. Beyond it the cliff face was bright vermilion which faded to crimson where the cliff's shadow fell. On the nearer side the sun shone on an arching precipice of deep purple veined by wide streaks of turquoise blue and apple green, blood red and dove grey.

We wished 'buenas tardes' to the friendly fisherman as we re-passed him and once more we faced the desert sands. Now we had to compete with time for the sun was getting down the sky and we did not care to be in the desert when the chill evening fell. The lowering sun clothed the waste in still more wonderful colours and I understood why the Arizona desert is called 'painted'. Although on our homeward journey we never once picked up our outward tracks, our sense of direction did not fail us and we came out on the cove where the ship lay as darkness was descending. A loaded lighter was afloat and setting out for the barque in readiness for the morning's work and we were just in time to scramble aboard and to give the lancheros a hand with the big sweeps.

Next morning I spoke to the Mate about the lightermens' shortage of food and, acting as interpreter with my halting Spanish, I told him that they asked for the use of the ship's boat and a coil of new rope. My command of their language was insufficient to discover their purpose but the Mate was curious enough to acquiesce. Two of us rowed the boat ashore with the Mate and a new coil of two-inch rope. The lightermen's foreman held one end of the rope and asked us to row out from the shore for the length of the rope and then to haul it in very slowly. We rowed off the beach and paid out the rope as we went. When we came to the end we hauled it in slowly and at every yard or so a big crab, about eight inches or more across his back, clung to the rope with all his feet and claws. As soon as the crab came out of the water he let go, but one of us had a hand under him and tossed him smartly into the boat. By the time we were back to the beach the rope was coiled down in the stern sheets and there was a huge pile of crabs in the middle of the craft. A unique method of crabbing.

The lancheros danced with joy to a chorus of 'Gracias, muchas gracias, Senores!' as we unloaded the crabs but we kept two or three dozen for ourselves. The cook was enticed into cooking a bucketful for us forward while doubtless the steward made an attractive dish for those aft. At the end of the day's work we stood along the rail with a crab or two each, cracked the shells by blows from the backs of our sheath knives and scooped out the delicious flesh. Very welcome it was for as we were far from civilisation, we were on sea-going rations, mainly salt horse and biscuit, while we loaded this ballast at the head of Pisco Bay.

The following Saturday we had quite an adventure which might well have brought the voyage to a sudden end. We had finished work at midday and after our dinner and half an hour of reading, mending, or yarning, all hands had turned in for a quiet sleep. There was nothing to do. We could not get ashore without swimming for it and anyway the inhospitable country did not appeal to many of us, and we rested as sailors do, when they can. Almost everyone in the ship must have been asleep. Officially, one of the apprentices was on anchor watch and he should have been on deck, but because of our sheltered position and the absence of any possible marauders, the watch was no more than a pretence.

I was awakened at about four o'clock by the sound of running feet and shouts and curses. I looked out of my porthole and I saw the headland of the little cove slipping by. There was quite an unusually stiff breeze blowing and I stepped out on deck to find that the ship was drifting rapidly out of the bay, her cable taut across her bows. As I ran forward the chain swung in and hung almost up and down. In deeper water now, lightly loaded and with the drag of her anchor released, she came broadside to the wind and went off at good speed if in bad style, back for Pisco. We soon uncoupled the windlass gypsy and the Mate let off the brake. The cable roared out, the anchor took the bottom, dragged for a few fathoms, then held and brought her up.

Shingle is never a good holding ground and the cable was short so that we would not lie too far off the beach. There was some misplaced confidence in the degree of shelter that the cove offered, for at times, and especially in the afternoons, the south wind would freshen considerably. This, together with the short cable, had caused the barque to drag.

I believe that it was the Second Mate who had noticed the drag of the anchor and it appeared that by good chance he was the only one aboard who was not sound asleep. There was a deal of grumbling in the focsle that her movement had been discovered. Several men bemoaned the fact that it had not happened at night when all hands would certainly have been asleep.

'Why worry?' they said. 'There's sandy beach an' shaller water fer miles along the coast. With this wind we'd go ashore nice an' gentle about near enough to Pisco jetty an' then we'd be shot of the lousy sonofabitch of a bug ridden barge. We couldn't be paid off 'ere. We'd 'ave ter be sent back ter

England as passengers in bleedin' luxury, an' paid off there. That'd cause the Old Man ter shit 'isself.'

Soon after this the ballast loading was completed and we bent the topsails. The following day this small spread of sails was enough to bowl us along to our anchorage off Pisco at a much better speed than when we were towed down.

At Pisco there were letters for us and news of the ship. We learned that she was to discharge all her coal here, which, as we had loaded so much ballast, was not surprising. Then we were to proceed to Callao for orders but it was freely rumoured that guano would be our next cargo. Two of the hands had been shipmates with this beastly freight before and they told gruesome tales of how it affected the men who worked it. We discounted much of this but we were soon to discover for ourselves.

During our stay at Pisco I had several annoying but amusing encounters with the Skipper in the matter of lamp glasses. Up to this time the chimney on our focsle lamp had borne a charmed life. All through the passage out, in spite of cold draughts and a wildly rolling vessel, daily cleaning by a none too careful apprentice or ordinary seaman, it had come to no harm. In Australia, though drunken men had come in and lurched violently and flung their arms wide in vehement gesticulation, the old lamp had continued to give its weak but steady light. Again, across the South Pacific with its wild storms and spray-drenched air, its heavy rain on our none-too-watertight deckhead, nothing but smoke had marred its pristine clarity. The port watch had not been so fortunate. A stray spot of spray or a drop of sweat from the iron plates in the deckhead had often found theirs and they had had some half a dozen new lamp chimneys.

We had not been at anchor in Pisco Bay very long when, one evening as we lounged in the focsle on bunks or sea-chests, there was a faint 'ping . . . tinkle' and the glass collapsed. We could find no reason for this but it was thoroughly ruined and we despatched an ordinary seaman aft to the steward to request another. He returned with this very

227

necessary article. A week later this glass broke in the same inexplicable way and it was at once renewed with the injunction to 'be careful'. This one also cracked and broke during the following week and we had a message with the renewal to say that 'there weren't any more in the ship and if this one gets broke, you can't have another'. It did 'get broke' ten days later and the boy who was sent aft for a replacement came forward without it. He said that the Old Man himself had come out and said that we could not have one.

There was a discussion round the copy of the Articles posted forward and armed with the knowledge that it was incumbent on the ship to 'provide the seamen's quarters with adequate illumination', I was deputed to go aft to beard the lion.

The Skipper raved and swore. He declared that we were grossly careless. We played the bloody fool. We couldn't look after a little lamp glass, etc. etc. I quietly reminded him that the ship was bound to supply us with this necessity. He knew that I was right and that he could not refuse us but he was damned if he was going to admit it. After a long and vain argument he gave me a chimney for our lamp largely because I was determined not to go away without one and I think that he realised this.

In the course of the following week the darned thing cracked and a piece the size of a crown fell out of its side. Not wishing to insist while the glass was at least serviceable, we stuck the piece back with the aid of some brown paper and a smear of condensed milk. This served its purpose though the lamp flickered and smoked a good deal. This lasted a fortnight but on the Saturday evening following, as I lay reading by its feeble light, it suddenly and unreasonably collapsed. I took the fragments aft and asked for a new glass.

On Saturday evenings the Skipper used to open the 'slop chest' and the crew bought tobacco and cigarettes and matches and such articles he supplied, at a price, and these were charged against their pay. When I went into the saloon, several men and boys were making their purchases. I took my place in the queue and when my turn came and he saw and heard what I wanted, the Old Man's expression changed, shall I say from that of an interested business man to that of an exasperated parent. He squared his shoulders and filled his lungs and roared.

'It's no use, Brookesmith! I SHALL NOT GIVE YOU ANOTHER LAMP GLASS! You've had one each week now for I don't know how long. If you can't look after them you'll have to go without!'

'But ...'

'NO! You CANNOT have another! Next please.'

I stood aside and I waited patiently for the business to conclude. He glared at me once or twice but he said no more till the last man had gone. Then, the better to express himself, he stood up and banged the table.

'You can't have any more lamp glasses! There aren't any more on the ship, and I can't buy any more ashore!'

'Surely, Mister,' I replied, 'it is possible to purchase these things in Pisco? There is no gas or electricity there and every house is lit by paraffin lamps.'

Obviously his ignorance of conditions ashore was considerable for he was quite taken aback by this and he stumbled to recover himself, but he stuck to his guns.

'Er ... er, I tell you I can't buy them ashore. Th-th-ere aren't any for sale.'

'Then sir, let me go ashore tomorrow, and I'll buy you a gross,' I said eagerly.

'Oh rubbish! I haven't got one. You can't have one. If you can't be more careful you can go without. How do you suppose the Company are going to go on buying lamp glasses for you to break up, eh?'

'But, we didn't break them, sir. They broke of their own accord for some quite unexplained reason. We're very puzzled to know why. You know that the ship is obliged to supply ...'

'FIDDLESTICKS! I can't MAKE glasses. What d'you suppose I'M to do? Here,' and he grabbed the tall glass from

229

the ornate brass cabin lamp, 'take this and I'LL go without. I'LL be in the dark!'

'Thank you,' I said and much to his surprise, I took it and I marched out of the saloon with the spoils.

To our delight, the glass fitted our lamp and strange to say, after this we did not have any more breakages. I believe that we did have one more chimney before we completed the voyage but that was many weeks after and the tall and stately glass did good service on our little tin lamp.

Some three weeks after loading the ballast, we discharged the remainder of the coal and we saw the last bag go overside with a heartful cheer. Some one said, 'That's the last of those fossilised turds!', to general laughter.

Now followed a period of considerable and more varied activity. Some of us were down in the dark and dusty bowels of the ship to sweep out the hold and to prepare it for our new cargo. Others more fortunate were aloft in God's fresh air to bend the sails and to free the gear for her run of one hundred miles up the coast to Callao. We spent the weekend there but we could not go ashore. I wanted very much to visit Lima and I pleaded with the Skipper but no amount of persuading would soften his heart. I said that I wanted to get some films for my camera. I had some films to be developed and if they were not, the passage through the heat of the Tropics might well spoil them. I claimed that they were very important. I assured him that I would not spend more time ashore than I could possibly help. He only looked at me coldly and said, 'NO!' I suppose I couldn't expect him to be very kindly disposed towards me.

My old ship *William Mitchell* was in port discharging grain from Australia and one evening her boat came out to us. I had a chat with the apprentices who rowed her and the Captain had a word for me. She was to load guano at some islands down the coast and we left the next day to load a similar cargo at the Pescador Islands, twenty miles to the north.

We were towed there by a diesel engined tug that blew

230

smoke rings into the calm air with staccato reports from her squat funnel. It was one of those glorious clear days that are frequent on that coast in the summer months and it was not long before we sighted the barren islets that were white with thousands of years' deposit of guano. The rocks lifted sheer from the sea but to no great height. Perhaps the highest would be two hundred and fifty feet. I could see no beaches and no place where a boat could land and the Pacific's restless rollers swirled and broke at the feet of the cliffs. In one place the swell surged into a cave and shot out of an opening above in a column of snowy spray that showered down like brilliants in the sunshine. On the largest island a landing stage had been erected high out of reach of the heaviest seas. Here a whaleboat swung from davits and a rude crane was rigged to take stores and men ashore and to unload the unsavoury products of their labours into lighters below. Here also was an office and a dwelling of sorts where the señor in charge lived while above on the hillside, rough shelters of corrugated iron and gunny sacks told where the peons who gathered the filthy harvest lived in extreme discomfort. Under the lee of the island but out of sight of the little settlement, our anchor was dropped in twenty fathoms of water.

We were five miles from the mainland which rolled away from guano-covered headlands to desert uplands of those wonderful colours that rose and rose for many miles inland to the towering heights of eternal snow. By day, the islands and the hills along the shore shone white from the dazzling sun reflected from the deposits of guano but at evening, when the desert took on those marvellous colours that we had observed further south, the countless millions of birds returned to their roosting places, and in the few minutes between daylight and darkness their black bodies crowded wing to wing and completely blotted out the signs of their ages of habitation.

Unbelievable hordes of birds lived on the teeming life of the sea there. They flew off to their fishing in the mornings

231

in great clouds and streams that stretched from horizon to horizon. They were mostly shags and cormorants with a high proportion of gannets. When they passed close to where the barque lay, the noise of their pinions was deafening and it was difficult to hear one another shout above the roar of those innumerable wings. They fed on the sardines that abound in those waters. One day these little fish shoaled about the ship and their close-packed bodies formed black patches in the sea. I dropped a bucket on a rope into one of these shoals and so dense were they that I picked up more fish than water.

Mackerel, bonito, and albacore drove lanes through them while the clouds of birds overhead shut out the sun. As they wheeled and screamed, their cries and the beat of their wings completely drowned other sounds. Then, when the myriads descended to dive and swim after their prey, the noise of them striking the water was like the thunder of huge seas breaking on a rocky shore.

The men who brought the guano out to us in lighters caught many mackerel which they split open and placed around the edges of their craft to dry in the sun. After an hour or so they ate them as they were.

The populous sea was of continual interest and in strange contrast with the barren land ashore. Seals and sealions abounded and it was entertaining to see one of these animals come to the surface with a big fish across its jaws, throw it in the air with a quick toss of its head, catch it again head first and swallow it at a gulp.

Some days an army of porpoises could be seen advancing in a vast crescent. Some of their numbers scattered ahead and on the flanks of this formation and these drove fish into the arc. There must have been many thousands for the curve would be a mile or more in length. Their sleek bodies could be seen leaping and darting in pursuit of their prey but always they kept formation.

Though shags, cormorants, and gannets made up the vast majority of the birds, there were many other varieties. There were some strange birds that swam under water and leaped like fish clear out of the water and back again. These were penguins of course, and it was only because of the cold current from the Antarctic that they and the sea-lions were to be found here, only a few degrees south of the Equator.

There were many pelicans and there is something indescribably droll about these big slow birds. They always seemed to wear an indignant expression as if to say 'Don't you dare laugh at me!' In flight they were most amusing. They took off with their long beaks and necks outstretched, kicked madly at the water with their wide feet to get them airborne and then as they commenced to fly, they brought back their heads with a folding motion as if their bodies flew on faster than their heads, till their necks rested along their backs and their long beaks jutted out over their snowy breasts. They would fly in line ahead, rarely more than a dozen in a flock. Their leader would be about three lengths ahead and the others with little more than their own length between them. We thought that it was Old Dad who led and his harem and family that trailed after. They flew only a foot or so above the water with a slow beat of their wings. The leader would make six beats and then glide for a period of three. The next in line would start to glide and then recommence his flight one beat after the one before and so on down the line. This was an invariable procedure. When Dad in front spied fish, he would rise to a height of fifteen to twenty feet. Each bird would fly on in his deliberate manner to the point where the leader had risen and then he (or she) too would rise. When they were all in the air, and not till then, they would concertedly turn on their sides, stretch their necks and fall rather than dive, thoroughly ungracefully, and make most terrific splashes as they struck the sea. They came to the surface with heads and tails of fish sticking out along their beaks and the pouches underneath were distended. There would be strange stirrings in these pouches and one could imagine them sorting out the meal with their tongues and heading the little fish all the right way before sending them

233

down below. This done, off they went on their unhurried way.

We appreciated these diversions, for loading guano is a pretty ghastly business. It smells of concentrated ammonia but over and through it is the overpowering sickly stench of dead things. It was mainly dry and dusty but amongst it all were many feathers and the bodies of long dead birds which their comrades had trampled as flat as pancakes and which the combined action of the climate and the guano had dried to the consistency of leather.

Lighters brought the stuff alongside in bags of 100 kilos each and we cut the mouths of the sacks and emptied the contents into the hold. When tall peaks of it had risen under the fore and after hatchways, for those ships had only one hold and no athwartship bulkheads, the ballast was dumped overboard, the shifting boards were cleared and we took shovels below to trim the muck. We shovelled away at the reeking stuff. Soon our eyes watered. Then the backs of our noses felt seared and raw. Something in our heads was swelling and swelling and it must soon burst. Our throats became hot and dry. We gasped for air and rushed for the open hatch. Fresh air rapidly caused the discomfort to go but it was noticeable that when we returned to the job, we could not stick it for more than a quarter of the time that we did at first. We would retire for more gulps of air then force ourselves back to the stink again until at last it became too much. One simply had to get out and up on deck and away from the foul stuff.

Even now, after all these years, I can again feel, when I think of guano, the sting in my eyes, the burning at the back of my nose, the horrible bursting feeling in my head, the drumming in my ears and the desperate, gasping desire for air. I have heard that it can cause men's noses and ears to bleed but I never experienced it nor have I seen anyone suffer to that extent.

In loading the filth we did all we could to avoid going below to trim. We made hatches of the ventilators. We

234

pulled up deck planks and loaded through the openings thus made but whatever we did there was always some to be levelled off. We found that we could do best by sticking it as long as we could without a break and then coming on deck for as long a spell.

The fine dust of it hung in our hair and eyebrows and it coated us with a grey powder. I well remember the first time that I tried to wash it off. I had come from the hold at the end of that first day and my hair and beard were full of the smelly foulness which also lay thick on my limbs. I drew my bucket of water and took it forward. I peeled off my singlet and trousers and plunged in my head. I grasped the soap and started to lather but it would not go. The shit formed into sticky mud which clung between my fingers and around my nails. As I rubbed my face and beard the mud stuck in my whiskers and was more unpleasant than dough. No amount of rubbing would shift it. It got worse in my matted hair. It smelled. Tom mentioned its origin and laughed till he cried. In desperation I leaped on the rail and dived into the sea.

When I came to the surface I rubbed irritably at my hairy face and to my intense surprise it was clear and clean. I looked at my hands. They were as clean if not cleaner than they had been for weeks. I turned on my side and swam round the ship with long easy strokes. I climbed up the jacob's ladder and called, 'There you are boys! Here's the original salt-water soap!' That is the truth of it. No matter how grubby you may be, a handful of guano and a tub of salt water will clean you up like nothing else. Not that I would expect the idea to become popular!

After that we all bathed in salt water. This must have pleased our parsimonious Old Man for sweet water had to be brought from Callao and it had to be paid for. He must have expected to purchase barrels of it for our daily bath but now there was all that salt water by the cubic mile, and all for nothing. All that was required was for an apprentice to pump up a few buckets from the ocean and even that was not necessary for me and a few others. The end of the working day saw us come up from the dusty hold, peel off and dive straight over the side. No soap, no rubbing, no scrubbing, and one came up as clean as a babe.

We laboured on at loading the muck. The old donkey engine wheezed and coughed and the level of the stinking lousy guano rose in the hold. It *was* lousy too. Scorpions four to five inches long were found there with countless spiders of a peculiar appearance that gave us a painful bite. They were about the size of a pea but lozenge-shaped with a weird black mark on their backs that looked like a Chinese character. If one picked one up and rolled it between finger and thumb it felt tough and rubbery. When crushed, their blood or whatever it was in their bodies, showed black as Indian ink.

In Pisco, the First Mate had gone ashore with his watch and I gathered that they had had a fairly hectic time of it. He had returned in the small hours with a duck. No one knew how he had come by it but there it was. Someone said that he had won it in a raffle! This duck thoroughly enjoyed the spiders. They may have thought that the iron ladder that led up from the hold held promise of better things and they came up one after the other and peered over the hatch coaming. When the duck stood up and stretched his neck, his bill came just to the edge of the coaming. He stood there for hours and took in the little strangers as they appeared over his horizon.

For weeks the work went on. I made one of a party of three which worked at a big ventilator shaft which went down midway between the fore and main hatch. A dolly winch was worked by three Peruanos and it swung aboard one bag at a time. One of us landed and unslung the bag, one cut the mouth, and I picked up the one hundred kilos and shook it down the hold. As fast as I cast aside one empty sack, another was there at my feet and all day long it was stoop and lift and shake, stoop and lift and shake. Fifty tons a day we three handled and at the end of it we dived over the side and swam round the barque. The food was

236

poor and there was none too much of it. The water left much to be desired. Conditions were awful but I don't suppose that I was ever again as fit as I was then.

The work that we put in was as nothing to that of the poor Cholos on the islands. A number of them were pure-blooded Indians recruited from the hinterland but many of them were the scum of Lima and of Callao and some were convicts. They carried the heavy sacks high on their shoulders round the steep sides of the rocky hills, over rough tracks where the least slip meant being dashed to death on the jagged rocks at the waters edge. Hounded on by their overseers, they trod with their burdens as sure-footed as goats, grunting, sweating, and complaining. From dawn till dark they worked, and when I saw them, weary and worn, clothed in indescribable rags, their bare feet and legs covered with horrid open sores from the bites of spiders and scorpions, I marvelled at their stoicism. They were getting their hell on earth.

One day, as a lighter was being made fast alongside, one of the men on her shouted up to us, 'Grande huelga en Inglaterra!' He passed me a Lima newspaper and I read in Spanish of the General Strike in England. There was much discussion pro and contra in the focsle.

CHAPTER XIX HOMEWARD BOUND

Now we learned that *Kilmallie* was not to go home by way of Cape Horn. She was bound for London and she was to be towed through the Panama Canal. If ever I prayed, I then and there gave up a silent prayer of thanksgiving when I heard the news. I had dreaded the possibility of such a passage in that ship. There was less rope in her rope locker than could be found in many a tramp steamer and much of the running rigging was sadly in need of renewal. A great deal of it was that which had been rove off on her previous voyage. Since then she had been laid up for four years so it could not have been less than five years old. Her sails were old and much patched. I was sure that there were not overmany provisions aboard and I doubted that our stingy Old Man would lay in ample stocks. Added to this was the fact that a big proportion of our crew were poor seamen who could not be depended on in an emergency. I did not care to think of making a winter passage round Cape Horn in company with such indifferent sailors. There were only three men in our watch whom the Skipper would allow to steer. Peter, who was a real sailorman, told me quite seriously that he would jump over the side rather than make such a passage with such shipmates.

239

'Here, hold on,' I said. 'There's only you and young Paddy and I who can steer now. What do you suppose would happen to us if *you* left the old tub? Apart from that none of them can tuck a splice or make a decent knot.'

'Vell,' he said, 'you'd never get de sheep home anyway. So vot vould it matter?'

I spoke to the Second Mate in some glee that we were avoiding the Cape Horn route and I was amazed to find him disappointed. He thought that sailings ships were made to round old Cape Stiff and it didn't seem right to him that this one would not. That there were so many other considerations he just could not or would not see. I asked him if he had never been round and in future he wanted to say that he had. He didn't answer and I walked away.

Romanticism can be a fine thing in its way and I suppose that there is cause to regret the passing of the sailing ship in the minds of some men, but I have never let my mind be so clouded by the glamour that surrounds these ships to forget that there was so much of misery and privation in the life aboard them. The idea of putting the ship to fearful risk and her company to certain hardship, cold, and semi-starvation, and of turning one's back on one of the greatest triumphs of civil engineering, solely because 'these ships have always gone the Cape Horn road' appalled me. Traditions die hard — like salt beef.

I was glad that the decision did not rest with one so restricted in vision for it is doubtful if the barque *Kilmallie* would ever have reached her destination if she had headed south from the Pescador Islands.

Much has been written and said of late by old timers who lament the disappearance of sail. They deplore the fact that there is no British sailing ship in which British lads may put in full time on long ocean voyages to train for the sea. I agree that it is a wonderful training, but for what? It entails so much of wet and hunger, cold and misery, and back-breaking, brutalising toil, which cannot be justified. Is it necessary or advisable that youngsters should go through this purgatory

240

to train them for a life where mathematical, electrical, and mechanical knowledge is of far greater importance than physical strength and the ability to parcel and serve, to tuck a splice, to strop a block, or to cross a yard?

Of course it is fine to sit in the comfortable saloon of a steamer while the purring turbines are pushing her along or the throbbing diesels which you can hardly feel are thrusting her through the ocean without any effort on your part, and to talk of the days when you were in sail. Of the night when the half-deck was washed out and you had no dry clothes or blankets. That first time you stowed a royal on your own. When off the pitch of the Horn the galley was swamped out and you had no hot food or coffee for days. You stood by on the poop, red-eyed from lack of sleep, cold and bone-weary and so hungry that you could chew your boots. Yes, it all sounds well and people say admiringly, 'What a life!' You glow a little. But would you go through it again from choice? Not bloody likely.

Life is like that. We forget so soon and the passage through the delightful Trade Wind area wipes out the memory of the cruel grey Cape Horn seas.

On 16th June the loading was completed, the decks cleared, and we made ready to bend sail. The sail locker in that vessel was in the forward 'tween decks and it was separated from the cargo by wooden gratings only. It seemed that all the worst smells of our foul cargo had collected in the locker and rotted there. A wave of nauseating gases rose from the hatch when it was opened. The Second Mate and I went down that little hatch under the focsle head to get out the sails in order. We tried to breathe as little as possible as we struggled with the stacks of sails that were made up into long sausages of canvas and rope. All we had to do was to pass one end up to those on deck but we could not stick it for long enough even for that. The air was impossibly foul. Our very lungs felt raw and our eyes wept. Soon came that frightful drumming in our heads. Then came a feeling of desperation and we positively fought our way out of it to the

241

deck where we fell gasping and retching. I hoped that this was all some horrible dream from which I would soon wake.

Eventually one of the crew went and passed a rope's end through the clewiron of the nearest sail. We took it in turns to hold our breaths, make a rapid dash to pass the rope, fling the end up on deck, and scramble up the ladder after it. Thus we took all the sails out of that stinking place and sorted them out in the fresh air on deck.

It was sheer joy thereafter to be up on the yards in air as pure as could be expected in the lee of the birds' dung heaps and to be doing real sailors' work again in bending sails for the homeward voyage. Even on the t'gallant yard we would get occasional sickening whiffs as some trick of air currents wafted the gases aloft from our disgusting freight.

By the evening of the 18th, all sails were bent and the barque ready for sea. The first thing next morning, the Mate strode along the deck and yelled, 'All hands! Man the windlass!'

With sixty fathoms of chain to come in, we hove round the capstan to the tune of many shanties sung lustily and enthusiastically.

'Hurrah!' we sang, 'Hurrah, me boys, we're home-ward bound! With a load of stinkin' shit, we're home-ward bound!'

Now that we were actually started on the homeward passage, relief if not joy was predominant and it evinced itself in the many facetious and ribald remarks that flew around and across the circle of heaving, sweating men. Cheerily we braced our toes to the planking and thrust our shoulders against the heavy bars. Link by link the cable rasped through the hawse-holes while we sang of the naughty life and naughtier adventures of that maid from Amsterdam.

With forty fathoms out the Mate called: 'Avast heaving! Set fore and main topsails and t'ga'nts'ls!'

We laid capstan bars on the deck and gave up pushing to pull as we put our weights to sheets and halliards. Old Sails led us in 'Reuben Ranzo' and to the interesting song of his life, the yards rattled aloft. The sails on the mainmast were

242

put aback and we returned to the focsle head to resume our trudge. With twenty-five fathoms still overside we were adrift. As the barque's head fell off the yards were swung and she headed north with a little wind on her quarter. As she got clear of the lee of the islands, quite a swell rolled in on her beam and she behaved drunkenly with only a light breeze and so much chain and a ton or two of anchor over her bows. I wasn't at the wheel but she must have been difficult to steer.

We staggered round the reeling focsle head as we leaned on the bars to heave up the hook. Now uphill and now down we went and we were thrown this way and that as the ship wallowed in the seaway. We gripped at the deck planking with our bare feet and gradually we brought the anchor within range of the cathead.

Now the barque was steady and we had the anchor catted and fished by 1.30 p.m. when all hands, save the man at the wheel, adjourned for dinner. After this welcome break the courses and all the fore-and-afters were set, the yards were braced sharp on the port tack, and to a freshening breeze we stood out to sea. The Mate called, 'Clear up the decks! Starboard watch below,' and we left the port watch coiling all down.

I went up on to the focsle head and I looked away to the weather quarter to where a blue-grey smudge was fast disappearing and there were no regrets in my heart. I haven't left many places without the thought that I would like to come back some day but I didn't want ever to see those lousy muck-heaps again.

For several days a breeze that maintained its direction but varied its strength drove us to the northward. Sometimes she heeled along at a smart seven knots. Again she stole along at a quiet three. The sea was calm and the weather was pleasantly warm though the sky was continually overcast. Altogether it was a very restful time after the past four months. In spite of the all-pervading stench, we were happier to be at sea. The smell was quite bad in our focsle and we were puzzled why this should be. Then we realised that a part of our forward

243

bulkhead was one side of the wooden ventilator shaft through which we had loaded so much of our cargo. There were gaps between the planks which formed quite an escape route for the many stinks down below. With long strips from old newspapers and condensed milk as an adhesive, we sealed these and breathed a less polluted air.

One night we were treated to a most remarkable phenomenon of which I had read but the actuality is difficult to describe. I never thought that I would be grateful for being called from a sound sleep when I had a 'farmer' in the middle watch, but I thanked Tom for waking me. The night was calm though slightly overcast and there was just enough wind to keep the sails asleep. The barque slipped along at about three knots through a sea of milky light. Clear to the horizon where the clouds stopped short at its brightness, the whole ocean positively glowed. About the ship was a ring of bright fire that became a wave of scintillation at her forefoot, bathed the length of her scarred sides in lovely sparkling radiance and became great blobs of brilliance in the eddies at her stern. A big fish swam by and with its wake, formed a bejewelled fiery snake. Every breaking wavelet was a shower of diamonds. It was strangely beautiful and the soft effulgence which rose from the glowing ocean had a semblance of fairyland.

The waters here abounded in fish and we had some good sport and very welcome fresh food. One day the bonito were in shoals around the bows and Tom and I had great fun. We took it in turns with the line and he had caught three and I had a couple when he caught a small albacore. A few of them joined the bonito and I was delighted for though they were small, I had always wanted to capture one of these fiercely fighting fish. I tried for one but the difficulty lay not so much in catching the albacore as in avoiding the bonito who made concerted rushes at the lure. At length I hooked one and I swelled with pride as I hauled up twenty-five pounds of leaping vitality.

I was at the wheel one day when the Old Man was on the

poop and he talked with me about fishing in many parts of the world for he too was a keen fisherman. Suddenly we heard a violent splash to leeward. We looked but saw nothing but some disturbed water. As we stared, a mantua, a large member of the skate family, eight to ten feet wide and as many long, leaped many feet into the air and fell back to the water flat on its tummy to make a sound like a cannon shot. I understand that they have a way of doing this periodically to rid themselves of parasites.

The morning after, when I was at the wheel from four till six, I saw a big dorado alongside and after I was relieved and was working aloft, I could see four of them swimming round the ship. After eight bells I hurried through my breakfast and repaired with my line to the jib-boom end. It was not long before they came hungrily to my lure and I hooked what I thought was the biggest. He fought with all the power of his vigorous body but I managed to forestall his wild rushes and to keep his head out of the water as much as I could. After twenty-five minutes of twisting, threshing, and worrying, he lay comparatively still. I lifted him foot by foot till I could drop him in a sack which a shipmate held. He was a beauty and he measured four feet eight inches in length. I don't know how much he weighed but it was quite a job to lift him with one hand and he must have gone all of fifty pounds. Everyone remarked on his size and the Skipper said that it was the largest he had seen caught in all his fifty-five years at sea. A big one that *didn't* get away — and he tasted good.

The fish were a continual source of interest to me and I often stood on the focsle head in my watches below and watched them for hours. Even when working aloft, my eyes were ever lifting for signs of life overside and there was constant entertainment.

A number of big dorado hung about the barque for days here and they harried the poor little flying fish no end. I hooked one particularly large one which gave me a terrific fight for ten minutes or so before the hook tore from his mouth and he broke away. I admired him and I thought

245

that he deserved his freedom. He stayed with us for a few days and he was readily identified by the scar that my hook had made on his upper jaw. He must have felt upset for he did not go chasing after his grub with the same enthusiasm as the others. He surprised me by demonstrating that affection does exist between cold-blooded creatures. I had never before credited fish with having any kindly feelings towards their fellows — and who, having seen their cannibal habits, could readily do so?

A big female (the sexes are easily distinguishable by the shape of the head) had been swimming near us during the late afternoon. In the first dog watch I made an attempt to capture her. She was quite eager to take the hook and she made several rushes at it. Each time my sick friend forgot his wound and came with a burst of speed to head her off and always he got there first. Once he actually thrust his head into her flank and pushed her away from my lure. I gave up trying to catch her. It didn't seem fair.

From my point of view, that fine weather passage up to the Gulf of Panama was enjoyable for the fishing and the meals that it produced. Of course there was any amount of work to do and as sailmaker's mate I plied palm and needle under the break of the poop or I swung aloft on the yards with marlin spike, serving board, spunyarn, and tarpot. Again we hauled and pulled at braces as we altered course round the western bulge of South America's coast while the old hooker lumbered along before the light breezes, the bugs bred and bit and the guano stank to high heaven. It was delightful weather and the winds were continually fair but it was hot and stuffy in the focsle and I was never a great one for sleep anyway. So I spent many a daytime watch below perched out at the end of the jib-boom. Over the tops of the waves I dangled my hook wrapped with its white rag and I tried to get the dorado and bonito to believe that it was a flying fish, and with some success. The fish made very good eating and were a more than welcome variation to our salted and dried provisions.

246

The life of the sea existed by a continual and terrible struggle. The flying fish were the sport of them all. There were some like little white moths, an inch or so long that fluttered out of the crests of the waves in panic fear of the mackerel and bonito. The bigger fish chased the mackerel and the flying fish which grew up to a couple of pounds in weight. There went a dorado, a brilliant streak, his back half out of the water, or he leaped from the low crest of the long swell as he tore with amazing speed after a fear-racked, pop-eyed flying fish but a few inches from his nose. At length the little chap could fly no more and he splashed into the sea. The dorado gave one last leap, a gulp, and he smiled with satisfaction as he gracefully moved his powerful body in search of more prey. Sometimes the intended victim was more artful and he gave a rapid right-angled twist to his flight as he returned to the water. The dorado would bring up short and swish round in small circles in frustration and dismay. It would not be long before some other poor little devil would be hounded to death. If the dorado did not catch him, a frigate bird would swoop down and take him in flight.

A day or so after we crossed the Line, some heavy rain fell and we collected water in every available vessel and then we stripped off and stood out in the warm downpour with a bar of soap and had the first good fresh-water bath that we had had for months. All hands seized the opportunity to wash a collection of clothes but the rain persisted for several days and sodden clothes swung damply in every sheltered place where we brushed against their clammy wetness.

Here a number of huge moths alighted on the ship. They were as much as six or seven inches across their spread wings which were of the most wondrous colours and patterns. It was a surprise to see them there for we were over a hundred miles from land.

Now we pushed on to the north and east before winds that grew lighter and lighter till their strength was negligible and often we lay becalmed for hours on end. On the sixteenth day at sea we sighted Las Perlas Islands. The luxuriant vegetation and the intense green of the grass were a delight to eyes tired of the monotony of sea, for we had seen no land since the barren coast of Peru. We drifted there in the Gulf of Panama for a couple of days in a perfectly flat calm. The sea around was thick with fish of brilliant colours among which bigger fish disported and cormorants dived and fed. A tree trunk drifted by and beneath it the sinister shapes of two sharks lurked. Nearby a water snake lifted its yellow head. The sea here was full of living things and as the barque lay with slack sails we saw much of them and she collected a deal of them, for her bilges were heavily overgrown with weeds and barnacles which made a welcome home for crabs and shellfish and myriads of diverse marine life.

At midday on Wednesday, 7th July, eighteen days after we had left the Pescador Islands, a light wind found us and sent us along in the right direction, but at a bare one-and-a-half knots. At 2 p.m. a tug was sighted steaming out to us from Panama. Shortly a powerful sea-going tow-boat, almost as long as ourselves, ranged alongside. Her Skipper, a big beefy man clad in only a singlet and white duck trousers, roared in familiar nasal tones that he had been sent out by our Agent to tow us in. He proceeded to pass us his hawser.

We took the heavy wire rope in over the bows, made it fast to the fore deck bitts, passed a lashing, and at once manned downhauls and buntlines and soon had all the sails up in their gear. The last buntline was scarcely belayed when I said to Tom, 'Come on! Up the main,' and we were on the t'gallant yard before the others were over the top. We were picking the sail up on to the yard when there was a frightening bang from the deck and we looked down to see the after bitt flung clear across the deck and fetch up at the starboard bulwark with another loud report. The towline wound round the remaining bitt and came up on its lashing which quickly carried away and the tug went off on its own. Fortunately everyone was in the rigging by this time and clear of both the flying lump of iron and the murderous wire as it snaked over the bows. As the towboat came round to give us his

248

wire again, we all ran down from aloft and this time we got a better lead by taking the towing line through the hawse-hole instead of over the focsle head as before. It was now made fast on the starboard bitts.

Again we ran aloft and we made sure that we put a good harbour stow on the sails. We would show the Yankees that, though they called us 'lime-juicers' and the towing bitts weren't as strong as they ought to be, we were good sailors (?). While aloft we passed close to leeward of the island of Toboga and the wind carried to us the scent of flowers. How we filled our lungs with it!

We rigged and lowered the gangway and then there were the decks to be cleared and all ropes to be coiled down and while this went on the port doctor came aboard. The medical officer's launch was handled cleverly as it came alongside. Without taking a line or making fast in any way, its speed was regulated to coincide with ours and the health officer simply stepped on to the platform at the base of the gangway. The boat immediately sheered off. It reminded me of the trim sailing cutters that used to operate outside San Francisco Harbour and which I had had the pleasure of seeing when I was in the tanker *Orowaiti*. One would come sailing at speed up to the companion way. The helmsman would put her head into the wind and spill the sails at just the right moment. The pilot would step on to the gangway, the cutter's helm would be put over, the sails filled on the other tack and off she would sheer.

Pratique was granted and the tug signalled to us to cast off. She hauled in her big towrope and came round to make fast alongside. The big Skipper stepped off the wing of his bridge and greeted our Old Man with a 'Good-day Cap'n'. He stuck his thumbs in his waistband, looked aloft, glanced back at his tug, spat overside and said, 'Say, Cap'n, it sure must be strange to you to see a big towboat like this alongside yore funny li'l ship!' and he grinned amiably.

The Old Man's face was a picture. He swelled with indignation. Could not trust himself to speak. Made one or two

249

choking gasps and turned away with a snort.

The tugboatman strolled down to the main deck to super-intend his black seamen as they made fast. His twelve-inch manila line was far too big to be taken round our bitts satisfactorily, and he, understandably, did not trust them. He gave instructions for the rope to be passed round the main-mast. The Old Man came bustling down from the poop.

'Here!' he called. 'You can't do that! You'll pull the mast out of her!'

The towboat Skipper looked at him with interest. 'Say, Cap'n, if that rope pulls the mast out of her, it's *time* it came out! Go on boys.'

With the tug secured on her quarter she was pushed along at eleven knots, faster than she had ever sailed. By 5.30 p.m. she was moored to the buoys at the Canal entrance, and ready to be towed through at six the next morning. One of the black deckhands from the tug looked at me, held his nose and said, 'Say, mistah, she shuah niffs.'

It was a calm and peaceful tropic night and I stood on the focsle head and enjoyed that last pipe before turning in. I watched the shore lights and the deep purple sky. I again gave heartfelt though silent thanks that we were to pass from one ocean to the other in this sunny clime rather than battling with winter gales off the pitch of Cape Horn.

At six sharp the tug was by us and was soon made fast. We cast off from the buoy and passed through miles of swampy jungle to Miraflores Lock. Through this engineering triumph we went through more miles of low-lying land to Pedro Miguel Lock. Thence through the famous Culebra Cut, since re-named, out on to Gatun Lake. The heat was intense and no wind stirred. All hands were 'standing by' and there was nothing we could do save take advantage of the fresh water in which we floated by collecting it in every available container and by bathing ourselves with reckless extravagance. It was too hot for the effort of washing clothes and even bathing grew absurd for the exertion of drying oneself brought on a generous perspiration that made one wetter than before. We

250

crept listlessly about the decks or leaned limply at the rail with that peculiar flabbiness of muscle which one experiences in extreme heat. We watched the green hills and the driftwood and the alligators. We grumbled at the sweat that poured into our eyes.

The only light moment was provided by Taffy who was reading a month-old newspaper in the shadow of the focsle. He suddenly threw it down in disgust and cried:

'It says 'ere: "Nine 'undred miles as the crow flies." Now indeed, did effer you 'ear of a crow that flew nine 'undred miles?'

By late afternoon we were at Gatun Lock. We descended these wonderfully-constructed steps to the level of the Atlantic Ocean and were towed out past Colon with the dying day.

It is impossible to forget the Panama Canal. It is inspiring to see the silent power of those great lock gates; the wild swirl of water as the sluice gates are opened; the quietly powerful electric 'mules' that tow mighty ships from one lock to the next. One has a feeling of wonder and of pride in man's achievement when one looks back from the sea-level cut to see a huge passenger liner lifted high up great Gatun's three-stepped stair.

CHAPTER XX   NORTH ATLANTIC

We steered by the tug's stern light as it rose and dipped ahead and we were towed twenty-five miles to sea. Dark lowering clouds brought no breath of wind to temper the sweltering heat. We lolled about and gasped and feebly cursed. When the tug cast us off, we had to pull and drag at halliards and sheets and set sail. Sweat poured from us and even Old Sails's cheery voice singing out to 'heave and raise her!' could not put any punch into our slack muscles. With throats as dry as dust and bodies streaming with sweat, we hoisted the yards, sheeted home the canvas, hauled on braces to trim the yards, but no wind stirred.

By this time it was nearly midnight and for what was left of our watch below, I sat on the edge of my bunk and wrote up my log. Today it shows the stains where perspiration dripped and where my sweaty hands brushed the paper. Relief from the steaming heat came as I wrote and I felt a faint draught from the open porthole. Then came the Mate's voice from the deck as he called his watch.

'Port main brace!'

This was followed by the pad of bare feet and the calls of the men. The breeze grew to a fresh and steady Trade and all next day we lay close-hauled to it and made good progress

253

to the northward. The sea was of deepest sapphire blue which golden masses of gulf weed intensified. With every watch the wind grew more fitful and drew aft so that we made a better course but the passing days brought weather that was now calm and now squally, and fierce sudden storms blew up out of cloudless skies.

One afternoon the squalls became increasingly more frequent and violent. I came from my trick at the wheel at two o'clock and, as it was Sunday, I took the opportunity to do some washing. Clad only in a pair of shorts, I was hard at it when a particularly heavy squall struck the barque. It brought hard driving rain, shrieked and howled in taut rigging and laid her hard over. Above the din I heard the Old Man's stentorian shout and as I skipped aft there was a terrifying banging and slamming from aloft. The Old Man was yelling to haul down the mizzen topmaststaysail and as it was full of the strong wind we had a hard pull to get it down. We left a couple of the boys to make it fast and we hurried forward to find that the thunderous roar from above came from the free weather clew of the fore upper tops'l from which the chain sheet and the downhaul had carried away. The sail flapped wildly and the heavy iron clew banged and rang on the steel yard. That clew, with a fathom of chain lashing and flying would have broken and maimed terribly.

'Haul it up!' shouted the Old Man, when men were already manning the buntlines and I was lowering the yard. The sail was half-way up in its gear when the rotten old ropes parted and the sail blew out with one mighty flap and great masses of it flung away to leeward. From mast to yardarm there were only the bolt ropes and a few tattered pieces of canvas. We climbed aloft to take in the remnants and from then till six o'clock we on the yard didn't come down to the deck. We made the framework fast along the yard as best we could and then went up and stowed the two t'ga'nts'ls.

Eight bells had now gone and it was rightly our watch below, but as we made to go down, the Old Man came forward and gave instructions to bend another sail. So I passed a gantline about the sorry bundle of rags and we cast off the remaining sheet and the earrings, cut the rovings and sent it down. The wind had now died away and the warm rain fell in steaming torrents on my bare back. I think that I was as wet with perspiration as with rain but I felt no discomfort. There was too much to do. The replacement sail was already up from the locker and laid along the deck and while the other watch made it ready to go up we repaired the broken chain with a split link and had it all right to shackle on by the time the sail was hauled up to the yard. Not till the sail was stretched out along the yard, rovings secured it to the jack-stay, buntlines, leechlines, downhauls, and sheets made fast, and the sail ready to be set, did we come down on deck. As we did so, four bells of the first dog watch went and it was once more our watch on deck. Now all hands hoisted the yard and set the sail.

That was the last of the squalls for a while and the wind blew steady and strong all through that night and the next day. Bright sunshine gladdened the world when I relieved the man at the wheel in the forenoon and an island about ten miles in length was fairly close on the weather bow. The barque was sailing full and by, and as I kept an eye lifting to the weather clew of the upper t'ga'nts'l, I spared a glance for the island. It was in the form of a low peak whose gentle slopes were thickly wooded. As we passed along its shores, we opened out a little bay and a white painted house in the midst of a grove. Below it was a landing stage to which a boat was tied and I could see a few figures moving about. It seemed to me that those people's lives must be very pleasant in such a fertile lovely spot and I wondered what was the name of the island.

The Old Man stepped out of the charthouse, stared at the land and turned and grinned at me.

'Nice little island,' he said.

'Yes,' I said. 'Seems a very charming spot. What is its name, please?'

He turned and looked at me in amazement that anyone

255

could care or that it could matter what its name might be. Then he looked a bit blank and said:

'I . . . I . . . don't know,' and he stumped forward.

He was one of the old school who knew his way about the world. His natural and acquired knowledge of the sea was such that he had a certain contempt for those seamen who depended on fearfully accurate instruments, but he, like old Captain Slocum in his little sloop *Spray* could have success-fully navigated the globe with no more precise record of time than that provided by a dollar clock. A remote island in the West Indies was no concern of his. He was not bound there and the fact that it was near his course bothered him not, so long as it was not close under his lee or directly in his way.

He reminded me of a tale I had heard in Australia about Slocum when he was at anchor inside Sydney Heads to wait for a favourable wind to take him north. Near to him the Moravian Mission schooner was also anchored and he got into conversation with the good brothers. As they showed much interest in his craft and his voyage, he invited them aboard and showed them his boat and his old sextant, his lead line, and his chronometer, which was in fact a dollar clock. They in return asked him aboard their ship and they showed him their sextants and beautifully accurate chronometers, their fathometer and all the latest aids to navigation. He was suitably impressed and, as he left, he said, 'Wal, I guess you sky pilots don't trust much to Providence.'

About this time we were all getting short of fair weather clothing. There had been little opportunity to renew our 'wardrobes' in Pisco and none at all in the islands of the Pescadores. We wore the minimum and they of the lightest, but thin singlets soon rot in hot weather when perspiration is heavy and washing infrequent. I had given up wearing anything but a pair of dungaree trousers or shorts. While I went about the ship thus, comments were made but nobody seemed to mind. When, however, I appeared at the wheel so garbed, the Old Man goggled. Of course it must be remem-bered that to deep-water men of his day the poop was a

256

sanctus sanctorum and one should always be properly dressed to appear there. He said nothing directly to me but he told Sails and others that he had 'plenty of clothes in the slop chest, and you should tell Brookesmith.'

Most, if not all of us had long decided that we would buy no more clothes from the slop chest. We knew fairly well what the penny-pinching old Skipper must have paid for the articles in his stock for we had bought similar articles ashore. His rate of profit seemed unreasonable to us. Seamen get used to being robbed and a moderate return we could bear, but rather more than cent per cent looked a bit stiff to poor sailormen. Even our tobacco price was loaded. Whatever one may think of present-day prices, increased as they are by swingeing taxes (and of course our baccy was duty free) I had never in those days paid more than three shillings and six-pence for a pound of plug tobacco when at sea. Here we were stung for five shillings. I was determined that I would shock his sensibility no end and I'd break all the outworn customs of the sea before I'd let him deplete my payday for which I had worked so hard. Others thought the same and shirts with the most amazing patches were general. Some were repaired with old canvas that the wear and tear of the roaring forties had made soft and pliable. Many were patched with pieces of dungaree of many hues and even burlap was used. As Jock described them, 'A patch on a patch an' a bluidy patch o'er all.'

Flour came aboard in 50-lb bags of good linen and I thought that I could make myself a singlet from one of these. I persuaded the steward to give me one rather than follow his usual practice and make it into a tea towel. I washed it thoroughly and I cut holes in the bottom and sides for head and arms and I hemmed them up neatly. I had quite a dinky little garment which proclaimed in bright colours to our little world the virtues of somebody's flour. I wriggled myself into it with some difficulty and I wore it for a watch and proudly at the wheel. But, it came off to a struggle and uproarious merriment for it took two strong men and my own wriggles to remove it. Regretfully I passed it on to a shipmate with a less robust figure.

There was no sign of any appreciable fall in the temperature and we sweated through day after broiling day. Only the Gulf Stream and a few light airs took the barque through the Yucatan Channel. The sea lay calm and gleaming and the sun blazed down. The sails hung flat and motionless save for a gentle flap as she rolled on the slight swell. At times it was so calm that they hung without a shake. If it had not been for the strong current we'd still be there. There were continual thunderstorms all round us and vicious blasts of hot wind would come after a thunderclap, push her along a bit, perhaps take a sail with it. It would go careering on within a minute to leave us idly rolling as before. I think that our awful cargo rotted the sails, which anyway were far from new, for she lost many as we sailed up through the Caribbean and the Gulf of Mexico. If we had sailed for the Horn and had managed to get round we would have had to set our blankets on the yards to get us home.

One gust that lasted no more than thirty seconds blew out half of the fore lower topsail. In bad weather this would have been the last sail to be stowed and was of our stoutest canvas. Another topsail was lost later and several fore-and-afters were blown to shreds.

One night a quick puff blew a hole in our mainsail through which a horse and cart could have been driven. That, I think, could have been avoided. It was the hurricane season and the belief was held that the Old Man was a trifle panicky. Distant thunder rumbled and growled and lightning flashed all round the horizon. The air felt thick and heavy. The barque was stealing along full and by, with barely enough wind to keep the sails quiet, when a big dark cloud came up on our quarter. The Skipper, ever anxious, was pacing the poop and he immediately gave orders to shorten sail. We had stowed the spanker and were hauling up the mainsail when the squall hit us with screaming wind and stinging rain. The sail, half up in its gear, gave one mighty flap and the lee leech split from

258

head to foot. The bunt was a great gaping hole lately occupied by a square of canvas that flopped into the sea half-a-cable's length to leeward. The Skipper bawled to lower the t'ga'nts'ls and the Second Mate dashed to the main and I to the fore and the yards rattled down. We bunted up the sails and were up on the main yard furling what was left of the course when the squall passed. The rain stopped. The gale dropped to a light breeze.

It is possible that if the mainsail had been left set and drawing, it would have survived and the ship could certainly have carried it. One wild flap when it was loose in its buntlines was more likely to damage it than additional pressure when it was set and quiet. A dense cloud approaching or the shadow of a squall on the horizon was enough to get the Old Man shouting to shorten sail. By the time that the sails were up in their gear the sky would clear and they had to be set again. All of which meant so much of hauling on ropes, furling or loosing canvas and hoisting heavy yards in that sweltering heat. One very dark night of calm, I had been relieved at the wheel and I was descending the poop ladder when I heard a squall close aboard. The Skipper was at the break of the poop and he yelled to me to lower the fore upper t'ga'nts'l. I nipped forward as the barque heeled to the hard wind. I still had a turn of the halliard on the pin and I had not lowered the yard at all when it was all over and we were becalmed again. I just belayed the rope and went forward. There wasn't a breath of wind.

There was a heavy sticky feeling to the air. At every masthead we saw a blob of blue flame that crackled and swung. At each yardarm swayed a glowing haze of light. At every place on mast and yard where iron or steel projected, or where a broken strand of wire pointed from lift or clewline, blue sparks darted and spluttered. It was weird and beautiful in the extreme.

Through this sweltering heat and straining effort our thirst was cruel. Our water ration was wholly inadequate for such conditions. Apart from a cup of coffee at breakfast and one of tea in the evenings, seven of us shared half a bucket of water a day for washing and drinking. It is easy to realise that in such circumstances with the temperature something over 100° in the shade when shade could be found, washing was simply not done with *that* water. We were able to wash for we had filled the two wine tuns abaft the foremast with fresh water from the Panama Canal. The Americans in the Canal Zone had warned us against drinking this water because there was a real danger of infection and moreover it smelled high. The smell wasn't so bad if one siphoned out a bucketful and left it in the open air for half an hour. We sweated and thirsted as we hauled at halliards, sheets and tacks. As we clambered aloft to lift and secure heavy wet sails, unbent rags from the yards and bent on sails, hoisted the heavy yards, dragged at braces to pull round unwilling spars to every variant air, the thirst was agony.

In spite of requests from men of both watches, we could get no more than our 'whack' of water. It was little wonder that our focsle tank was always nearly empty for any one of us could have drunk all the water that went into it each day. In that heat and possibly because of our unspeakable cargo, for the gases were always with us, the tank went foul. I upended it one evening in the dog watch and I emptied the dregs into a bucket. There was an inch of water in the pail. It was black and it stank. Because of the work we had to do in the stifling heat, I thought that it was only just and reasonable that we should have some extra water at that time. Under the most unfavourable conditions it was hardly likely that we should spend more than three months on the passage to England. We had left the Pescador Islands with six months' supply of fresh water in the ship's tank. As I looked at and smelt the filthy muck that I had poured from our focsle tank, my thirst burned the more and I boiled with indignation. I seized the bucket and strode aft.

The Old Man was alone on the poop. I knew from the steward that *he* had one full bucket each day. I went up to him and said quite politely:

'Excuse me, Sir, but could we please have some extra water?'

'Certainly not!' said he. Then, 'What for?'

'Because we don't get enough to drink.'

'You get your whack, don't you?'

'Yes Sir, but we have to work hard and it's fearfully hot. Would it not be possible for us to have an extra bucket now and again? We're all terribly dry.'

'No! You're always asking something unreasonable!'

'But surely, this isn't unreasonable, Sir.'

'It is! You can have no more.'

This was too much. I lifted the bucket up to his nose and said:

'Smell it! That's what we have to try to drink, Sir.' I slammed it down on the deck at his feet.

'Well,' he answered, 'I . . . I have to drink it.'

'Well bloody well drink that!' I said furiously, and with my foot I pushed the bucket at him. He gaped and stepped back a pace, and I, disgusted at his petty meanness, emptied the dirty water over the side and stamped forward.

Six weeks later, as we were entering the Channel after over a fortnight of cool weather and our focsle tank was cleaned and half-full, he stopped me as I was leaving the wheel and said, 'You can have some extra water now, if you like, Brookesmith.'

'Thank you, Sir,' I answered, I hope respectfully, 'but it would have been doubly welcome in the Caribbean.'

So we drifted on. Sometimes we had fair breezes, sometimes foul. Yards were braced now on this tack and now on that, anon with them laid square but never were they for long in any position. At times the wind held for a whole watch and hopes ran high that we would soon get clear of the heat and the calms. It would die away either quietly and undemonstratively, or with a last gasp that laid the barque over and sent us scurrying aloft to furl, or yet another sail went flying to leeward in tatters. All through it we sweated and grumbled and thirsted but we got on with the job and made fun of our own and each other's troubles while the bugs and the scorpions crawled about our noisome cargo and the duck grew fat on their loathly bodies. At least one hatch was always open for ventilation and we were never able to forget the presence of our stinking freight.

We sighted the Cuban coast, and one night we saw the loom of the lights of Havana. Then Key West lay away to port. Here there was a steady head wind and the barque was put about every four hours as we tacked our way through the Florida Straits. I doubt if the poor old tub would ever have done it without the help of the Gulf Stream for she could never lay very close to the wind and with her bottom so foul she was trebly sluggish and she went to leeward like a crab. She made it, in time, and not long after we left Grand Bahama on our quarter she headed up fairly well on the starboard tack but on Sunday 25th July, we were only off Palm Beach.

The next day a fresh easterly wind brought with it the long roll of vast stretches of deep water. I started the day well by catching a big dorado which was very game and as I perched at the end of the jib-boom he gave me an anxious half-hour before I 'landed' him.

I was preparing him for the cook when a big tanker overhauled us and caused some consternation by giving us warning of a hurricane brewing in the vicinity. When, at midday a rain squall appeared to windward, the Old Man had us stow t'ga'nts'ls, mainsail and foresail, and all the fore-and-afters except the jibs and the mizzen staysail, and he had her put about on the other tack.

The rain passed with only a capful of wind and the sky cleared. We looked to the lashings of everything on deck and we renewed and secured and doubled them as necessary. There was an air of expectancy about the ship although the atmosphere was clean and fresh and not heavy and dull as it usually is before a hurricane. At 3 p.m. the tanker *Charles Pratt* of Bayonne overhauled us and slowed up close on our beam. She signalled us the good news that the hurricane had passed over the Bahamas and far to the south of us. We set

262

our sails again and stood on for the north as close to our course as the wind would let us lie.

The breezes came unfavourable and continued to freshen so that a couple of days later we were lying hove to under two lower topsails and reefed mizzen staysail to a strong gale. At midnight, at the first stroke of eight bells, as all hands turned out to muster aft, there came a loud bang from aloft and away went the windward half of the fore lower topsail and we watched it fade into the distance. Even with all hands aloft it was no light task to clew up and make fast the rags that were left by that gale. Then it was decided that we should stand around on the other tack, so we all had a solid pull on the braces and as something of a sea had now got up we became wet as fish into the bargain. Fortunately it was warm and the wetness was easy to bear. For twenty-four hours it blew a hard gale with some really violent squalls. Two very heavy ones came the next evening and the accompanying rain stung like driven sand and was so thick that the main topsail appeared as only a blur to the man at the wheel. It was here that Jock made the Old Man's face grow longer. He mentioned to the Skipper as he came on to the poop to take his trick at the wheel that when he had been in the logwood trade he had been in a barque that had been hove to for three weeks in these parts.

Some pretty little terns were flying about the ship for we were not very far from Bermuda, and the wind was giving them a hard tussle. One little chap flew between the main and mizzen masts and as he got to the weather side of the vessel, a gust caught him and hurled him against one of the main backstays. His poor broken body fluttered into the grey seas and a scrap floated just whiter than the wave crests.

We came on deck next morning to find the ship still with the yards braced hard on the backstays, but sailing on her course and with the foresail set. The port watch had unbent the damaged topsail and we had a hard-working watch. In that four hours, we bent a new topsail, set it, set fore upper topsail, main upper, mainsail, fore and main lower t'ga'nts'ls.

We shook the reef out of the mizzen staysail and set it and then we set the main upper t'ga'nts'l. By this time it was eight bells and all hands stamped along the deck to set the fore upper t'ga'nt'sl by hoisting its yard. As we went below, the port watch were setting the spanker and all her canvas was spread once more.

That was 29th July and it was the morning of 11th September, after more than six weeks of uncertain winds, that we sighted the Lizard light. When breezes blew hard, they came from ahead. When they blew fair they were no more than light zephyrs. There were days after days of oily calm and torrid heat when the barque stood up straight on a flat ocean and the sails hung loose and lifeless. I spent many a watch below perched at the end of the jib-boom while I angled for small dorado and other strange fish with a trout fly!

The passage across the North Atlantic was uneventful and my log for this period of the voyage is a record of light and variable winds, of rain and mist and of weather that only grew colder. There was one period, off the Grand Banks, when we ran with square yards at about six knots in thick mist that lasted for four days. All that time apprentices relieved one another each watch to keep the foghorn sounding its mournful wail till it broke down with one blood-curdling howl just as the fog cleared. Until we were off the south of Ireland that was the best favourable wind we had if one may except a few hard gusts which lasted but an hour or two. They brought flurries of rain, gave us some sail drill with the wet hard canvas, and got up enough sea to give us an occasional ducking.

On 7th September, *Kilmallie* crossed her outward course with square yards before a good stiff breeze. On that day the Mate's duck laid an egg and, fortunately for me, I found it. That egg, with three others, remained a secret between me and the duck. I like raw eggs.

Four days later we were in the English Channel. Steamers were always in sight while the sea was dotted with the

264

picturesque sails of fishing smacks. One, a Brixham trawler named *Inspire*, came close under our counter when we were sailing at only a knot or so. Our Old Man offered them a plug of tobacco for some fresh fish. They were making for their grounds and they had none aboard but they offered us some newspapers which the Old Man refused. Refused! When none of us had seen an English paper for months and we had been out of touch with the world since we had left Panama two months before! He could not be bothered to take a newspaper aboard and said, 'It doesn't matter.' Could you beat it?

A freshening westerly took us up Channel in good style. It was bright and cheerful and there were many ships about. Obviously we were an object of interest and many passenger ships altered course to get a better view. Doubtless she looked quite a picture as she bowled along in the sunshine with all sails set but they must have suffered a rude shock when they got down wind of her.

The Isle of Wight was abeam on the 12th and on the 14th the pilot boarded us off Dungeness at ten o'clock in the morning. A tug was to meet us in the Downs and as she stood on for the South Foreland, the wind faded. It was a glorious day as she completed her voyage under sail. Though the breeze was scarcely enough to put a popple on the water, it and the tide were in her favour as she passed Folkestone and Dover. The sun shone gaily from a cloudless sky and the old white walls of England looked as inspiring and splendid as they always do.

There was no sign of a tug when we arrived off Deal in the evening so the hook was dropped. Sails were furled for the last time and we prepared to spend the night there. An hour later the tug hove in sight and all hands immediately manned the windlass. We stamped round the focsle head to cheerful shanties and hove up the anchor, the towboat made fast, and we went off for what we thought was the last lap of our long journeyings.

The wind freshened from the west and the tide was against us from the North Foreland so that little progress was made through the night. Southend was abeam soon after daybreak. After more hours of plugging against the head wind, we reached Gravesend and prepared to take the river pilot aboard. To our dismay, there were no further orders. We were towed back to the end of the reach and down went our anchor.

Of course we grumbled. Didn't we have good reason to grouse when, after a good run up Channel, we had to lie lost and forgotten here? We didn't even get fresh provisions and were imprisoned in the ship in this out-of-the-way corner of the river when we had planned to step it out in the high places and have good food and drink.

We consoled ourselves that it was interesting there as we watched the ships of all sizes, shapes, and nationalities come and go. Jock had spent some time in the British coastal trade and he knew a lot of the coasters and the flags of the different Lines. He had a yarn to tell of each, of how they fed and lived aboard, of the places they visited and of fair weather and foul round these shores. Then the well-known Medway barges with their big brown spritsails would come sailing by as they tacked up the narrow waterway and made the most of every trick of current and twist of shore. They were loaded to their gunwales and handled with consummate skill.

There was plenty for us to do. All sails were unbent, labelled, and stowed below. All running rigging that would not be required was also sent down and labelled and stowed, and the barque was made ready to discharge her cargo. The owners must have saved themselves quite an expense, for if we had gone straight to our moorings, a shore gang would have had to be paid for this job and at a much higher rate than we had. Perhaps that was the idea.

The day after our arrival, the Finnish barque *Penang* came to her anchor below us. She also had come from Callao by way of Panama and we learned that she had made a similar passage to ours, i.e. eighty-eight days. I was surprised that she had not made better time for this tall craft should have shown us a clean pair of heels in any weather. A good proportion of the light winds that had been blowing across the Atlantic during the previous two months must have come our way.

Penang looked a picture as she sat on the water like a bird. Her graceful hull and lofty towering spars were all fresh white paint and she looked, as she was, a lady of the sea.

After three days, orders came for us to go up river to Charlton Buoys. Now we stamped round the windlass once more to rousing choruses. Cherrily-oh we went as all hands painted rosy pictures of life ashore and how we would spend our pay. Clink . . . clink . . . clink went the pawls and in time with them we sang of how mightily glad we were that we would not again lean our chests against capstan bars in that ship. It would not be long before we had other bars to lean against when we had left the old barky and her bugs and stinks for good.

Through the late afternoon and evening she was towed up the river to Charlton and tied up alongside the old *Monkbarns* on which ship our Second Mate had served his apprenticeship. Two old ladies of the sea had come together for a last word before they went to their final rest. *Monkbarns* was bound out next day for the shipbreaker's yard and, not long after, *Kilmallie* was sold to the same fate.

I wonder did they exchange experiences and fight their battles over again as they lay there together through that night with the gentle wind in their rigging and little waves whispering along their old scarred sides?

It was 10 p.m. when we were all secure. The Mate called, 'That'll do men!' and our contract with the barque and her owners was completed.

It was too late and I was too weary to think of going ashore at that time so I turned in. How glad I was that this was the last time that I should sleep there fitfully and restlessly while beastly creatures tried to eat me alive in this bug-ridden relic.

Next morning I packed and carefully cleaned and disinfected my sea-chest. My thoughts were on hot baths, good food, and clean sheets. A boatman took me and my chest ashore. I sent my gear off to the Sailors' Home and with no slightest regret I turned my back on *Kilmallie*.

I went to the Memorial Sailors' Home in Salmon Street which had recently been opened and I booked myself a room. I asked for a bath and I was shown to a pleasant cubicle which contained a bath, soap, and towels. I filled the bath with water as hot as I could endure and I washed and scrubbed and wallowed. I pulled the plug from the waste pipe and rubbed myself down as the water drained away. I put the plug back again and filled the bath. I got in and soaked and soaped and scrubbed again and again. Marvellous!

AFTERWORD

When I look back after all these years, I always think of that time in sailing ships as a marvellous experience. Something that I should hate to have missed. There was so much of strength and of good companionship; so many skills that were learned and which have since been of advantage to me in so many ways; so much fun and so many happy memories. I suppose that I learned a lot about men, though I learned little about women. Sally (and that wasn't her real name) was an ideal and I got what I deserved. Whether or not I should have said goodbye to her is something I'll never know, but she was absolutely right to forget me.

In both *William Mitchell* and in *Kilmallie* I met unforgettable people, some of whom I feel beside me at times and some others that I'd rather forget. Always there was a sense of endeavour and a challenge to the elements and a pride in pitting one's strength and determination against the odds.

To look forward; with the necessity to conserve energy I can visualise the development of many-masted fore-and-aft rigged ships which could carry much of the world's sea-borne trade. These could be very efficient sailing ships which could make good passages on all trade routes. I have no doubt that there are men to crew them who would accept that it would be a hard life and who would be prepared to face up to it, but I cannot help feeling that the greatest difficulty would be to find for those ships crews that would face hardships and dangers with a laugh and a cheerful word and a "growl you may, but go you must".

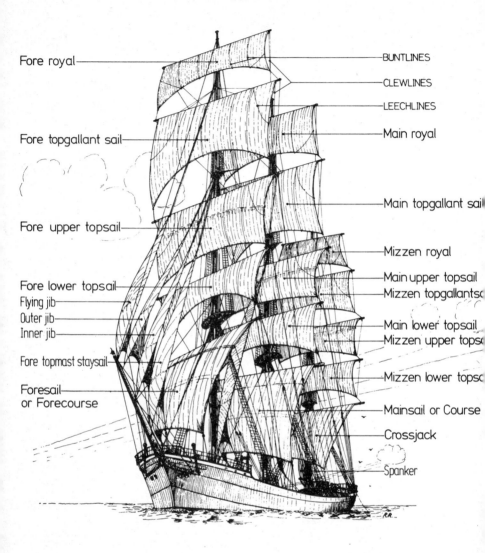

Fore royal

Fore topgallant sail

Fore upper topsail

Fore lower topsail
Flying jib
Outer jib
Inner jib

Fore topmast staysail

Foresail
or Forecourse

BUNTLINES

CLEWLINES

LEECHLINES

Main royal

Main topgallant sail

Mizzen royal

Main upper topsail
Mizzen topgallantsail

Main lower topsail
Mizzen upper topsail

Mizzen lower topsail

Mainsail or Course

Crossjack

Spanker